Battleground Europe

HE RHINE CROSSING

h US Army & 17th US Airborne

Battleground series:

Battleground Europe

THE RHINE CROSSING

9th US Army & 17th US Airborne

Andrew Rawson

Pen & Sword
MILITARY

First published in Great Britain in 2006 by
Pen & Sword Military
an imprint of
Pen & Sword Books Ltd
47 Church Street
Barnsley
South Yorkshire
S70 2AS

ISBN 1 84415 232 4

A CIP catalogue record for this book is
available from the British Library.

Typeset in Palatino

Printed and bound in the United Kingdom by CPI

Pen & Sword Books Ltd incorporates the imprints of Pen & Sword Aviation, Pen
& Sword Maritime, Pen & Sword Military, Wharncliffe Local History, Pen and
Sword Select, Pen and Sword Military Classics and Leo Cooper.
For a complete list of Pen & Sword titles, please contact
Pen & Sword Books Limited
47 Church Street, Barnsley, South Yorkshire, S70 2AS, England
E-mail: enquiries@pen-and-sword.co.uk
Website: www.pen-and-sword.co.uk

CONTENTS

ACKNOWLEDGEMENTS

Operation VARSITY, 21 Army Group's crossing of the Rhine, rivalled Operation OVERLORD in size. Yet while the opening of the Allied campaign in the summer of 1944 is widely written about, there are few books covering the events around Wesel nine months later; the battle that marked the beginning of the end of the war in Europe. This book covers the American part of the Operation, codenamed FLASHPOINT, Ninth US Army's crossing of the river south of Wesel during the early hours of 24 March 1945 and the subsequent desperate battle with *116th Panzer Division* in the Wesel Forest. The American part of XVIII Airborne Corps' operation is also covered. The British and Canadian part of the operation, including the crossings at Xanten and Rees, the Commando raid on Wesel and the British landings around Hamminkeln are covered in a companion volume by Tim Saunders.

Airborne troops, the revered elite of the Allied forces, are widely written about and feature in many modern films but the daylight landings between Wesel and Hamminkeln, where British and American paratroopers and gliders landed on top of the German anti-aircraft gun positions, are rarely covered. So

Somewhere in England – C47 Skytrains each with a Waco glider tethered alongside.

Ready to go.

while the 101st Screaming Eagles and the 82nd All American Airborne Divisions are the favourites of many historians, the exploits of the 17th Airborne Division, nicknamed Thunder from Heaven, are largely forgotten. Hopefully, this book will redress the balance and visitors to the battlefields of Europe will take a little time to understand why the crossing of the Rhine should be remembered.

Several people helped me to collect information for this book, and my research would have been incomplete without their assistance. All the staff at the US National Archives in Washington DC, made me feel particularly welcome and did what they could to make sure that my visit to the USA was both productive and enjoyable, however, a number of people deserve a special mention. David Giodarno, gave me a invaluable tour through the printed documents and continued to keep an eye on my progress as work developed; his assistance was invaluable. Beth Lipford's guided me through the archives indexing system and made sure that I received the documents I wanted, while Holly Reed made available the photographs I required in the stills department. Tom McAnear also worked hard to find and copy the maps I wanted in the cartography room. They all made sure I had the documents I needed before my departure date; customer service is certainly uppermost in the minds of the staff at the NARA.

Back in the UK I would like to thank Roni Wilkinson at Pen and Sword for initially suggesting the idea and drawing together my words and illustrations to produce the book you hold in your hands. Finally, I would like to dedicate this book to my teenage son Alex who is rapidly becoming as interested in discovering the battlefields as I am; let us hope that his generation witness another sixty years and more of peace across Europe.

Chapter 1

THE ADVANCE TOWARDS GERMANY

Allied troops returned to the continent, dropping from planes and gliders or hitting the coast in landing craft on 6 June 1944, in one of the largest operations of the Second World War, Operation OVERLORD. Little did anyone know that a similar sized operation, again involving landing craft and airborne troops, would herald the beginning of the end for Nazi Germany nine months later as Field Marshal Bernard Montgomery's 21 Army Group crossed the Rhine between Arnhem and Düsseldorf.

Following the collapse of the German Armies during the Battle of the Falaise Gap in August 1944 and the subsequent advance across France and Belgium, it looked as though the war could be over in a matter of weeks. As the Allies raced towards the German border, the main problem facing their Supreme Commander, General Dwight D Eisenhower, was keeping his Armies supplied. Huge stocks of ammunition, fuel and food were mounting along the Normandy coast but both 21 Army Group's commander, Field Marshal Bernard Montgomery, and 12 Army Group's commanding officer, General Omar Bradley were in danger of outstripping their supply lines.

Hitler had issued orders to the garrisons holding the ports along the northern coast of France to hold out as long as possible to give the engineers time to destroy the harbour facilities needed by the Allies. Throughout July and August 21 Army Group failed to take a major port before explosives had ravaged it, leaving the Allies reliant on the Red Ball Express, endless columns of lorries carrying supplies across France. But the overland route was reaching the limit of its range. As winter approached, the Allies' problems would mount as bad weather and high seas threatened to close the temporary harbours along the Normandy coast. Hopes for a deepwater port facility were raised at the beginning of September when Antwerp fell into Montgomery's hands. However, German troops still held the forty-mile long Scheldt Estuary linking the city with the sea.

Eisenhower was forced to prioritise his plans to accommodate the supply situation in the face of rivalry between his two Army Group commanders. On the Allies' northern flank, 21 Army Group had charged across Belgium to the Dutch border and Field Marshal Montgomery was confident that *Fifteenth Army Group* was on the verge of collapse. Meanwhile, General Omar Bradley was anxious to exploit the successes on his own front in the Rhineland. First US Army was heading towards Bonn and General Courtney Hodges hoped to force a way across the Rhine and seize the Saar coalfields beyond. Meanwhile, General George Patton's Third US Army had advanced to the south of Luxembourg and was rapidly closing in on the river near the city of Koblenz.

All three commanders wanted to spearhead the way into Germany but the limitations of the supply lines meant that Eisenhower could only sanction one offensive and after careful consideration he adopted Montgomery's plan for a single narrow thrust across Holland. First Airborne Army would lead the attack, dropping three airborne divisions between Eindhoven and Arnhem, to capture the bridges across canals and rivers on the road to the Neder Rein (the Dutch name for the Rhine). An armoured column would advance through the corridor of airborne troops and cross the Rhine at Arnhem, opening the way into northern Germany. The plan was bold and surprise was the key to the operation's success.

On the afternoon of 17 September planes and gliders filled the skies over Holland heralding the start of Operation MARKET GARDEN and within hours many of the bridges were in Allied hands. After the initial surprise, German troops in the area reacted far quicker, and with far greater numbers, than intelligence sources had suggested and by the end of the first day the operation had begun to falter. The 101st (Screaming Eagles) and 82nd (All American) Airborne Divisions faced fierce counter-attacks as they fought to keep the road, which soon became known as Hell's Highway, between Eindhoven and Nijmegen. The anticipated rapid advance towards the Neder Rein never materialised leaving the 1st Airborne Division outnumbered, outgunned and isolated on the north bank of the river around Arnhem. After attempts to relieve the beleaguered British paratroopers failed, the survivors withdrew across the river, leaving 21 Army Group holding a narrow salient. The

General Dwight Eisenhower, discusses 21 Army Group's future plans with Field Marshal Bernard Montgomery.

attempt to cross the Rhine by surprise had failed; the next time Montgomery planned an operation to cross the river he was going to be prepared.

Hopes for a rapid drive into northern Germany had been crushed and Eisenhower faced a long winter as the supply situation deteriorated. Over the next three months British and Canadian troops fought to clear the Schelde estuary to open Antwerp while the Americans fought fierce battles for 'Bloody' Aachen and the Hürtgen Forest, putting pressure on the slender Allied supply lines.

As the German Armies consolidated their positions along their border, Eisenhower's generals proposed new plans for the advance into Germany. While Montgomery wished to continue where Operation MARKET GARDEN had ended, Bradley's plan for a pincer movement through the Rhineland was chosen, leaving Montgomery in a subsidiary role while the First and Third US Armies advanced towards the Rhine.

The dual offensive left the rest of General Bradley's line on the defensive, stretched thinly in some sectors such as the Ardennes, an area of wooded hills in southern Belgium. Although General Bradley's headquarters thought it was highly unlikely that the Germans would counter-attack, on 16 December three Armies struck the American lines with large armoured formations in Hitler's last gamble to turn the tide of the war.

After overrunning large parts of the American line, the *panzers* advanced rapidly through the Belgian forests, while the poor weather stifled the United States Air Force. As the Germans pushed deep into the Ardennes, the GIs began to fight back and heroic stands at places such as St Vith and Bastogne helped to slow the *panzers* as reinforcements moved forward to stem the breakthrough. After a week of panic the skies cleared and Allied air superiority helped the soldiers on the ground turn the tide, bringing *Sixth Panzerarmee* to halt short of their first main objective, the River Meuse. By the end of December the crisis had passed and while Bradley's men fought to reduce the huge bulge in their line, plans were underway for a return to the offensive.

The start of 1945 brought new challenges as the First and Third American Armies drew close to the Siegfried Line but once again there were differences of opinion on how to enter Germany. Eisenhower wanted to try to trap thousands of German troops behind the Siegfried Line and decided to renew a pincer attack with Montgomery taking the leading role. While 21 Army Group advanced south between the Maas and Rhine rivers, General Hodges' First US Army would push north towards Bonn.

The Allied offensive began at the beginning of February but hopes for a rapid breakthrough were quickly dashed by poor weather and First US Army's offensive moved forward at a snail's pace. The advance came to an abrupt standstill in front of the Röer when German engineers sabotaged reservoirs along the river, turning it into a raging torrent.

As the Allies slowly cleared the west bank of the Rhine, Eisenhower could not avoid the economic problems facing Germany as he considered his options for crossing the river. By March 1945 the Ruhr on Germany's north-west border was the powerhouse for Hitler's armaments industry. Before the war the

GIs hug the ground for cover during Ninth Army's advance to the Rhine.
111-SC-335574

The main highway bridge across the Rhine on Ninth Army's front lies in ruins on the outskirts of Wesel.
111-SC-323577

area had produced over half of Germany's coal and steel but once the Russians had seized Silesia in the east and the Seventh US Army had captured the Saar on the French border, it was Hitler's only source of raw materials. Eisenhower's new plan was for 21 Army Group to lead the final assault into Germany, crossing the Rhine north-west of the Ruhr near the town of Wesel; the attack would be the beginning of a drive deep into northern Germany.

While 21 Army Group planned for the final thrust into Germany, a dress rehearsal was taking place on Ninth US Army's front. On 28 February landing craft crowded with men, closely followed by amphibious tanks, crossed the Röer River and marked the start of Operation GRENADE. As Allied troops began to advance east towards the Rhine *Generalfeldmarschall* Gerd von Rundstedt wanted to withdraw behind the river and regroup but Hitler was adamant that no one would retreat; every inch of Germany had to be fought for. The Führer's order bore no relation to the true situation and as resistance collapsed, large parts of von Rundstedt's Armies fell back across the river ahead of the Allies. In the panic that followed thousands of soldiers were cut off on the west bank as they clung onto their positions.

Hopes for a crossing over the Rhine were dashed each time the Allies drew close to the river as German engineers successfully destroyed dozens of bridges in the face of the advancing troops. All along the Rhine magnificent structures, some hundreds of years old, toppled into the swirling waters as carefully prepared explosives detonated when the last German soldier had crossed.

Chapter 2

PLANNING OPERATION VARSITY

Field Marshal Montgomery had been studying the problem of crossing the Rhine ever since the failure of Operation MARKET GARDEN the previous September. The river would have to be crossed at some stage and as early as October Eisenhower had encouraged staff from the First Canadian, the Second British and the Ninth US Armies to confer and plan the forthcoming operation.

Behind the front, engineers set to work designing and training with new river crossing equipment, looking for ways to adapt seagoing landing craft to river work. Naval Unit No 3 arrived in Ninth US Army's area equipped with two types of craft; the Landing Craft Medium known as LCMs and the smaller Landing Craft (Vehicle and Personnel) or LCVP. Experiments on the River Maas in Holland showed that both were suitable for river crossings and the LCVP, a small craft capable of carrying either twenty-four men, four tons of supplies or a small vehicle, would be ideal for carrying the first waves across the river. The larger LCM, measuring over fifteen metres long, was able to carry one medium tank or sixty men. A harbour craft company equipped with ten-metre long Seamules also participated in the trials. When Montgomery put forward his first outline to Supreme Allied Headquarters (SHAEF) in November, one thing was certain, he would need a large number of amphibious craft to cross the Rhine in force. A survey showed that existing stocks fell short of the required number and Eisenhower petitioned suppliers in the States to step up production and eliminate the shortage of boats and bridging material.

The German offensive in December halted planning for several weeks, but once the crisis had passed experts from all three Army groups met at SHAEF Headquarters to hear Eisenhower outline his plans for the first time. 21 Army Group would lead the offensive on Germany, crossing the Rhine to the west and east of Wesel before driving deep in enemy held

General William Simpson, or Texas Bill as he was known in his West Point days, Ninth US Army's four star general.
111-SC-194191

territory; the two remaining Army groups would cross the river at the first opportunity.

As soon as Montgomery heard the news he began to formalise his planning and at the end of January General Moore, Ninth US Army's Chief of Staff, attended a meeting at 21 Army Group Headquarters. He was astonished to find that his services would not be needed during the initial attack as Montgomery intended to allocate the whole of his front to General Miles Dempsey's Second British Army; the Americans would provide a Corps of two infantry divisions to fight under the British. The unexpected proposal came as a shock; it suggested that US troops had been relegated to a subsidiary role in one of the most important campaigns of war.

The outline strategy appeared to have several flaws and as soon as Moore returned to Ninth Army Headquarters, General William Simpson took steps to revise the plan with General Dempsey. Simpson believed that if Second Army monopolised all of the crossings west and east of Wesel it would be difficult to pass Ninth Army's mass of men and equipment through Second Army's bridgehead when the attack developed. Dempsey agreed with Simpson, each Army needed to have its own sector, Second Army to the west and Ninth Army to the south-east of Wesel. Montgomery relented, agreeing with his subordinates' suggestions and 21 Army Group's new directive issued on 4 February assigned an eleven-mile stretch of the river south-east of Wesel to Ninth Army. At long last detailed planning could begin.

Despite the tensions between Montgomery and Simpson during the planning of Operation VARSITY, it is all smiles during a visit by General Omar Bradley. 111-SC-197799

Airborne troops were included in 21 Army Group's plans for the first time on 9 March. The intention was to drop XVIII Airborne Corps to the north of Wesel, enlarging the bridgehead to a depth of six miles at a single stroke, while disrupting the German chances of counter-attacking. To begin with, 21 Army Group's plan envisaged using three airborne divisions, but Montgomery decided to scale the airborne operation down to two divisions when a survey revealed a shortage in transport aircraft and suitable runways. He was not prepared to repeat the mistakes of Operation MARKET GARDEN, where valuable troops were tied up guarding the drop zones during the critical hours following the landing. By dropping all the airborne and glider troops together, General Matthew Ridgway's men could concentrate on holding their perimeter while medium bombers dropped supplies on the landing grounds.

The plan was for 6th British Airborne Division to land in the north, taking the town of Hamminkeln, while 17th Airborne Division dropped to the south. The main objective was to establish an all round perimeter, seizing bridges over the Issel Stream on their eastern perimeter as well as Diersfordt Forest, an area of wooded high ground overlooking Second Army's crossing site at Xanten to the west.

Dropping the airborne troops close to the river meant that the link up with the ground troops would occur before the Germans could bring the full weight of their reinforcements against the lightly armed paratroopers. It also meant that 17th Airborne Division could immediately count on artillery support from the opposite side of the river while it established a perimeter north of Wesel.

Airborne landings had always preceded the ground attack in previous operations, but on this occasion General Dempsey suggested a different approach. If the paratroopers landed in advance of the river crossings, Second Army's artillery could not shell the area ahead of the river crossings and following experiences in Normandy, night landings had been ruled out as too dangerous. Dempsey's answer was for XVIII Airborne Corps to land on the morning after the land assault, eight hours after the last crossing had started. It was a hazardous proposal in the short term, however, the long-term effects would be extremely beneficial. The link up with troops advancing from the Xanten bridgehead would occur at an early stage, creating a bridgehead six miles deep by the first day. It had to be tried.

As the planning forged ahead, Montgomery ordered the building of eight new temporary bridges across the Maas River, a potential bottleneck on his supply lines. The attack would require a massive amount of materials, estimated at 540 tonnes per day for each division, and Ninth US Army alone had twelve divisions. 21 Army Group could not afford to run short of supplies once Operation VARSITY had begun.

Surprise at Remagen

During the first week of March the Allies were chasing the retreating German Armies towards the Rhine and despite Hitler's order to hold every inch of German soil, thousands of men were forced to retreat and seek safety beyond the Rhine. Engineers had ample time to prepare the bridges along the river for demolition and on several occasions American and British troops saw huge structures collapse in clouds of smoke and dust as they approached. In spite of the chaotic nature of the retreat, it appeared the German engineers were organised; that is until the afternoon of 7 March.

On First Army's front 9th Armoured Division was pushing towards the Rhine hoping to trap parts of Fifteenth Army as it fell back in disorder between Bonn and Koblenz. On 7 March one of Combat Command B's armoured task forces, based around 27th Armoured Infantry Battalion and elements of the 14th Tank Battalion, was closing on Remagen and although a huge rail bridge crossed the river in the town, few expected it to be standing by the time American troops arrived.

The rapid retreat had created confusion in the German command and plans to defend Remagen had failed to

The surprise capture of the Ludendorff Bridge at Remagen sent shock waves through the Allied and German High Commands.

materialise, leaving only a few dozen men to protect the engineers as they prepared the Ludendorff Bridge for demolition. With no one to stop them, the American Task Force advanced through the town and as Company A's commander, Lieutenant Karl Timmerman, gave the order to cross the railway bridge, on the opposite bank *Hauptmann* Friesenhahn threw the switch controlling the primary circuit. Nothing happened. Either shrapnel or sabotage had damaged the wiring but as the GIs prepared to cross, Friesenhahn fired the secondary charges. This time there was an explosion but only half the charges had detonated and although the bridge had been seriously damaged there was still a route across. In the confusion that followed Timmermann's men ran over the bridge and fanned out on the far bank while the rest of the battalion followed. The news stunned everyone – the mighty Rhine had been breached by accident rather than design.

As US troops poured across the river, the German High Command struggled to recover from shock, sending reinforcements to try to eliminate the tiny bridgehead. Hitler was furious and reacted with typical vengeance, sacking *Feldmarschall* Gerd von Rundstedt and several other senior officers connected with the fiasco. He also approved the execution of four junior officers; a fifth officer held by the Americans was condemned to death in his absence. As the Germans looked for scapegoats, First US Army took steps to expand its bridgehead, sending every available man towards Remagen while engineers built pontoon bridges to relieve the bottleneck; the race to expand the hold on the east bank of the Rhine was on.

Von Rundstedt's replacement, *Generalfeldmarschall* Albert Kesselring, set about trying to contain the Americans in the Westerwald, a series of wooded hills and ravines east of Remagen, while the *Luftwaffe* tried in vain to destroy the bridges. One reserve deployed against the Remagen bridgehead was the *11th Panzer Division*, a significant move in more ways than one. The *Panzer Division* would have been ideally placed to counter-attack 21 Army Group's planned bridgehead at Wesel; the capture of the bridge at Remagen had indirectly increased the Montgomery's future chances of securing a bridgehead in the north.

After the Germans had bombed, shelled and finally fired V2

rockets at Remagen, the Ludendorff Bridge toppled into the Rhine on 17 March. The collapse was not a direct result of enemy action but the culmination of heavy traffic, engineering works and near misses had seriously weakened the damaged structure. The loss of the bridge made little difference. Several pontoon bridges had already been built and they were more than capable of supplying First Army's bridgehead. American troops had already seized the hills overlooking the river and Kretzhaus and Notscheid, key road junctions in the Westerwald, bringing the Germans' chances of reaching the river to an end; it meant that First US Army could start to plan its drive deep into the heart of Germany.

The final plan

While all eyes had been focused on Remagen, Montgomery continued to plan Operation VARSITY. Securing a sizeable bridgehead on the east bank of the Rhine demanded a large-scale assault rivalling the size of Operation OVERLORD and Montgomery's plan involved five separate operations starting with the first river crossing at 21:00 hours on 23 March and culminating with the airborne landings thirteen hours later.

The attack would begin with Operation TURNSCREW on Second Army's left flank and 51st (Highland) Division aimed to capture Rees and the high ground overlooking the crossing point before daylight. An hour later 1st British Commando Brigade would begin Operation WIDGEON, a crossing west to Wesel, while 200 bombers from RAF Bomber Command reduced the town to rubble with 1,100 tons of bombs.

The third stage of Operation VARSITY would start at 02:00 hours, with the rest of Second Army and Ninth Army crossing

Major General Leland Hobbs, 30th Division's leader.
111-SC-205532

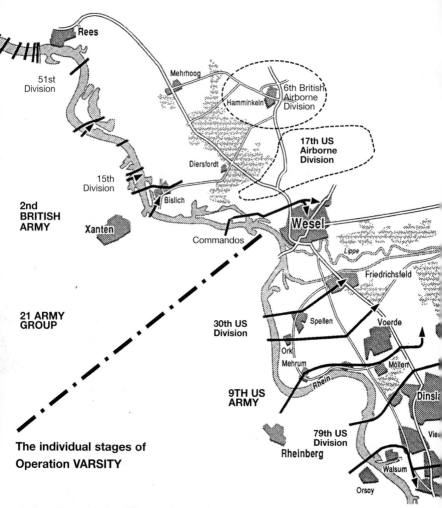

51st
Division

Rees

Mehrhoog

Hamminkeln

6th British
Airborne
Division

17th US
Airborne
Division

Diersfordt

15th
Division

Bislich

**2nd
BRITISH
ARMY**

Xanten

Commandos

Wesel

Lippe

Friedrichsfeld

**21 ARMY
GROUP**

30th US
Division

Spellen

Voerde

Ork

Mehrum

Möllen

Rhein

**9TH US
ARMY**

Dinsla

79th US
Division

Vie

Walsum

**The individual stages of
Operation VARSITY**

Rheinberg

Orsoy

**Major General Ira Wyche (centre) escorts the British Prime Minister,
Winston Churchill, across the Rhine on 25 March.**

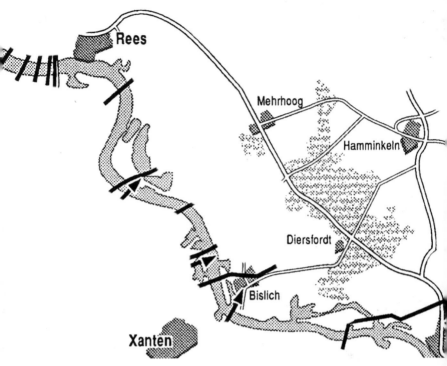

Major General William Miley discusses 17th Airborne Division's plans with First Airborne Army's Chief of Staff. 111-SC-203302

the Rhine in close succession either side of Wesel. In the centre of Second Army's front 15th (Scottish) Division would launch Operation TORCHLIGHT, crossing the river at Xanten to the west of the town. Simultaneously, General John B Anderson would open Operation FLASHPOINT, sending the first of XVI Corps' divisions across the river south of Wesel. 30th Division, led by Major General Leland S Hobbs, would push east to cut the Wesel–Dinslaken railway at the earliest opportunity as a prelude to an advance through Staatsforst Wesel, an area of wooded hills, south of the Lippe river. 79th Division would start to send troops over the river an hour later and Major General Ira Billy Wyche's men would link up with 30th Division and seize Dinslaken, forming a protective flank along the Neue-Ernscher Canal on the southern flank of 21 Army Group's front.

While the ground troops pushed east of the river, the final phase of the attack would begin at 10:00 hours on 24 March. XVIII Airborne Corps, with the 6th British Airborne Division and the 17th US Airborne Division, led by Major General

23

William Bud Miley, would land between Hamminkeln and Wesel, seizing Diersfordt Forest and establishing a perimeter along the Issel Stream.

The rapid series of crossings would hopefully keep the Germans on the defensive and the final blow, the Airborne landings, would hopefully throw *Army Group H* into confusion. In the first twenty-four hours Field Marshal Montgomery was hoping for a bridgehead twelve miles wide, extending from Rees in the west to Dinslaken in the east, and stretching over six miles deep; large enough to hold off anything the Germans could throw at it. Montgomery later summed up the scale and importance of the operation:

> *My intention was to secure a bridgehead prior to developing operations to isolate the Ruhr and to thrust into the northern plains of Germany. In outline, my plan was to cross the Rhine on the front of two Armies between Rheinberg and Rees, using the Ninth American Army on the right and Second Army on the left. The principal initial object was the important communications centre of Wesel. I intended that the bridgehead should extend to the south sufficiently far to cover Wesel from enemy ground action, and to the north to include bridge sites at Emmerich: the depth of the bridgehead was to be made sufficient to provide room to form up major forces for the drive to the east and north-east.*

Chapter 3

NINTH US ARMY PLANS
OPERATION FLASHPOINT

General Anderson's XVI Corps, which had recently participated in the drive from the Röer, had been earmarked to lead Ninth Army's assault across the Rhine and although the Corps was a relatively new formation, the two assault divisions, the 30th Old Hickory Division and the 79th Cross of Lorraine Division were both veterans of the campaigns across Western Europe.

Major General Ira T Wyche had commanded the 79th since its first campaign in Normandy, liberating Cherbourg three weeks after D-Day. Major General Leland S Hobbs had also led 30th

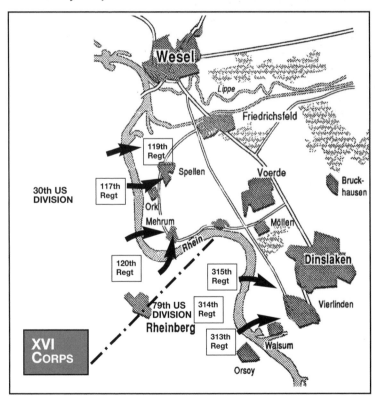

Generals Simpson and Anderson look stern during a meeting with Field Marshal Montgomery; General Bradley and General Alanbrooke, Montgomery's Chief of Staff. 111-SC-203441

Division since Normandy and its first taste of action was in the bloody battle for St Lô against the *116th Panzer Division.* General Simpson had Brigadier General John M Devine's 8th Armoured Division, nicknamed the *Thundering Herd,* waiting in reserve to exploit the breakthrough made by the infantry. 35th Division and 75th Division would follow in the wake of assault divisions, expanding the bridgehead while XIX Corps waited ready for the breakout. Ninth Army's final Corps, the XIII, held the west bank of the Rhine facing Düsseldorf, south of the crossing sites.

30th Division held the left sector of XVI Corps front, an area five miles wide, extending from the Lippe canal to Mehrum. A dyke protected the east bank of the river but the flood plain beyond was flat, open farmland dotted with small villages, farmhouses and orchards. To be successful, Major General Hobbs' men would have to advance two miles while it was still dark, engaging the Germans' main defensive line along two railway embankments before they could regroup.

The ground climbed steadily beyond the railways, rising into a high wooded ridge seven miles east of the Rhine where a partially built highway, one of Hitler's planned *Autobahns*, ran along the edge of the Staatsforst Wesel, a five mile deep area of thick woods. General Hobbs' men would have to advance through the forest along a network of trails while their supporting armour was confined to the handful of roads. 8th Armoured Division would have to wait until the infantry had cleared the woods before it could launch its attack between Dorsten and Kirchellen, two towns twelve miles beyond the river.

79th Division held XVI Corps' right flank and the meandering nature of the river put its front two miles east of 30th Division. General Wyche's men would cross an hour later to account for the difference, reducing the chance that German counter-attacks might drive a wedge between the two divisions. Once again a large dyke ran along the far shore across the full length of the sector and beyond the embankment. Wyche's men faced open farmland dotted with villages, small woods and factories.

The delay to 79th Division's crossing had added one extra problem. The assault battalions only had three and a half hours of darkness to clear the villages beyond the dyke and form a secure flank along the Neue-Ernscher Canal. General Wyche had arranged to shell the area south of the canal with white phosphorous shells at first light, creating a smokescreen across the division's sector. The chemical smoke would cover his reserve battalions as they moved towards the division's final objective, the town of Dinslaken.

The Air Campaign
While preparations on the ground were growing towards a climax, a relentless bombing campaign was being waged on Germany. The Allies had enjoyed air superiority for the majority of the campaign in north-west Europe and by the end of 1944 the *Luftwaffe's* presence in the skies had virtually ended. During the second week of February the American, British and

Canadian Air Forces began a bombing campaign across north-west Germany, attacking rail bridges, viaducts and canals in support of the forthcoming operation. Over the weeks that followed, Allied bombers carried out 1,792 sorties, dropping 31,635 tons of bombs on targets extending from the southern side of the Ruhr in a huge arc up to the port of Bremen on the North Sea coast. The main target was the German transportation system and as the Allied bombers destroyed bridges and railways, one by one the routes leading towards Germany's industrial centre and 21 Army Group's area were cut. Operation INTERDICT NORTHWEST GERMANY carried on relentlessly and by 21 March reconnaissance planes reported that ten out of seventeen bridges had been destroyed while five others had been seriously damaged. Meanwhile, after giving air support to 21 Army Group's advance to the Rhine, 2nd British Tactical Air Force and the 29th US Tactical Air Force joined the campaign to seal off the Ruhr. Between 11 and 21 March fighters and fighter-bombers carried out over 7,000 sorties directed against the road and rail systems of the Ruhr.

Infantry Planning

Battalion commanders in 30th and 79th Division were briefed about the forthcoming operation on 9 March and a few days later the two divisions moved to Nijmegen in Holland to begin training on the River Maas. After rehearsing on dry land, the GIs moved onto the river and the landing craft coxswains helped the soldiers as they practised entering and leaving their assault craft. New elements were added to the training each day and the programme culminated in a full dress rehearsal carried out at night.

The planning for Operation FLASHPOINT had been carried out in meticulous detail at the highest levels and steps were taken to ensure that every GI knew what to expect. Briefings and planning meetings were staged daily and the arrangements made at 314th Regiment's headquarters were typical:

A sand table 8ft by 6ft was prepared covering the actual crossing of the Rhine. Each house, road and railroad track was represented by pieces of wood and the river and woods by coloured dyes. Each grid square on the 1/25,000 map was blown up to one foot by one foot. Upon completion each battalion was allotted sufficient time so that their platoon leaders could be

Signallers practise laying cables with the help of a DUKW.

Officers study their objectives with the help of a sand table.

present at the table for an orientation. Each company was
allotted two hours each for its officers.

Thousands of maps covering the east bank of the Rhine had been produced and each squad leader was issued with the street plans of the villages en route to his objective. Aerial photographs were also issued in large numbers and several battalion commanders were flown over the crossing sites to view their objectives. Nothing was being left to chance; by the time the GIs were moving to their embarkation points along the riverbank on the night of 23 March, every man knew what was expected of him.

Although observation posts along the river sent back daily reports of troop movements on the far bank, General Hobbs and General Wyche wanted first hand information about the condition of the shoreline and the German defensive works on the embankment. 75th Division had failed to get patrols across the Rhine but as soon as 30th and 79th Division moved into their assembly areas on the west bank, plans were made to send men to the far bank.

120th Regiment was due to cross opposite the village of Mehrum on 30th Division's right flank and its patrolling regime was repeated all along Ninth Army's front. Lieutenant James Butler led a five-man patrol across the river during the early hours of 20 March. They pushed off the shore from Ettroig and their boat was swept 400 metres downstream before it touched down on the far shore ten minutes later. After waiting motionless for a short time, they scrambled ashore noting that the shoreline was ideal for assault craft. Crawling inland, Butler's men penetrated the German lines to a depth of 600 metres, finding nothing to cause concern. After returning to their boat, the patrol drifted back to the safety of the west bank before it was light.

The following night Lieutenant Michael Esquivel led a second patrol and again they crossed without being seen. While two men stayed by the boat, Esquivel pushed inland to investigate a second dyke that had been built to protect Mehrum during winter floods. After crawling past a line of foxholes, moving so close that they heard the sentries whispering, the three men crawled over 500 metres, finding a second line of outposts along the dyke. One German soldier challenged the group but Esquivel's men froze and stayed silent

Sherman tanks line up in the streets of Rheinberg behind Ninth Army's front. 111-SC-201895

in the darkness, leaving the guard to carry on his patrol. Lieutenant Esquivel had seen enough, the dyke did not present a serious obstacle to infantry, he could withdraw to the boat and return to the far bank.

Patrolling all along XVI Corps' front gave Generals Simpson and Anderson the information they needed to plan the final details of the attack. Observation posts and reconnaissance planes completed the picture and as D-Day drew near Generals Hobbs and Wyche could chose their crossing points and plan the first stage of the assault with confidence. The only question remaining was how ready were the Germans?

The meandering Rhine varied from 300 to 500 metres wide where XVI Corps planned to cross and although it could be turbulent along the shoreline, where sandbanks lay lurking beneath the surface, the speed of the river was only five miles per hour. A minimum draft of three metres in the main channel meant that the planners could include all the medium landing craft and small assault craft, and the patrols had proved that the far shore was usually an ideal mix of sand and gravels, suitable to land on. The flood dykes rose to five metres high and on 120th Regiment's front a second winter dyke had been built some distance from the river to protect the villages, however, they were passable to both infantry and tanks.

17th Airborne Division's flight plan is explained during a final briefing.

The Countdown Begins

As the assault troops practised and planned for the forthcoming assault, the build up of supplies along the west bank of the Rhine was reaching a climax. The engineers had worked around the clock to construct new railheads and a network of roads leading to the riverbank along Ninth Army's front and in places bulldozers had been forced to demolish buildings so that lorries could carry landing craft down to the water's edge.

Over the past two weeks 37,000 British and 22,000 American engineers had been preparing for the crossing, stockpiling thousands of tonnes of ammunition, fuel, bridging equipment and food in camouflaged dumps; over 138,000 tonnes had been stored in Ninth Army's area alone. The concentration of men and materials behind 21 Army Group's front was going to be one of the largest ever assembled and while over one million men trained and worked to make Operation VARSITY a success, Ninth US Army assembled 2,070 guns while 3,411 artillery pieces rolled into position in Second British Army's and First Canadian Army's sectors.

It was impossible to conceal the build up of men and equipment on the west bank of the Rhine but deception and camouflage were used wherever possible to try to deceive the Germans waiting across the river. Dumps and camps were camouflaged while dummy installations were built in other

Tonnes of supplies and ammunition were stockpiled and then camouflaged on the west bank of the Rhine. 111-SC-203428

parts of 21 Army Group's front to try to draw attention away from the real crossing sites. As a final touch, hundreds of generators covered the river with a twenty mile long smoke-screen during the ten days before D-Day.

While operating in Germany the Allied soldiers had for the first time to accept that they were not liberators and civilians had to be evacuated from the assembly areas to reduce the chances of spies reporting troop movements. Ninth Army had also taken steps to conceal the arrival of 30th and 79th Division, (the *Wehrmacht* rated both as *Schwerpunkt* or attack divisions) and their movement towards Rheinberg would arouse suspicions in the German intelligence service. Communication teams remained behind as the two divisions made their way towards their assembly areas and busied themselves passing false messages to give the impression that neither divisions had moved. As an added precaution officers and men were ordered to remove divisional patches and paint out vehicle markings to fool spies.

As the ground troops moved towards the Rhine, the Allied air campaign began to intensify during the final seventy-two hours and the Eighth US Air Force changed to military targets, concentrating on airfields and barracks, paying particular attention to airstrips used by jet aircraft. The 9th US Bombardment Division joined in the aerial assault, directing 2,000 medium bombers against the communication centres, rail yards and flak positions north of the Ruhr. The Royal Air Force's Bomber Command attacked targets north of the Rhine and over the course of three days the combined might of the Allied air forces flew over 11,000 sorties. One bombing mission on 21 March scored an unexpected success. It demolished part of First Parachute Army's headquarters and severely wounded *Generaloberst* Alfred Schlemm. Although Schlemm stayed at his post throughout Operation VARSITY, his health deteriorated and he was forced to retire on 28 March; his injuries no doubt affected his ability to command at a crucial time.

While the Air Forces pounded targets across north-west Germany, 21 Army Group continued to assemble and by nightfall on 23 March 750,000 British, 330,000 American, 180,000 Canadian, 15,000 Polish, 7,000 Belgium, 6,000 Czech and 1,700 Dutch troops were in position; Operation VARSITY was a truly multi-national affair.

The Germans

In spite of 21 Army Group's attempts to keep the build up of troops a secret, First Parachute Army's staff on the opposite side of the Rhine knew that the Allies were preparing to cross. It was impossible to disguise the fact that over one million men, hundreds of vehicles and thousands of tonnes of supplies were being moved close to the river. Even so *Generaloberst* Johannes Blaskowitz, Commander of *Army Group H* did not know the answer to two burning questions. Exactly where would the Allies cross and when?

Tension mounted as rumours about the imminent Allied assault spread and on 20 March General Blaskowitz ordered a high state of alert. He correctly guessed that the Allies would attack between Emmerich and Dinslaken and had spread his limited resources to cover every eventuality. First Parachute Army's artillery fire increased as D-Day approached and as the guns searched for targets on the far bank, patrols tried to cross

Generaloberst **Johannes Blaskowitz knew 21 Army Group was going to attack across the Rhine in the Wesel area; the question was when?**

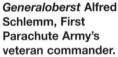

Generaloberst Alfred Schlemm, First Parachute Army's veteran commander.

General der Fallschrimtruppen Eugen Meindl would have to contend with Second British Army crossing the Rhine to his front while XVIII Corps landed to his rear.

the river to find out what 21 Army Group was planning; hardly any returned. Despite Allied air superiority, *Luftwaffe* pilots flew lone sorties low over the Allied side of the river looking for evidence of the build up.

First Parachute Army would face the brunt of 21 Army Group's attack and the injured *Generaloberst* Schlemm, a veteran of operations in Crete, Russia, Italy and the Reichswald, had three infantry corps to hold his sector. His only reserve was a depleted armoured corps. II Parachute Corps held the front opposite the British crossing sites at Emmerich and Wesel. *General der Fallschrimtruppen* Eugen Meindl's command was the strongest of Schlemm's corps, having three divisions, 6th, 7th and 8th Parachute Divisions, and although each only had around 3,500 men they were still expected to be worthy opponents. *General der Infantrie* Erich Strabe's *LXXXVI Korps* held the riverbank from Wesel upstream to Dinslaken. 84th Division, a weak formation of only 1,500 men led by *General der Infantrie* Heinz Fiebig, held the riverbank either side of Wesel.

Generalmajor Heinz Fiebig's 84th Division held the riverbank either side of Wesel.

General Anderson's XVI Corps faced the southern sector of *LXXXVI Korps*, held by 180th Infantry Division. *LXIII Korps*, commanded by *General der Infantrie* Erich Abraham, held the area opposite the southern flank of XVI Corps. The Hamburg Division, a makeshift formation of old men and teenagers led by a few battle weary convalescing soldiers, held the front opposite 79th Division. 2nd Parachute Division held the Rhine south of the selected crossing sites.

XXXXVII Panzerkorps, comprising the *116th Panzer* and *15th Panzergrenadier* Divisions formed First Parachute Army's reserve; a sizeable force on paper but the trials of the past six months had considerably weakened both formations. Allied intelligence believed that the *Panzer Division* only had seventy tanks while the *Panzergrenadiers* had fifteen *Panzers* and twenty-five self-propelled guns. Independent armoured units added another forty tanks and a heavy anti-tank Battalion was also reported to be operating in the area. The armoured reserve brought the total strength facing 21 Army Group's twenty-two mile sector to around 85,000 men and 150 armoured vehicles.

Although the Germans lacked men and tanks, one type of weapon they had in abundance was the anti-aircraft gun. During the days leading up to the attack the number of artillery and anti-aircraft weapons on the east bank of the Rhine had increased significantly. *Generaloberst* Blaskowitz had correctly anticipated that the Allies would use airborne troops to expand the bridgehead but he believed that the landings would take place deep behind his lines; the miscalculation meant that many flak weapons were positioned ten miles north-east of Wesel, some distance from XVIII Airborne Corps' landing grounds.

Even so, the number of anti-aircraft weapons waiting for the paratroopers grew daily as Blaskowitz moved guns from Holland into First Parachute Army's sector. In the days leading up to Operation VARSITY the number of 20mm calibre weapons in *Generaloberst* Schlemm's area increased from 153 to 712, while another 114 heavy weapons, including several batteries of the feared 88mm flak guns, were positioned in the fields around Hamminkeln and Wesel.

The tension mounted as the Allied air attacks increased and on 20 March *Generaloberst* Schlemm asked General Strabe for a report on the anti-aircraft defences between Wesel and Dinslaken. Two days later the order was passed to 180th Division's headquarters: the details were still being compiled as XVIII Airborne Corps flew overhead.

Patton steals the limelight

With all the attention being lavished on 21 Army Group's planning, there was a hint of resentment amongst the rest of the US Army's hierarchy. Despite the fact that the Americans had four times as many troops as the British in Europe, Eisenhower had chosen Field Marshal Montgomery to lead the drive into Germany. The crossing at Remagen on 7 March had brought some light relief to SHAEF's headquarters as they contemplated the forthcoming crossing of the Rhine, but as the date for 21 Army Group's attack drew nearer, 150 miles south of Wesel General George S Patton, Third Army's flamboyant leader, was planning to steal Montgomery's limelight. Patton was furious that he was not allowed to advance across the Rhine, leaving his men waiting along the river, while the preparations for Operation VARSITY swallowed up massive amounts of supplies and equipment. He refused to wait and, without consulting General Bradley, devised a plan to sneak across the river before Montgomery.

There would be no massive air offensive, no shattering bombardment and no Airborne troops in Patton's plan; just infantry and an assortment of assault boats kept in Third Army's area for minor river crossings. The two chosen places were in 5th Infantry Division's sector at Oppenheim and Nierstein, upstream of the town of Mainz and within striking distance of Frankfurt. The location had been chosen because the meandering river presented 5th Division with a natural staging

General George S Patton.

area needing only a small number of troops to protect the bridgehead. It was a risky plan and one likely to create waves in the Allied High Command if it succeeded. Patton did not care about upsetting Montgomery and ordered Major General

Stafford Irwin to cross on the night of 22 March, twenty-four hours ahead of 21 Army Group.

While the anxious GIs crossed the Rhine in their flimsy assault boats, no doubt cursing their leader's impatience, the German reaction was minimal. Irwin's men reached the far side with light casualties and stepped onto dry land; Third US Army had crossed the Rhine. It appeared that the Germans were as stunned as the Allies and as men and equipment flowed onto the east bank, the chances of eliminating the bridgehead diminished by the hour. Ferries carried tanks and tank destroyers across the river while engineers built a treadway bridge and by mid afternoon the whole division was on the far bank.

Delighted by the coup, Patton called General Omar Bradley, 12 Army Group's leader to pass on the news, mischievously pointing out that he had crossed without any assistance, an obvious dig at 21 Army Group's meticulous preparations. On the afternoon of 23 March, only hours before Operation VARSITY was due to start, Bradley reported Third Army's bridgehead to the press corps, repeating Patton's jibe at Montgomery. The news no doubt confused *Feldmarschall* Kesselring and the German High Command; for a second time American troops had crossed the Rhine with ease.

As a final show of defiance Patton ordered his driver to pause momentarily as he crossed the Rhine a few days later. Stepping from the jeep onto the pontoon bridge, Third Army's controversial leader stared at the river below before relieving himself; it was Patton's own comment on the great river's defensive capability.

Chapter 4

XVI CORPS CROSSES THE RHINE

The final countdown

At darkness fell on 23 March convoys of trucks moved towards the Rhine, guided by military police working to detailed schedules. Infantry moved halfway on board lorries, walking the final six miles to the assembly positions, while 2 ½ ton trucks carried their heavy weapons down to the crossing sites. Motorised elements followed different routes to the river to avoid the attentions of the German artillery:

March units not to exceed 25 vehicles; ten minutes between serials; 60 yards distance between vehicles in open country and 20 yards distance between vehicles in towns and cities; slowest vehicle will lead each march unit; head of column speed 17½ mph in daylight and with lights at night and 10 mph in blackouts; maximum speed any vehicle 25 mph, halts for 10 minutes every two hours.

The movement of thousands of men called for a highly organised traffic control system controlled by communications cables laid along the route. Signallers could plug into the network at any point and transmit messages by wire or radio to keep the convoys moving.

Each group of men and vehicles had been allocated a number and serials waited at a

This GI is wearing the twin tube inflatable life belt, a lifesaver if an assault boat overturned.

41

Soldiers wait anxiously for their turn to carry the assault boats down to the water's edge.

safe distance until their transport was available. Flexibility was the keyword and the order of serials could be changed if the situation on the far bank changed and Regimental Executive Officers worked alongside the Beachmasters, coordinating operations on the riverbank. Once the initial crossing had been made, General Hobbs and General Wyche were reliant on a steady flow of men, tanks, vehicles and supplies to the far bank to have a chance of succeeding.

The priorities for the first stage of the operation had been given to anti-tank guns and Weasels, small amphibious vehicles stocked with ammunition. Tanks and tank destroyers would be needed in the push east and amphibious Sherman DD tanks, (named after the Duplex Drive propeller system that powered the tank through water) would follow the infantry, while rafts carried M24 Chaffee light tanks and tank destroyers across the river. As soon as the bridgehead was secure, landing craft could begin to operate on the river, delivering communication vehicles, ammunition jeeps and $1\frac{1}{2}$ ton prime movers to the far bank. Bulldozers would then cut roads through the floodbanks to allow DUKWs, (amphibious lorries) to operate a ferry service across the river, taking ammunition, fuel and food across to the far bank and returning with the wounded.

The final artillery barrage
As XVI Corps assembled opposite its crossing sites, the first stages of Operation VARSITY had already begun and 51st (Highland) Division encountered stiff resistance as it crossed opposite Rees on Second Army's front. 1st British Commando Brigade had managed to cross the river to the west of Wesel and

The devastating results of the RAF's bombing raid on Wesel.

General Eisenhower and his Deputy, Air Marshal Tedder, accompany Montgomery and Bradley during a final visit to Ninth Army's headquarters.

was moving along the riverbank towards their objective as 200 bombers reduced the town to rubble.

As midnight passed, a three-quarter moon illuminated the Rhine, casting an eerie glow through the thick smokescreen drifting across the river. As the final hours passed, General Eisenhower and General Simpson mingled with crowds and both were impressed by the GIs' professionalism and enthusiasm as they passed on encouraging words; Eisenhower later recalled that the men were 'remarkably eager to finish the job'.

As 01:00 hours approached the two commanders could do no more and moved to the church that would act as their observation post during the vital hours of Operation FLASHPOINT. With one hour to go the bombardment suddenly intensified as over 2,050 artillery pieces opened fire, creating a continuous roar of noise as over 1,000 shells a minute hit the German positions across the river. Meanwhile, the Allied Air

44

Forces were making their own contribution and 1,500 bombers were on their way to hit airfields beyond the Rhine, stifling the *Luftwaffe* during the critical early stages of the operation.

The intensity of the bombardment gave the men waiting along the river a degree of confidence and as they looked back at the western sky, ablaze with gun flashes, many must have thought that no one could survive the barrage of shells hitting the far bank. Only time would tell if it had succeeded in breaking the Germans' morale. A few hours later Lieutenant Colonel Norman King heard

Eisenhower watches the spectacle unfold.

first hand what the men across the Rhine thought of the Ninth Army's preliminary bombardment:

> *They had never seen anything like it, and it completely stunned, scared and shook them.*

30th Division's crossing

Each battalion had fifty-four storm boats, large enough for seven men, and thirty double assault boats capable of carrying fourteen men. The companies chosen to lead the crossing formed close to the west bank, sheltering behind the dyke and as the minutes ticked by, buckled double-tube life preservers around their waists. As H-hour approached the noise of the artillery, machine guns, mortars and howitzers rose to a crescendo as the assault troops pulled their boats from their concealed positions and dragged them down to the river's edge. Gasping as they waded into the cold water, men steadied the boats as their comrades climbed aboard and as soon as the last man had scrambled inside the pilots fired the motors into life and set out across the river. The assault was underway.

In the left sector of 30th Division's front, 2nd Battalion led 119th Regiment's assault and as the first wave crossed opposite Spellen, tracer bullets fired overhead to guide the boats through the smokescreen to the far shore. The German reaction was negligible and two minutes later the first wave of boats grounded on the opposite bank. As GIs ran across the exposed beach the second wave was in the water, crossing in the larger and slower double M2 boats, guided across by flashlights and

Gasps and curses as the GIs wade into the cold water and scramble into their crowded assault boat.

luminous markers set up by the first men ashore.

Colonel Russell A Baker listened carefully to the radio as Lieutenant Colonel McCown reported on progress across the river. The assault was looking promising. 2nd Battalion's crossing had been far easier than expected as the following radio signals show:

02:18   First wave went over in time; second wave is on its way. So is Thomas' bunch.

02:20   Notify Beston to take care on other side, there are Schumines and S-Mines over there.

02:23   Second wave is gone.

02:33   Third wave is gone.

02:40   Fourth wave gone.

02:41   Whole outfit is over. Stewart is on his way to Alligators.

It had been a complete success and 2nd Battalion had only lost two boats to hostile artillery fire.

2nd Battalion fanned out beyond the dyke and while Company G headed north towards the locks at the mouth of the Lippe Canal, the rest of the Battalion cleared a group of farmhouses overlooking the crossing site to the south. Many Germans were taken by surprise and an hour after the first soldier had stepped on the east bank of the Rhine, Lieutenant Colonel McCown was able to report that his first objective had been secured; opposition had been negligible.

1st Battalion led 117th Regiment's assault opposite Ork in the centre of 30th Division's sector while 3rd Battalion helped to carry the storm boats to the water's edge. From the moment the first wave boats hit the water, radio reports gave Colonel Walter M Johnson a running commentary as the operation unfolded:

02:10   *1st Battalion informs that initial wave has reached east bank of Rhine and second wave has jumped off.*

02:37   *1st Battalion report right platoon of Company B has cleared first obstacle (dyke) and Company is reorganising to proceed as planned.*

02:38   *1st Battalion CO reports all his Battalion has completed crossing of the Rhine River and are now reorganising to proceed as planned.*

After reaching the top of the dyke, Company B worked its way south along the dyke clearing German outposts covering Ork and by 03:30 hours 1st Battalion was moving towards the hamlet where the garrison was sheltering from the American barrage. 1st Battalion moved forward as soon as the artillery increased their range and at 05:00 hours Colonel Johnson was pleased to hear that Objective Judy had been taken with minimal casualties. One hundred and fifty prisoners had been taken and as one company commander later commented "there was no real fight to it, the artillery had done the job for us".

The bend in the Rhine on 120th Regiment's front meant that Colonel Branner P Purdue planned to send two companies across at the same time. Company G would cross on the left, clearing the curve in the river, before advancing over the two dykes to assault objectives north of Mehrum. Meanwhile, Company F would make its assault 1,000 metres upstream, attacking the southern end of the village.

Despite the extra number of men and boats entering the water, the Beachmasters made sure that both companies hit the water on time. As the minutes ticked by Colonel Branner P Purdue was pleased to hear that men had reached the far bank in both sectors; it seemed that everything was going to plan. As the GIs swarmed ashore, the German artillery responded with indirect fire, shooting at pre-planned points with little effect.

One German artillery observer captured on the dyke overlooking Mehrum, pointed out this battery had been ordered to only fire five rounds a day and stockpile shells ready for the forthcoming assault. The plan to shell the American soldiers as soon as they hit the beach fell foul of the Allied bombardment; shellfire severed the telephone link to the battery and the observer had been captured before communications were restored.

Thirteen minutes after H-hour, Colonel Purdue was pleased to hear that Company F had secured the first dyke. Captain John Jacobsen's crossed the second dyke only to come under fire from the outskirts of Mehrum. As soon as the machine-gun platoon had silenced the German bunker, the rest of the company charged down the embankment into the village. A second enemy machine gun opened fire on the mortar platoon as it moved forward but the crew surrendered following a burst of fire from Sergeant Sellers BAR; a second rifle pit was captured a few minutes later bringing Sellers' haul of prisoners to twenty-two. The rest of Jacobsen's men moved quickly into the village.

As Company F stormed the southern end of Mehrum, Company G was experiencing difficulties crossing the river downstream of the village. Captain Charles W Moncrieff's men were supposed to capture Objective Bill, a bridge over the Momm Stream north-west of the village, but hardly any of the

Assault boats and Alligators begin to ply their trade on the river, ferrying men and equipment through the smokescreen.

boats had reached the assigned landing point. The curvature of the river was disorientating and some pilots accidentally steered back towards the friendly shore without realising. In the confusion of smoke and noise the GIs were met by the next wave of soldiers as they charged ashore. Other boats mistook a sandbar in the middle of the river for the far shore and returned for their next load, leaving the men stranded midstream for some time.

Although Captain Moncrieff was amongst the missing, Lieutenants Arthur Saal–field and Charles Pike rounded up two groups of stragglers and headed for their objective. Pike's group stumbled on an enemy post as they headed along the dyke and the young officer was killed in the fight that followed leaving Private Earl A Otto to lead the group to the rendezvous point. As the minutes ticked by Lieutenant Saalfield waited in vain for the rest of his company to arrive and eventually decided to attack Objective Bill with the men to hand. As the group moved inland over the winter dyke, scouts reported that a patrol was guarding the bridge and if they did not move quickly Saalfield's small group might not be able to take their objective. With no time to spare the GIs broke into a run, overpowering the guards before they realised what was happening.

As the group reorganised, Sergeant Boures reconnoitered the road into Mehrum and found a German outpost at Check Point Able 8, a crossroads on the northern outskirts. Charging forward, firing his BAR from the hip, Boures welcomed the sight of the four guards raising their hands; they had not fired a shot. With his first objective secure, Lieutenant Saalfield led the depleted Company G north-east across the fields towards Objective Abner, the hamlet of Wurm-Gotterswick.

Company E had crossed the river close behind Company F and, while Jacobson's men engaged the German troops holding the east end of Mehrum, moved west along the dyke to attack the opposite end of the village. The pincer movement had immediate results and as GIs closed in from both sides, the garrison surrendered leaving Objective Betty in Lieutenant Colonel Cantey's hands. Despite the initial setbacks 2nd Battalion had taken all of its objectives and Colonel Purdue was able to order 3rd Battalion across the river.

All along the line resistance had been lighter than expected as the Germans reeled in the face of the crushing bombardment

Lorries carry LCM landing craft to the river so they could start ferrying tanks across.

Powered assault boats guide a raft and its tank over the Rhine.

and the well-executed attack by the assault battalions, however, 30th Division faced a race against the clock and as the first three battalions consolidated their objectives, the next phase of Operation FLASHPOINT was underway on the west bank. Beach masters guided men to the embarkation points as the second wave of Battalions moved forward and wave after wave of men crossed the river in a mixture of storm boats, assault boats and LCVTs. Meanwhile, armour was on its way to support General Hobbs' troops. Amphibious DD tanks entered the water and began to swim across the Rhine while huge lorries carried landing craft to the shore and engineers brought rafts to the water's edge ready to take Light M24 Chaffee tanks across. Meanwhile, 1153rd Engineer Combat Group was busy moving pontoons towards the river ready to begin work.

The Second Phase

Having cleared the dyke and the first line of villages on the far shore, it was time to send the second wave of battalions across the river and link up the three small bridgeheads. On 30th Division's left flank the second phase involved a coordinated attack by 119th Regiment and 117th Regiment against Spellen, large village overlooking the centre of General Hobbs' front. Although 2nd Battalion had captured the locks at the mouth of the Lippe Canal on 119th Regiment's left flank with ease, the plan was beginning to unravel in front of Spellen. 3rd Battalion had crossed on time and had assembled in woods ready to assault the north end of the village, Objective Patty, as early as 04:35 hours. However, although Lieutenant Colonel Stewart was ready, no one else was.

In 117th Regiment's sector, 2nd Battalion's crossing had been a fiasco. Several assault craft had failed to start and the occupants had to wait until other boats became available, meanwhile, many of the pilots became disorientated out on the river and deposited their load of men in the wrong place. For the second time that morning GIs milled around on the shoreline while their officers tried to herd them to their assembly point. It would take some time to round up the stragglers; time General Hobbs did not have. To make matters worse the riverbank in 119th Regiment's sector was too soft for tanks and the landing craft pilots had been ordered to take the M24 Chaffee's upstream into 117th Regiment's sector.

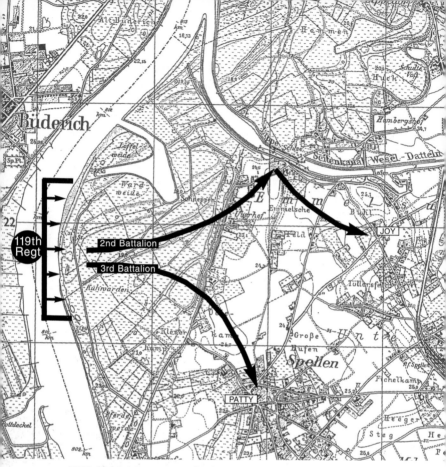

119th Regiment secures Spellen and 30th Division's left flank along the Lippe Canal.

After waiting for an hour for news from 117th Regiment, Colonel Baker felt he could wait no longer; 3rd Battalion would have to attack Spellen on its own. Moving quickly across the fields towards Objective Patty, Colonel Stewart's men made good progress to begin with, penetrating the outskirts of the village before the alarm was raised. However, as the Germans tumbled out of their shelters the GIs were soon pinned down, unable to advance any further. They needed help from the south.

Two hours passed before 2nd Battalion recovered from its disaster on the riverbank by which time a company of amphibious Duplex-Drive tanks from 743rd Tank Battalion had arrived in 117th Regiment's sector. At 06:30, two hours later than planned, the second phase of 117th Regiment's advance was underway and as Shermans and infantry moved out of Ork heading into the southern outskirts of Spellen, codenamed Polly, German resistance collapsed. Although the 200 strong garrison had been able to hold its own against one attack, the arrival of American troops to their rear broke their morale. With dawn approaching the village had been cleared just in time and as the prisoners were herded towards the river, Colonels Baker and Johnson ordered their reserve battalions across the Rhine for the next phase of the operation, the advance to the Wesel–Dinslaken railway line.

On 119th Regiment's front 2nd Battalion had started to move forward at first light and was already closing in on Objective Joy, two bridges on the division's left flank, when aerial reconnaissance planes reported a lot of enemy activity on the far side of the railway. 2nd Battalion alone faced a company of German engineers armed with four machine guns and tanks had been seen roaming beyond the railway. It looked as though 30th Division advance was about to come to an end. Only one company of 743rd Battalion's DD tanks had managed to reach

117th Regiment captures Ork before moving north towards Spellen.

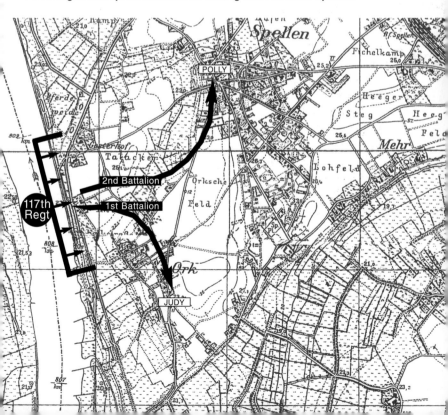

Prisoners start to pour in as XVI Corps expands its bridgehead.

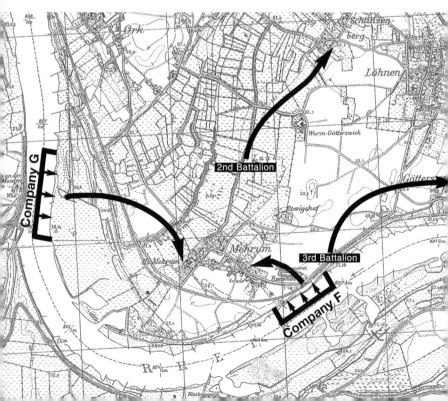

120th Regiment's two-pronged assault on Mehrum.

the east bank and Colonel Duncan was expecting to have to wait until noon before his M24 Chaffee tanks would begin to cross. The rest of 119th Regiment and 117th Regiment faced a tough battle for the underpasses.

While the rest of the division had been focused on Spellen, Colonel Purdue was having his own problems getting the rest of 120th Regiment across the river. While 2nd Battalion advanced north-east from Mehrum towards Schanzenberg, codenamed Blondie, 3rd Battalion was supposed to advance along the riverbank towards Objective Daisy, Götterswickerhamm. However, yet again moving troops across the Rhine was proving to be a problem and Major Chris Mac McCullough's men were still stranded on the wrong side of the river.

3rd Battalion was in position on the west bank on time but as the minutes ticked by neither the LCVPs nor the Alligators designated to ferry the battalion across the river had arrived. The LCVPs had been launched downstream and missed the crossing point as they sailed up river. Frantic radio calls eventually located the missing boats but as they sailed back to the rendezvous point, Major McCullough was informed that the Alligators had also failed to arrive. Although the Alligator officers had been shown the route to the loading point and tapes marked the cross-country sections, the column had managed to miss a turning in the darkness. They reached 3rd Battalion an hour later than planned and found Major McCullough's men operating a shuttle service with assault boats as they tried to cross the river to join the rest of the Regiment.

There were more problems ahead. One of the Alligators carrying Company K sank midstream, leaving the unfortunate platoon to swim the rest of the way. The rest of the Company was scattered along a wide stretch of the shore and it was some time before the disheveled GIs found their way to the assembly area where Captain Harold Plummer was waiting.

The LCVPs designated to carry Company L's leading platoon turned up late and it was some time later before Captain Earl Wilson found the demarcation point. Company M and Company L landed together on the far bank but disaster struck as the men organised on the move and advanced over the dyke in close formation; a shell hit Company M's machine-gun platoon killing two and injuring another nine, including the platoon officer. Company I also experienced difficulties as it brought up

Soldiers file down to the water's edge to wait their turn to cross.

the rear. One LCVP suffered engine failure midstream but after Lieutenant John DePutron had ordered his platoon to abandon ship the motor fired into life. The crew headed back to the shore to pick up another load, leaving twenty-five men to swim to safety.

The succession of delays had set Colonel Purdue's schedule back by two hours and while Major McCullough waited for the rest of his Battalion to assemble, Company K headed east towards Götterswickerhamm. As Captain Plummer's men moved along the riverbank, anti-tank guns and machine guns opened fire from the outskirts of the village but while the rest of Company K dived for cover, two individuals ran forward. Private Campbell sprinted ahead of his platoon shooting as he ran towards a machine-gun post shouting surrender; seven Germans complied with his request. On 1st Platoon's front Sergeant Owens ran towards a machine-gun nest, while his men gave covering fire. The sergeant jumped into the German trench and had killed an officer and two men before the rest surrendered. With the two outposts silenced, the rest of Company K moved forward to clear the anti-tank gun positions.

Moving into the heart of the village, Plummer's men found Germans holding many of the buildings and as they worked forward, clearing the houses with bayonets and grenades, it became clear that the garrison intended to make a stand. For three hours thirty soldiers, supported by an anti-tank gun and two machine guns prevented Company K advancing down the main street. It looked as though 3rd Battalion's advance had come to a halt until one individual found a way forward. Private Waldron ran and crawled forward while the rest of his platoon gave covering fire and eventually reached a commanding position overlooking a roadblock. As soon as he opened fire, the men behind the barricade took cover and the rest of Waldron's platoon charged down the street to clear the obstacle.

Although the main line of resistance in Götterswickerhamm had fallen, groups of soldiers continued to fight on as Plummer's men worked their way towards the eastern edge of the village. When a machine gun opened fire from an upper storey window overlooking the main street, Private Nyland ran forward dodging bullets and burst into the house; two grenades thrown up the stairs convinced the two men to surrender their weapon.

As Company K worked its way through the town of Götterswickerhamm, prisoners reported that SS men were leading the defence at the eastern of the village, explaining why the rest of the German soldiers in the town continued to fight on. By mid-morning Company K was exhausted and as soon as Company I was ready, Major McCullough ordered Captain Charles Shaw forward to regain the initiative. The added firepower turned the tide of the battle for Götterswickerhamm and once the SS leader had been killed, resistance ended; within a short time Company I had rounded up over 100 prisoners.

As 3rd Battalion pushed east a machine gun opened fire on Company L as it approached Möllen, codenamed Ruth. Several GIs were wounded but as the rest of the Company scrambled for cover Technician Pelkey ran forward to cut the barbed wire fence protecting the outpost while his squad gave covering fire. As soon as Pelkey was through the entanglement the GIs charged, killing all four Germans inside the emplacement.

Although Company L bypassed a second outpost, the machine-gun team inside caught Company K in the open as they followed. After four men had been wounded trying to reach the bunker, Sergeant Santella decided to take charge of the situation; Lieutenant Thomas Voorhis later recalled how his Sergeant risked his life to take on the German position:

> *Sergeant Donald J Santella, assistant squad leader, perceiving the enemy troops were holding up the advance, and acting entirely on his own initiative, carefully advanced about fifty yards over open terrain to a position from which he could effectively fire rifle grenades on the defending forces. When Sergeant Santella reached a woodpile about fifteen yards from the entrenchment he took careful aim and fired a rifle grenade into the trench, killing the officer in charge and wounding five others, one of whom subsequently died of his wounds. During the time Sergeant Santella was preparing to fire the enemy threw two hand grenades at him, neither of which wounded him despite the fact that they were thrown from such a short distance and at such a plain target. Immediately after he had fired his grenade Sergeant Santella ran from his position and jumped into the entrenchment with such speed that he succeeded in forcing the surrender of the remainder of the enemy force, taking ten prisoners.*

While Company K covered the Battalion's northern flank, Captain Earl F Wilson reported that Company L were pinned in front of log bunkers along the riverbank. Major McCullough had no option but to deploy his reserve, Company I, if he was to enter Möllen. Although rifle and machine-gun fire greeted Captain Shaw's men as they advanced, Lieutenant Peters managed to push his platoon across the railway. Before long the rest of the company followed, clearing the underpass on the outskirts of Möllen and entered the village. The most dangerous part of the attack had been completed but the Germans were far from beaten. Before long all three of Major McCullough's companies were embroiled in the battle for Möllen; street fighting would continue throughout the morning and well into the afternoon.

While 3rd Battalion fought for Möllen, 2nd Battalion had been advancing on the Regiment's left flank and when Captain Moncrieff finally caught up his Company at Wurm-Gotterswick he found Lieutenant Saalfield eager to press on to the Company G's final objective, Schanzenberg. He volunteered to take forty men forward while ten stayed behind with Captain Moncrieff to wait for Company E to arrive.

In the original orders Moncrieff planned to deploy the entire

Navy personnel were drafted in with their landing craft to help ferry heavy equipment across the Rhine.

company against the hamlet but Saalfield's small group pressed on undaunted, reaching the houses in spite of small-arms fire. Spreading out to give the impression that there were far more than forty men, Saalfield's GIs persevered and although progress was slow, three hours later the Germans withdrew from the village. On hearing the news, Lieutenant Colonel Cantey ordered Company E and Company F forward so the Battalion could prepare to attack Löhnen codenamed West Lana. It was 2nd Battalion's final objective.

In spite of the problems along 30th Division's front, by mid-morning the *Old Hickories* had seized all their initial objectives and were positioned to attack the two railway lines crossing north to south. The first railway ran along an embankment right across the division's front, posing a serious obstacle to tanks and other vehicles and both 119th Regiment and 117th Regiment would have to capture underpasses before their armour could advance to the next railway and a second embankment. Although General Hobbs realised he needed to coordinate all his supporting arms before attacking, there was a glimmer of hope on the division's right flank. Only the first railway ran on top of an embankment, and 120th Regiment already had men across, fighting in Möllen and anxious for armoured support.

The question was, could the tanks reach his men in time to make a breakthrough?

At first light a thick smokescreen engulfed the river as the storm boats, assault boats and LCVPs ferried the final wave of battalions across the river. As they assembled on the far bank engineers began to build a Bailey Bridge in 120th Regiment's sector. The sooner 30th Division removed its dependency from the Navy the better, and before long the need for a bridge was brought home to Major General Hobbs; the LCMs detailed to carry the tank destroyers across had been delayed, McCullough's men would have to fight on alone in Möllen for some time.

79th Division crosses the river

As 30th Division charged across the Rhine, 79th Division's GIs lined up on the west bank of the river near Rheinberg waiting for their turn to cross. The curvature of the river meant that the assault battalions would cross an hour later, at 03:00 hours, in the hope that the two divisions would meet near Möllen at the earliest opportunity. It also meant that the Germans on the far bank faced two hours of shelling rather than one.

General Wyche had chosen to make the crossing with two regiments side-by-side, each regiment using one battalion in the assault. They would attack on narrow fronts and the plan was to advance quickly behind the supporting barrage, bypassing centres of resistance. The deeper the assault troops could advance before dawn, the greater chance there was of disrupting the enemy's plans. If the leading battalions could cross the dyke and the railway beyond before first light, the reserve battalions would be able to mop up behind them. General Wyche had decided to mix storm boats and the larger assault boats to get the maximum number of men across the river in the shortest possible time; the slower craft would be given a head start so that every boat hit the far shore at roughly the same time.

315th Regiment, led by Colonel Andrew Schriner, would embark on A Beach on the division's left flank and land south of Stapp hamlet. The assault battalion would turn north-east towards Eppinghoven, linking up with 120th Regiment near Möllen. On the right, Colonel Edwin Van Bibber's 313th Regiment would leave B Beach $\frac{1}{2}$ mile north of Orsoy and land in front of Walsum. Moving quickly past the village, the assault battalion would advance to Vierlinden before forming a defensive flank along the Neue-Ernscher Canal; the second battalion across the river would take Walsum. 314th Regiment would bring up the rear, crossing via both beaches as soon as the far bank was cleared. Colonel Warren Robinson's men would then advance straight towards Dinslaken and seize the town.

Patrols believed that the Hamburg Division held the opposite dyke in strength, relying on sentries near the water's edge to warn of an attack. Anti-tank guns and anti-aircraft guns were

79th Division's crossing and rapid advance towards Dinslaken.

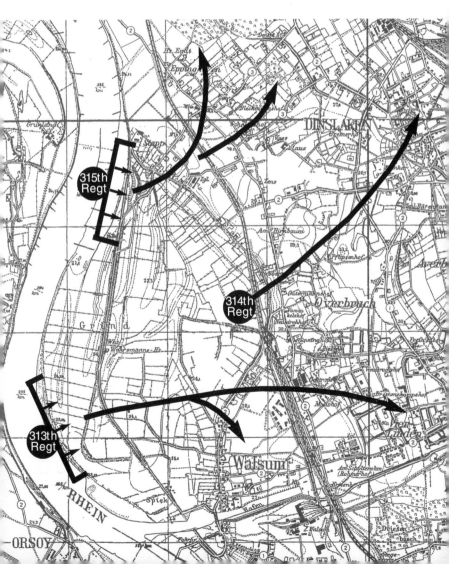

dug in upstream of the Neue-Ernscher Canal with commanding fields of fire of the front face of the dyke. A railway embankment just beyond the flood embankment was another likely line of defence and local reserves were garrisoned in the villages along the railway. The form of defence carried out by the Germans, Major Schwartz's *588th Regiment*, opposite 313th Regiment, was typical. *Leutnant* Weiss' company held the dyke while two more were dug in along the railway, the men of the fourth company were split between the other three. Despite his attempts to develop a coordinated defensive position, Schwartz could only count on two horse drawn 75mm anti-tank guns for support.

As zero hour approached the assault troops groped their way down to the water's edge carrying their boats while the barrage of shells hitting the far shore reached a crescendo. Tank destroyers and machine guns, positioned south of the crossing site, joined in the tremendous artillery barrage, in the hope of drawing the Germans' attention away from the beaches. At exactly 03:00 hours the first wave of boats, entered the water as .50 and .30 machine guns opened fire, drowning out the sound of the motors. The assault was on.

The men in the first wave braced themselves as the boats roared across the water, waiting in anticipation for the expected rattle of machine-gun fire from the German outposts. The

Another platoon of GIs makes the crossing.

artillery lifted their fire to the dyke as the boats approached the shore line and as the first wave of men jumped onto the east shore, it was obvious that the guns had paved the way with style. Only a few German sentries opened fire and they were overrun in the first few minutes. The lack of enemy artillery and mortar rounds landing in 79th Division's area indicated that the extra hour of shelling had completely shattered the German defences.

The main problem for Major General Wyche's men was navigation. By 03:00 hours a mist had started to form along the river and it thickened into a dense fog as it mingled with the smokescreen. Many crews became disorientated in the fog and failed to find their assigned landing points. Some coxswains had lost all sense of direction and returned to the west bank. The confusion caused some embarrassment to the men of one boat as they raced ashore and deployed into skirmish line expecting to encounter German sentries; the eager GIs were surprised to meet the next wave of friendly soldiers coming down to the water's edge.

Fortunately, the German reaction had been minimal and the first wave of troops crossed the dyke on time, moments after many of the howitzers and tank destroyers on the west bank had switched to the section of the dyke south of 79th Division's front to suppress the German guns there.

The initial, and most dangerous, stage of Operation FLASHPOINT had been completed (XVI Corps had only suffered sixteen casualties through enemy action crossing the Rhine) but General Simpson was under no illusions; now that the Germans knew where his men had crossed, the fighting was about to intensify.

Moving fast, the two assault battalions advanced towards their final objectives with the help of an unusual source of extra firepower; each battalion had 200 captured German *Panzerfausts* (single-shot bazookas), ideal weapons for dealing with emplacements and bunkers. On 315th Regiment's front 2nd Battalion headed north-east into Warnung Woods looking to open the road into Dinslaken while 1st Battalion advanced north along the riverbank into the village of Am Stapp. German resistance was sporadic, the attack had taken them completely by surprise, and Schriner's men were digging in on both objectives before daylight. 313th Regiment was equally successful on the southern flank. 2nd Battalion bypassed enemy strongpoints and drove deep into the German lines passing the phase lines, codenamed Kesselring, Quisling and Tojo, on schedule. The battalion entered Vierlinden before the alarm had been raised and 1st Battalion followed close behind, entering Walsum at the same time. The artillery had shattered the Germans' will to fight and by dawn Colonel Van Bibber was able to report that both villages had been cleared; it meant that 79th Division's flank along the Neue-Ernscher Canal was secure.

At daylight 89th Chemical Mortar Battalion opened fire with its 4.2 inch mortars, firing white phosphorous shells into the area south of the canal and before long the individual clouds of white smoke fused together to cover the division's flank with a thin haze. The effect was just what was needed, and while 313th Regiment dug in under cover of the smokescreen, the rest of 79th Division prepared to attack Dinslaken.

314th Regiment received the order to cross as soon as the plumes of smoke screened the crossing sites and assault boats and landing craft worked throughout the morning to shuttle all three battalions over the river. Sporadic artillery and mortar fire was the only response from the Hamburg Division but the shells hit nothing and by 13:00 hours 314th Regiment was at its assembly area on the east bank and ready to advance. 79th Division's operation had been a complete success.

Rafts operated a ferry service across the river during the early stages of the operation while engineers started work on a treadway bridge.
111-SC-203293

Chapter 5

17TH AIRBORNE DIVISION –
Thunder From Heaven

As 21 Army Group established itself on the east bank of the Rhine, preparations for the airborne landings north of Wesel were underway on airfields across France and England. Thousands of paratroopers and glider men of the 17th Airborne Division had begun to congregate alongside the lines of C-47 Dakotas and gliders parked nose to tail on runways around

Paratroopers help each other strap on their heavy load of equipment.
111-SC-203326

Paris while it was still dark. Although Major General Miley's men had seen action the previous December, during the later stages of the Battle of the Bulge, Operation VARSITY was the moment they had trained for; the young soldiers would be able to test their skills as airborne troops for the first time. The adjutant of the 507th Parachute Regiment summed up the mixture of apprehension and anticipation experienced by the paratroopers as they waited to take off:

24 March, dawn breaking clearly, found the 507th Combat Team gathered around their C-47s in crisp cool air that foretold the advent of a beautiful day – beautiful from an aesthetic standpoint and beautiful from a flying and tactical standpoint. In short, it was a good day for a jump. Groups were milling around their respective planes, checking last minute items of equipment, making last minute adjustments to parachutes and giving final bits of advice and instructions. The air was pregnant with tense expectancy, strained jokes cracked, they were greeted with brittle laughter and wisecracks bantered. This was it – D-Day – the biggest D-Day, the day for which countless hours of sweaty toil had been shaping us. The 507th was this day to take part in a jump into the Fatherland itself. The acme of every paratroopers dream was becoming an actuality.

By daybreak the two Parachute Regiments, 507th and 513th, were loading. The paratroopers pushed and cajoled each other into the cramped fuselages, sixteen men to a plane, as they struggled to carry their heavy loads (in some cases equivalent to the man's bodyweight). Platoons had previously occupied entire planes, keeping command integrity in the air, however once on the ground the men were scattered far and wide and this time the Airborne planners had decided on a different concept. The Dakota pilots would fly close together in patterns of three, (called the Victory V) and while one platoon occupied the front third of all three planes, a second platoon sat in the mid section while a third platoon filled the rear section. Training had shown that grouping in this manner allowed platoons to jump in a third of the time, greatly increasing the chances of regrouping on the ground.

Meanwhile, 194th Glider Regiment was loading its equipment and men into their CG-4A Waco gliders at three different airfields. Over 150 Dakotas were lined up along the runways ready to haul the gliders into the air on double tows,

Fully laden paratroopers climb on board their transport plane.
111-SC-253924

Waco gliders were capable of carrying heavy loads into battle, including jeeps and anti-tank guns.

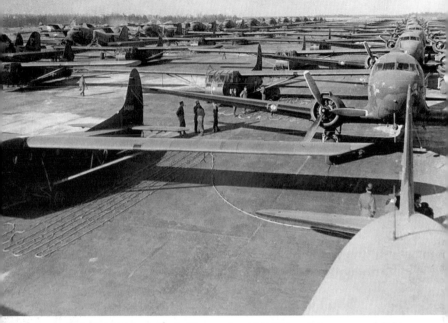

Dakota transport planes line up alongside Waco gliders on an airfield near Paris; each Dakota towed two gliders filled with men and equipment for 194th Regiment. 111-SC-203292

another new idea designed to reduce the number of planes required by the Glider Regiment. Once over the Rhine the Dakota pilots would cast off their cargo, leaving it to the glider pilots to steer the cumbersome Wacos as they glided towards the ground. In the past the paratroopers had gone into action first and the gliders had followed, gliding onto secured landing zones (except for small coup d'état landings). For the first time in airborne history an entire glider brigade was going to land on enemy held territory, territory covered with anti-aircraft guns; Operation VARSITY was going to be a trial by fire for the men of 194th Glider Regiment.

The first planes were airborne by 07:30 hours and began to circle as wave after wave of Dakotas joined the gathering formations over the French countryside. It took an hour to assemble the vast armadas of transport planes and gliders:

Off to the vicinity of Brussels for a rendezvous with the Glider trains and the 6th British Airborne column, a change of direction, off towards the Rhine and a destiny beyond prediction.

194th Glider Regiment takes to the skies.

A glider pilot waits for the moment when his Waco will be cast off, leaving him to guide the cumbersome machine to the ground.
111-SC-202650

Anxious faces on board a glider. The men have axes at the ready in case the glider doors jam when they hit the ground. 111-SC-203298

Looking out as far as one could see stretched the biggest sky armada ever assembled, literally thousands of aircraft, gliders, C-47s, C-46s and fighter cover of all sorts. A sight for those who dared the blue unknown, some successfully, others to dwell in posterity, as men who met the challenge, accepted it, and took the lot it dealt without a murmur.

Although there had been larger airdrops in Normandy and Holland the previous year, the men and equipment had been flown to the drop zones in several lifts; this time the two Airborne divisions would land in one continuous drop, requiring the largest airborne armada ever put in the air at one time by the Allies. 1,696 transport planes and 1,348 gliders carrying 21,860 men headed for Brussels followed by 240 Liberator bombers carrying supplies for the division. The armada was protected by 889 fighter planes and a further 2,153 fighters patrolled the skies across the Continent, keeping the

Luftwaffe at bay. A mass of bombing raids coincided with the airborne attack and 821 medium and 2,596 heavy bombers hit airfields, bridges and marshalling yards across Germany. With so much Allied air activity over the continent, German pilots were given little opportunity to interfere in Operation VARSITY.

As the two formations, each nine planes wide, united over the Belgian capital and headed north-east, the paratroopers and glider troops stared at the landscape below, wondering what lay in store for them. One Regimental diarist recorded his thoughts as the huge armada passed over Germany:

> *The panorama from the plane showed a beautiful European landscape, colourfully roofed hamlets, large industrial centres and cosy little farms. War seemed very far away. The twenty-minute warning was sounded; the men stood up and hooked up. It won't be long now. Suddenly as if a curtain had been lifted, the view changed. The countryside was beaten and grey, barren, a graveyard look. The smoke of battle wafted drearily upward, shots could be heard; we were approaching the Rhine.*

As hundreds of transport planes flew over the river the paratroopers inside made the final checks on their equipment, each confirming that the man in front was correctly hooked up and ready to jump. The glider men had no need for such checks. There was no room for parachutes in the cramped fuselages of their gliders; all they could do was brace their bodies and pray for a good landing. As the C47s cast off their tows and turned for home, the pilots took over control of their huge gliders and looked for a landing zone below.

Dozens of artillery batteries had spent the past hour shelling likely targets on 17th Airborne Division's drop zones and objectives, paving the way for the assault from the air, but as the planes approached the guns fell silent to avoid unnecessary casualties from friendly fire. The Germans showed no hesitation in targeting the planes flying overhead; every anti-aircraft gun in range, from 20mm up to 120mm calibre, pointed skywards and began to engage the approaching armada.

Tension on board the Dakotas and Wacos mounted as the pilots steered a steady course through the wall of flak. Men winced as shrapnel tore through the sky, sending planes hurtling towards the ground in flames. There was no turning back now; the final phase of Operation VARSITY was under way.

The battle for the drop zones

507th Regiment led 17th Airborne Division over the Rhine seven minutes earlier than expected, supposedly heading for Drop Zone W at the southeast tip of the Diersfordt Forest. The Regimental Diary describes the final moments in one of the Dakotas carrying part of the headquarters' company as it flew over the Rhine at 1,000 feet:

For an instance the big river flashed beneath us, ack-ack and anti-aircraft fire rattled and cracked about us. The green light. GO! A rush of air, a jerk, a look around and a jolt. Colonel Edson D Raff, commanding officer, was the first paratrooper to land on Heinie soil; we were on the ground and the 507th Parachute Regiment had been committed. [Heinie was the slang word for German beer.]

For thirty minutes wave after wave of planes flew over Wesel as thousands of paratroopers jumped out of their planes hoping to

A transport plane falls from the skies like a burning comet.

Manning a 105mm Flak gun.

Paratroopers brace themselves for the jump as flak bursts around their aircraft.

Go! Go! Go! Heavily laden paratroopers jump from their C46 Commando Transport plane. 111-SC-203393

Thunder from Heaven; thousands of paratroopers drop from the skies north and west of Wesel, many of them onto the wrong drop zones.

General Miley's men had to fight from the moment they hit the ground.

reach the ground safely; many would not.

The Dakotas carrying 507th Regiment's 1st Battalion misjudged their approach and dropped the battalion one mile west of Drop Zone W, on the wrong side of the Diersfordt Forest. The pilots of three planes carrying portions of the Regimental Headquarters were equally confused and dropped their loads to the north-west of the intended target. It was an inauspicious start for 17th Airborne Division; the question was how long would it take the paratroopers to assemble on their objectives? As the paratroopers drifted down, machine guns joined the aerial barrage and for a time it looked as though the decision to drop men on top of the German anti-aircraft batteries was going to fail:

> Several planes were destroyed in the air. At least one plane crashed on the DZ with all on board. Other planes burned after dropping their personnel. In some, the aircraft crew escaped; in others, charred bodies gave stark testimony to the devotion to duty performed by good soldiers. Some parachutists were hit during their descent; some were killed in their harness on the ground and others while scrambling off the field.

507th Regiment's original plan had been for 1st Battalion to form a defensive perimeter around Drop Zone W, creating a safe haven for the Regimental Headquarters and artillery. 2nd Battalion was to land next and immediately head west through the Diersfordt Forest, establishing a line on the far side of the

A 37mm Flak 43 in action.

507th Regiment was scattered either side of Diersfordt Forest and many paratroopers lost their lives before they reached the ground.

woods. 3rd Battalion would follow through the forest, moving north-west to take up positions on the right of 2nd Battalion and eventually link up with 513th Parachute Regiment, north-east of Diersfordt Castle. Having established a secure line along the perimeter of the forest, 3rd Battalion was to capture the castle

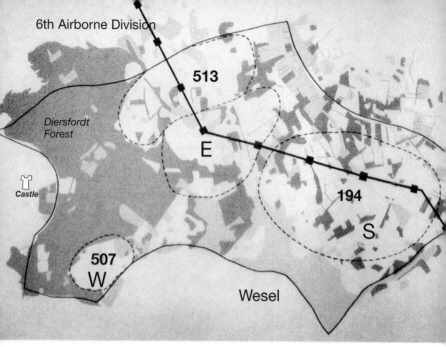

17th Airborne Division's drop zones north of Wesel.

clearing the way forward for the men of the 15th (Scottish) Division approaching from the Xanten bridgehead. However, plans meant nothing to the men who had landed in the wrong area and for the first few hectic minutes Colonel Raff's men fought where they landed, opening fire as soon as they hit the ground, while struggling to get rid of their parachutes. Fortunately, the German gun crews were equally disorganised, thrown into confusion as paratroopers landed in and around their gun positions.

1st Battalion's report has few details to tell about the first few moments after landing but the Battalion diarist accurately sums up the confused nature of the landings north and south of Diersfordt Castle:

> *Naturally all cannot be told, much will never be told. Individual acts of heroism, which are a natural part of the initial phase of an airborne landing, will go unsung. Many stories of heroic deeds will be repeated wherever two or more airborne soldiers meet for years to come. Much we will never know, as dead men tell no tales.*

Colonel Raff took charge of a large group of 1st Battalion north of the castle, gathering together around 200 men. Realising that he was nowhere near his expected landing zone, Raff directed his men to seek shelter in the woods until he had found his bearings. Shooting from the hip as they ran towards the trees, the paratroopers silenced five machine-gun posts along the edge of the wood and deployed under the thick canopy, finding a number of hidden field guns. The crews were quickly rounded up. Next on Raff's agenda was a battery of five 150mm howitzers stationed close by and before long the artillery men had been taken prisoner and the guns disabled; they would no longer shell the British bridgehead at Xanten. By now Raff's group had killed or wounded over 100 German soldiers and taken nearly 300 prisoners, including a colonel.

Having cleared his immediate area and found his bearings, Raff decided to locate the rest of his Regiment. A second group had gathered south of Diersforsdt Castle under 1st Battalion's commanding officer, Major Paul Smith. The paratroopers had headed for cover, engaging infantry, machine-gun posts and anti-aircraft crews in the woods east of the castle. Once again the Germans had been taken by surprise by the airdrop, failing to put up an organised resistance and within an hour of landing Smith's men were firmly established in Diersfordt Forest.

As Colonel Raff advanced south to locate Major Smith's position, it had become obvious that the castle was heavily fortified and machine guns, mortars and anti-aircraft guns in the grounds increased their fire as the paratroopers worked their way through the woods. As Major Smith's group approached from the south-east, two *Panzer V* tanks emerged from the courtyard and headed along the driveway towards the paratroopers. Men dived for cover as the tanks approached with guns blazing but one enterprising paratrooper disabled one passing tank with an anti-tank grenade. The crew of a 57mm recoilless gun (a new hand-held anti-tank weapon that had only been issued to the division a few days before) targeted the second *Panzer*, knocking it out as it drew close. As the rest of Raff's men looked on in amazement, the two tank crews bailed out of their stricken vehicles and surrendered. The recoilless weapons packed a powerful punch and for the first time paratroopers could hold their own against armour.

As the threat from the castle diminished, the two groups continued working their way through the undergrowth towards each other and by noon 1st Battalion had cleared both 2nd and

3rd Battalion's objectives; the western edge of Diersfordt Forest was secure.

While 1st Battalion struggled to find its bearings around Diersfordt Castle, pilots flying 2nd Battalion's Dakotas had more luck and dropped their loads above Drop Zone W. 1st Battalion was supposed to have cleared Flürener Feld but their miss drop to the left meant that the drop zone was still held by German troops. As the paratroopers drifted towards the ground, machine guns and rifles opened fire from the woods and houses on and around the clearing, killing and wounded many in the air. 2nd Battalion fought from the moment they hit the ground, pulling off their harnesses as they fired back:

> During this period the enemy seemed to be completely disorganised. Some gave up without a fight, although they had the advantage of prepared positions, combined with the fact that a paratrooper is comparatively helpless for some seconds after he hits the ground. Others fought hard and ferociously, inflicting casualties on the drop zone and in engagements immediately beyond the drop zone. Our positions were beginning to take form, but as yet the Germans did not seem to be maintaining any line.

The initial shock caused by the landing had worked in 2nd Battalion's favour and by the time the planes carrying 3rd

A paratrooper struggles to remove his harness while the rest of his platoon round up prisoners in the distance.

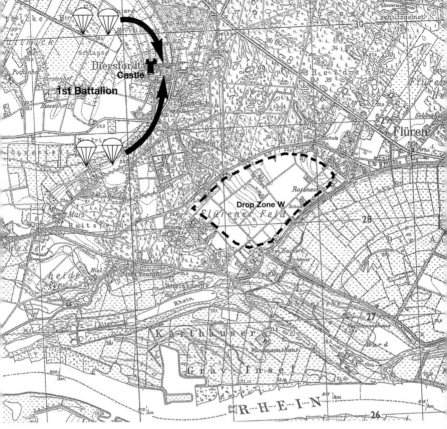

507th Parachute Regiment was scattered either side of the Diersfordt Forest.

Battalion were over the drop zone, many enemy positions around the perimeter of Flürener Feld had been taken.

Thirty minutes after the first men had landed on Drop Zone W the clearing had been secured and the two Battalions were ready to move out. A few light artillery pieces persisted in firing random shots at the drop zone but after leaving a screen of paratroopers to maintain the Regiment's perimeter, 2nd and 3rd Battalion were heading towards their objectives.

By midday, Colonel Raff had still not heard anything from the rest of his Regiment and decided that he could wait no longer; Major Smith's men would have to attack the Regiment's final objective, Diersfordt Castle. As the weary paratroopers prepared to advance, patrols on the battalion's eastern perimeter sighted columns of troops moving through the woods. Anxious moments passed until it was possible to see

Paratroopers round up a group of German prisoners on the edge of Flürener Feld.

that the approaching soldiers had first aid packs strapped to the front of their helmets, one of the identifying marks of an American paratrooper. At long last the rest of the Regiment had arrived.

With his fresh troops on hand, Colonel Raff ordered 1st Battalion to set up a defensive cordon while 3rd Battalion prepared for the final assault:

Company A was left as a base upon which to manoeuvre and Company I started to make a flanking attack to the northeast. 3rd Battalion, after taking over the job, systematically took over the castle as ours, and the last bit of resistance, consisting of a large group of officers holding out in an isolated tower, was overcome that evening. This strongpoint yielded approximately 300 prisoners, amongst whom were several high-ranking officers, including two colonels, two Mark V [Panther] tanks destroyed and two captured.

Subsequent questioning identified the castle as an important headquarters in *LXXXVI Corps* chain of command and Company G had captured several of General Straube's staff along with a number of senior officers of 84th Division.

While 3rd Battalion attacked Diersfordt Castle, the rest of the Regiment set about securing their assigned perimeters. 1st Battalion headed east through the forest, mopping up the remaining enemy posts around Drop Zone W, while 2nd Battalion secured the southern tip of Diersfordt Forest. After a discouraging start, the men of 507th Parachute Regiment had proved their worth.

The Dakotas carrying 513th Regiment followed 507th Regiment across the Rhine and headed for the landing zones in the northern sector of 17th Airborne Division's objective. 1st Battalion would land first, engaging enemy positions on and around Drop Zone E, before forming a defensive perimeter around the Regimental Headquarters and artillery. 2nd Battalion would be dropped next and head west through the Diersfordt Forest alongside the British paratroopers of 6th Airborne Division to the north before tying in with 507th Parachute Regiment on the western edge of the forest. The Regiment's 3rd Battalion had been allocated the eastern sector

507th Regiment had secured the southern outskirts of Diersfordt Forest by noon.

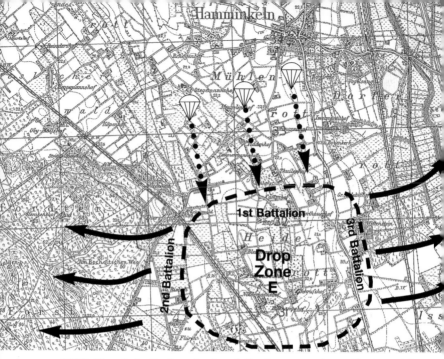

513th Parachute Regiment missed its drop zone but still cleared its objectives.

of the Regiment's zone and was expected to capture two minor bridges on the Issel Stream and link up with the British glider troops landing around Hamminkeln.

While 507th Regiment had suffered some confusion finding its drop zones, every one of the planes carrying 513th Regiment misjudged their flight paths as they came under heavy fire over the Rhine. By now the anti-aircraft crews were fully aware that an airborne landing was underway and showed the slow moving Dakotas no mercy as they flew low over Diersfordt Forest. The entire Regiment was dropped 2,500 metres north of Drop Zone E, in the area allocated to the 6th British Airborne Division. It would take some time before Colonel James Coutts and his Battalion COs realised what had happened; in the meantime his men would have to fight where they landed.

1st Battalion landed first and suffered heavy casualties from anti-aircraft and machine-gun fire before it hit the ground. The Battalion Adjutant, the Operations Sergeant and the Communications officer were all killed or seriously injured in the air, while the Commanding Officer and the S-3 Intelligence Officer both landed off target and were taken prisoner, (they

84

would be freed several hours later). The Assistant Communications Officer was also missing, he too would return to the battalion several days later.

Having lost a greater portion of the Headquarters Company the situation was looking bleak for the 1st Battalion until Lieutenant Cosner, the Headquarters Company Commander, took control. There was no time to organise as a Battalion so Cosner ordered the first three officers he came across to form informal companies. Lieutenants Melke, DeSilva and Keeler set to work gathering together as many men as they could find from the groups of paratroopers milling around the drop zone. They led them to the southern edge of the British landing zone to form a perimeter around Lieutenant Cosner's temporary, headquarters.

2nd Battalion came next, and again heavy fire from ground installations wreaked havoc amongst the Dakotas as they flew low overhead in tight formations:

At 10:10 hours the Battalion reached its drop zone and left the planes amid intense flak and small-arms fire from enemy troops on the ground. Several planes were hit and crashed immediately after all the men had left them. The Battalion hit as a group, but men were spread for a considerable distance in the length of the pattern. Small groups immediately started forming and mopping up on the Drop Zone and became the nucleus of the Battalion which was formed and reorganised within thirty minutes of landing.

Gun battles broke out across the drop zone and the paratroopers engaged enemy positions as soon as they hit the ground. Entrenched German infantry armed with automatic weapons and four field guns pinned down a platoon of Company E on the southern edge of the drop zone until Private Stuart Stryker rallied them and led a charge. Stryker was killed but his comrades overran the position and captured over 200 prisoners. Stryker was posthumously awarded the Medal of Honour. As the paratroopers congregated and closed in, German resistance collapsed and the Battalion found little to stop them entering Diersfordt Forest.

3rd Battalion landed in three main groups, again in the British zone south of Hamminkeln. All failed to realise that they had landed over a mile north of their drop zone and set off in a north-easterly direction, rather than south-east towards their

British and American paratroopers try to sort out the confusing situation on the drop zone south of Hamminkeln.

objective. Lieutenant Swem's group of fifty paratroopers realised their error after a prisoner identified Hamminkeln church allowing the group to set a new course for the Battalion assembly area. En route the group met up with Lieutenant Crowley, Company I's Executive Officer, and Lieutenant Phillips bringing the group total to eighty. Engaging enemy positions as they marched south-east the three officers were the first to reach the Battalion assembly area.

Lieutenant Colonel Kent rounded up 150 men before setting out on, what he thought was, the correct bearing. Before long he realised something was amiss. Hours of studying maps and sand tables paid off and within minutes Kent knew he had landed in the wrong area; the main landmark in the area, Hamminkeln church, was not where it should be. Ten minutes after setting off Kent had worked out his location and his group was heading in the right direction, clearing enemy anti-aircraft positions as it advanced. By 13:30 hours it had joined Lieutenant Crowley's group at the northern end of the Battalion assembly area.

The largest group, numbering 200 paratroopers, also headed off in the wrong direction under Major Anderson. It was over an hour before the Battalion Executive Officer noticed the error and after posting his men in an all round defensive perimeter, he set off to look for distinctive landmarks. For a third time Hamminkeln church solved the puzzle and by 13:00 hours the group was heading south; it eventually reached the rest of the Battalion four hours late.

At 12:30 hours Colonel Coutts found his way into 1st Battalion's perimeter where the number of troops from different commands was growing by the minute. With the help of Lieutenant Cosner's radio he soon learnt that the whole of his command had landed north of the correct drop zone and although elements of all three battalions were heading towards their respective objectives, 513th Regiment was scattered over a wide area. There was no time to lose, if the Germans counter-attacked soon, the Regiment could be overrun. Members of the 2nd Battalion were ordered to join the rest of the battalion as it cleared the Diersfordt Forest and by 16:00 hours Colonel Coutts was relieved to hear that contact had been established with 507th Regiment near Diersfordt Castle. Meanwhile, those belonging to 3rd Battalion were sent east to join the rest of the

A bloodstained paratrooper searches the horizon for landmarks as he tries to find his bearings.

Battalion along the Issel Stream to help establish outposts on the east bank. 1st Battalion's commanding officer had still not appeared and in his absence Captain Ivy took command with orders to prepare an all round defence in case the Germans counter-attacked Drop Zone E.

Despite landing under heavy fire on the wrong drop zone, 513th Regiment's Battalions had assembled and found their way to the objectives, taking over 1,100 prisoners as they overran dozens of enemy positions. Yet again the 57mm recoilless gun had proved itself, accounting for two tanks and a self-propelled gun; the Regiment had also destroyed two batteries of deadly 88mm guns.

194th Glider Regiment had the task of securing the eastern area of 17th Airborne Division's objectives, securing bridgeheads across the Issel Stream to the east of Wesel. 2nd Battalion would land first on Landing Zone S and secure seven bridges across the canal facing east, contacting 513th Parachute Regiment to the north, establishing a continuous defensive line along the canal. 1st Battalion would land next and head south-east to capture another three bridges on the stream, facing south, and hopefully contact the British Commandos in Wesel at an early stage. 3rd Battalion would bring up the rear securing

Glider pilots struggled to find a place to land and many fell foul of hedges, ditches and trees.

The pilot of this glider managed to make a safe landing and the crew wasted no time unloading a trailer full of ammunition.

the Landing Zone and take up positions ready to reinforce if the Germans struck back at the Regiment's line.

The first wave of Dakotas towing the Waco gliders carrying 194th Regiment crossed the Rhine at 10:26 hours and cast off their towlines four minutes later. Typically it took only three minutes to reach the ground but for many pilots it was three minutes of hell as the German anti-aircraft batteries opened fire on their cumbersome gliders. 2nd Battalion's gliders flew through a screen of smoke drifting up from the ground and ran into a curtain of flak as they made their final approach:

Several gliders were set on fire and streamed across the sky like a comet, to crash with all occupants, none of whom wore parachutes. Landings were made more difficult by smoke which had been laid down to assist in the river crossing by ground troops, and which obscured the ground until a very low altitude was reached. The initial resistance on most fields was intense and consisted of small-arms fire from rifles and machine guns, observed mortar fire and in some fields, fire from anti-aircraft guns of various calibres which were levelled in against the landing gliders. In one field alone seven gliders were destroyed by four 88mm guns on the perimeter before the occupants were able to leave the aircraft and go into action.

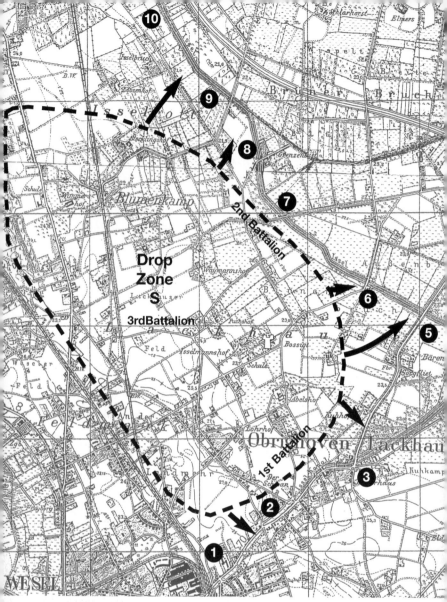

194th Glider Regiment secured ten bridges along the Issel Stream and Canal.

Company G's Wacos approached the ground first, heading for the fields surrounding the large château that Colonel James Pierce had chosen for his Regimental Command Post but as the gliders began to touch down it became clear that the buildings had been fortified (coincidentally it was a German Regimental

Command Post). One after another the gliders came under fire as the pilots struggled to steer towards a patch of open ground and as soon as they touched down the occupants scrambled out of the doors and ran for cover. Anyone trapped inside was unlikely to survive for very long:

Company G suffered heavy casualties immediately after landing, many men being wounded before ever getting out of the gliders. None of the landing fields in the area were large enough and most gliders tore down fence posts and went through wire fences but personnel were not injured in most cases. Many Company G gliders were in range of a 75mm field gun located at the designated Regimental Command Post and as fast as gliders landed in a field in front of this building a round of high explosive from this piece would set the glider on fire.

Glider troops gather together having had a lucky escape on the edge of this wood; in the background a dead paratrooper hangs from his tangled parachute.

The Commander, Lieutenant Colonel Stewart was an early casualty and Major Pleasant Martin was forced to run for cover in a nearby barn, where he gathered the Battalion staff and tried to make sense of the chaos on the landing zone.

While Company G spread out into the fields surrounding the château, Company F began to land and yet again the combination of enemy fire, smoke and obstacles on the ground wreaked havoc amongst the gliders as they hit the earth. However, as glider after glider skidded across the landing zone, spilling men and equipment onto the fields, the German anti-aircraft gun crews suddenly found that the tables were being turned against them:

> In the initial landing of the Battalion, most glider loads were forced to take up a fire fight immediately and the fact that gliders kept landing helter-skelter throughout the area rather than in a planned pattern was probably the biggest aid in overcoming the strong initial resistance. Enemy groups laying down fire in one direction would suddenly have another glider land in their rear and this continuous process so disorganised the enemy that they began to surrender in great numbers within thirty minutes after the first glider hit the ground.

Virtually every glider was hit by anti-aircraft fire either in the air or on the ground, and many were killed or wounded as they ran across the landing zone looking for cover. Two occupants of Glider No 25 had already been wounded before it skidded to a halt and Sergeant Dodge was injured as he clambered out of his craft. Unable to crawl far, Dodge ordered his assistant, Sergeant Reade, to gather their squad together and attack the château. A second group joined Reade's men as they advanced towards the complex of buildings and before long the two squads had rounded up the crew of the deadly anti-tank gun. Other groups began to move forward, taking dozens of prisoners in entrenchments surrounding the buildings. And before long 2nd Battalion had captured 145 members of 1052nd Regiment's Headquarters, including its commanding officer.

By the time Company E's gliders came into land, resistance was coming to an end on the landing zone and as soon as they had assembled, 2nd Battalion wasted no time heading towards the three bridges they had been allocated along the Issel Stream.

1st Battalion's story was the same. The Wacos carrying Company A led the way and came under heavy anti-aircraft fire

Amidst the tangle of debris Colonel Pierce's men prepare to move off towards the Issel Stream. 111-SC-202655

as the Dakotas cast off their tows; the volume of fire from the ground intensified to a crescendo as the gliders skidded to a halt:

> *Almost every glider was hit in the air by flak or machine-gun fire. The small fields caused many crash landings and several gliders were set aflame by enemy fire. After the landing the German guns continued firing on the gliders and personnel as they left their gliders.*

Wrecked British Horsa gliders and American Waco gliders lie side by side.

Although 194th Regiment secured its perimeter, landing gliders in enemy held territory was a dangerous undertaking.

Three gliders burst into flames and crashed on the landing zone killing everyone inside but the rest of the Company immediately went into action, overrunning German held entrenchments, most of them only yards away from where they landed. Company C and Company B each lost two gliders on the run in, but again, the glider men engaged the German troops as soon as they hit the ground. The glider carrying the Battalion's intelligence section crash-landed some distance from the rest and of the three survivors only two men managed to rejoin the rest of the Battalion. The Executive Officer was surrounded and after keeping a number of Germans at bay for some time with his pistol, surrendered when his ammunition ran out.

Every one of the Wacos carrying the anti-tank platoon crashed on landing as the pilots struggled to bring their overloaded craft down safely but with the help of axes and crowbars the crews eventually salvaged two guns from the wreckage. They would play a vital role in the hours that followed. 1st Battalion had no time to mourn their loss of their friends and as the medics set about collecting the wounded, the survivors headed for the bridges along the Issel Canal to the south-east.

3rd Battalion brought up the rear of 194th Regiment and once again the anti-aircraft batteries on the ground were waiting for them. The Battalion diary sums up the tense moments leading up to the landing and the furious battle that followed:

After the gliders were cut loose and began to descend the anti-aircraft fire became more intense and many gliders were hit and casualties were inflicted. The ground was partially obscured by smoke; however, there were few bad crash landings. The enemy was well deployed against airborne landings and nearly every field had dug in positions from which they could be swept by small-arms and machine-gun fire. These took the gliders under fire as they came in and swept them with fire as the men came out. It was at this stage that a great percentage of the casualties were sustained. The immediate areas had to be cleared out before equipment could be recovered from the gliders. Personnel remaining near the gliders were subjected to heavy small-arms and observed mortar fire. The men rushed for cover, orientated themselves and then proceeded to take the nearest enemy under fire. It was this bold and aggressive action combined with the continual pouring in of more gliders that overcame this main initial resistance.

Every few seconds a Waco skidded across 194th Glider Regiment's landing zone; some on fire as they hurtled into

These gliders found a safe landing zone on the fields south of Hamminkeln.

fences and trees, while others broke up as soon as they hit the ground but in spite of the chaos men survived and engaged the German positions. As the minutes passed the number of prisoners began to grow. Squads joined to form platoons, platoons joined to form Companies and after thirty minutes of mayhem every glider was down. Less than an hour after the first glider touched down all three battalions were moving towards their objectives; it was a remarkable achievement. As the surviving officers set up temporary headquarters, order began to emerge out of the chaos and by midday Colonel Pierce was able to tell General Miley that his Regiment had taken the landing zone and was well on the way to seizing their objectives along the Issel Stream. One final note in 2nd Battalion's Diary summarises the bravery that turned the chaos of 194th Glider Regiment's landing into success:

The fact that more gliders were not destroyed is due to the prompt and courageous method in which the members of the Regiment attacked and destroyed these [German] positions. Approximately 150 small battles were fought simultaneously on the landing zone in the first half-hour. Superb action by the glider pilots in bringing the ships down in the small fields saved many lives. Many men, wounded in the air or injured in crash landing, fought from where they landed rather than surrendering and aided greatly in establishing control of the initial area.

A later survey showed that 293 out of 345 gliders had been hit in the air by anti-aircraft fire; many others had been damaged by enemy action on the ground. Sending gliders onto enemy held landing zones was a risky operation.

On 1st Battalion's front Company A's survivors reached the Issel Canal at 11:00 hours, taking control of the three bridges at the eastern apex of the Regiment's objective. Company C had also captured three of the bridges on its objective in spite of heavy fire but a group of German infantry supported by mortars and artillery continued to hold Bridge 7 in the centre of the Battalion's sector; it would be several hours before Colonel Pierce's men captured the bridge.

2nd Battalion reached the Issel Stream on the Regiment's southern flank soon afterwards and had begun to engage the German outposts covering the bridges when a Panther tank appeared on Company F's front:

US Airborne forces in training. Firing a Browning MG, M1919A6, .30.

Landing craft on the east bank of the Rhine, off-loading men of the 79th Division near Orsoy.

General George S. Patton Third Army's flamboyant leader. He stole the limelight by crossing the Rhine twenty-four hours before the Ninth US Army.

2

A bridge across the Rhine in the area of General Patch's 7th Army. The barrier the the heart of Germany was being successfully 'bounced' along its entire length.

3

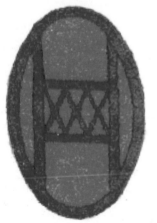

Top left: Shoulder flash of the 9th Army.

Left: 79th Infantry Division, 'Lorraine'. Inclusion of the Cross of Lorraine stemmed from service in France during the First World War.

Below left: 30th Infantry Division, 'Old Hickory'. They took the nickname of President Andrew Jackson, in whose home state, Tennessee, the unit was raised.

Top: The 17th Airborne Division 'Thunder from Heaven' was a new division activated in April 1943 at Camp Mackall, North Carolina.

En route to the objective at about 11:45 hours, a tank opened fire on the company. Bazooka gunner Private Weber got a miraculous hit on the tank at a range of 500 yards. The round must have penetrated the ammunition magazines, as the tank exploded and all but disintegrated.

Company G secured two more bridges on the Battalion's objective and by midday all but one of the ten bridges, Bridge 1 on the outskirts of Wesel, were in 194th Glider Regiment's hands.

Company E had also been busy rounding up 200 prisoners behind the Battalion's front; they also captured four 88mm guns. However as the Company closed in on its objective, closely followed by the support weapons company, patrols were alerted to a new threat; two more Panther tanks had escaped from Wesel and they were heading straight for 2nd Battalion:

At 12:45 hours a counter-attack led by two enemy tanks was made on the west flank of Company E. The anti-tank guns were on the move at this time and were not in position. One section immediately went into action in clear view of the tanks, suffering four casualties in doing so. They did, however, get effective fire on the tanks, knocking out one and scoring a hit on the second one. At this time Lieutenant Sheehy, after getting his section into action, personally took command of the other gun of the platoon coupled to a prime mover and with the squad took off in clear view of the tank. He attempted to get closer for a sure kill,

The new recoilless rifles gave General Miley's men the opportunity to fight back against armour.

depending on the fire of the other section to keep the tanks engaged. One tank was still able to move and withdrew at this time, going south along the far west flank of the Battalion.

The remaining Panther headed south to try to escape across the Issel only to find Company G barring the way. A patrol armed with a bazooka hunted it down and knocked it out.

By 13:00 hours Colonel Pierce was pleased to hear that his two battalions had established contact with each other along the Issel and were digging in on their objectives. However, the local German commander was determined to take at least one of the bridges to use as a base for future counter-attacks and during the course of the afternoon tanks made several attempts to break through 2nd Battalion's lines. The anti-tank platoon accounted for one tank while bazooka teams scored further hits on the marauding *Panzers*.

The story was the same to the north. 6th British Airborne Division had suffered heavy casualties during the initial drop north of Diersfordt Forest and around Hamminkeln but as the paratroopers began to assemble the German anti-aircraft crews began to surrender. By noon 6th Air Landing Brigade had secured Hamminkeln while 3rd and 5th Parachute Brigades were well on the way to clearing the northern perimeter of the Diersfordt Forest. General Ridgway's plan had worked in spite of the heavy losses over the drop zones; the bridges along the Issel were secure. It was only a matter of time before the ground troops advancing from the Rhine reached the paratroopers.

After salvaging equipment and ammunition from wrecked gliders this jeep heads off towards the objective towing a loaded trailer. 111-SC-203327

Chapter 6

XVI CORPS' ADVANCE ACROSS THE RAILWAYS

Both of General Anderson's divisions were firmly established on the east bank of the Rhine by mid afternoon on 24 March. On 30th Division's front both 119th and 117th Regiment were approaching the Wesel–Dinslaken railways, while 120th Regiment had one battalion across the first railway at Möllen. 79th Division had also rushed the German defences along the riverbank, securing both of its flanks before first light; the reserve Regiment was preparing to attack the final objective for the day, Dinslaken, a town with a pre-war population of 25,000, two miles east of the river.

Although the first German line had been broken, resistance could be expected to increase as the two German divisions in the area deployed their reserve of infantry and tanks against XVI Corps. Anti-aircraft positions formed an integral part of their defence line and both General Hobbs and General Wyche needed tanks and tank destroyers to support their attacks across the railways.

30th Division's fight for the railway embankments

As it began to grow light, the German artillery had begun to target the engineers working along the river and landing craft and rafts had to be brought forward to float the equipment across the river where the dyke afforded some shelter. As Major General Hobbs considered the consequences of the delay, 105th Engineers reported another difficulty. Landing craft had been unable to unload the tank destroyers where they were needed on the east bank; soft mud on the shoreline had forced the pilots to find a new landing site.

The first platoon of light tanks had been welcomed in 119th Regiment's area at 11:00 hours and immediately moved forward to 2nd Battalion in front of the railway embankment. A second platoon reached 1st Battalion on the south bank of the Lippe Canal an hour later and helped it advance towards Objective Joy

Armour pours into the bridgehead as XVI Corps prepares to attack across the Wesel–Dinslaken railway.

where patrols reported that the tanks could cross the railway. They were also quick to note that German infantry and anti-aircraft guns could be seen waiting in the woods on the far side of the underpass; it appeared that the Germans intended to take advantage of the bottleneck. As the engineers set to work, anti-aircraft guns across the canal opened fire on 1st Battalion's flank and while the mortar platoon fired smoke shells to screen the watercourse, two companies deployed to deal with the threat.

2nd Battalion reached the embankment thirty minutes later and Lieutenant Colonel McCown reported that he needed bulldozers to clear craters and barricades blocking the two underpasses on his front. As patrols moved over the embankment it was again obvious that infantry and anti-aircraft guns were waiting on the far side; three tanks had also been spotted waiting to target anything trying to move through the underpasses.

As the reports flooded into 119th Regiment's command post, Colonel Baker agreed to give the engineers two hours to finish their work, in the meantime the GIs would have to keep the Germans at bay.

117th Regiment's patrols reported mixed news to Colonel Johnson. The single underpass, Objective Katie, on the left of the

Regiment's sector, was blocked and 2nd Battalion kept the German infantry at bay while the engineers set to work. Meanwhile, the news from 1st Battalion's patrols was promising; tanks would be able to negotiate the embankment. Colonel Johnson sent his first armoured support, a platoon of DD tanks, forward and by midday 1st Battalion was across the railway. The DD tanks then retraced their steps to help the 2nd Battalion clear Objective Katie.

As the rest of the division prepared to cross the embankment, 120th Regiment set about clearing the villages astride the railway lines. 2nd Battalion was met by machine-gun and tank fire from the orchards and hedges around Löhnen but the show of strength was shortlived. As Company E worked their way forwards, a solitary *Panzer IV* withdrew, leaving behind a token rearguard; Captain Walter Wert's men quickly secured the village.

On 3rd Battalion's front Major McCullough's men were finally overcoming resistance in Möllen, and after Company L had cleared the riverbank and moved into the village from the south, Captain Shaw had Company I send patrols beyond the second railway line. It was soon apparent that there was no sign of the enemy on the Battalion's next objective.

By mid-afternoon both divisions had all three regiments on the east bank but the ferries continued to work around the clock. 111-SC-272416

Colonel Purdue was growing concerned by Major McCullough's desire to push on and expose 3rd Battalion flanks, but he quickly sought permission to probe beyond Möllen from divisional headquarters after McCullough had assured him that there was no sign of the enemy in the area. Major General Hobbs approved the plan when he heard the news from Major Eugene Thomas, Purdue's intelligence officer:

3rd Battalion went through Ruth. They're planning to attack
Mae and bypass most of the East Lana, West and East Jean.

The opportunity on 3rd Battalion's front was too good to miss. The chosen route involved advancing north-east before making a large sweeping arc through Bruckhausen, moving behind any Germans planning to make a stand around Voorde. Contact had just been made with 79th Division south of Möllen, securing Colonel Purdue's southern flank and it appeared that the time was ripe for making a deep push into the enemy rear.

Since midday engineers had been ferrying Company B of the 744th Light Tank Battalion across the Rhine on Bailey rafts. Alongside landing craft shipped a platoon of 823rd Tank Destroyer Battalions to the east bank and by mid afternoon the M-10 Hellcats had joined Company K in Götterswickerhamm.

Artillery shells targeted the column as it waited to move and as Captain Plummer's men scrambled for cover someone noticed a lone Piper Cub plane circling overhead; the only possible explanation was that the guns belonged to 79th Division. When news reached divisional headquarters General Hobbs immediately telephoned General Wyche for an apology; Wyche gave the caustic reply: 'We have battalions to spare to fire at anything in our zone.'

The mistake was quickly cleared up when the commanding officer of an artillery battalion admitted to thinking that the tanks were German; he had not realised that 30th Division had penetrated so deep into the enemy positions.

As soon as Company K remounted their tanks, Task Force Plummer moved out, finding the area beyond Möllen clear of enemy troops. The advance took the Germans holding entrenchments on the road to Bruckhausen, codenamed Objective Mae, completely by surprise and as tanks rolled by the GIs shot at anyone who tried to run. At the head of the column Sergeant McLeod spotted a group of infantry digging in on the outskirts of Bruckhausen, 1,500 metres to the north-east

Resistance collapsed across 30th Division's front beyond the railway, and
120th Regiment pushed deep into the German rear.

and while the rest of Company K rounded up their prisoners, he urged the tank commander to drive on. Many Germans tried to run as they spotted the tanks climbing the slope but it was too late, fifteen were killed or wounded and another forty were taken prisoner. Although McLeod had taken an important position, Captain Plummer was forced to recall his sergeant; the hill was beyond the limit of XVI Corps artillery. 120th Regiment had advanced over six miles from the river; the furthest of all the three regiments.

Along the rest of 30th Division's front preparations were under way for the assault across the Wesel–Dinslaken railway. Despite the show of resistance by infantry, tanks and anti-aircraft guns, 180th Division had been virtually destroyed by mid afternoon on 24 March. The only soldiers confronting General Hobbs' men were a mixture of rear echelon troops from Regimental and Divisional Headquarters and a few stragglers who had escaped the initial assault.

The assault across the first railway line had been timed for 15:00 hours and as soon as fighter-bombers had flown overhead, Ninth Army's guns across the river added to 180th Division's woes. As the final rounds of smoke shells erupted on the German positions, infantry swarmed over the embankment as Chaffees, Shermans and M10 tank destroyers roared through the underpasses. The next phase of 30th Division's attack was under way.

As XVI Corps pushed east, engineers started to build treadway bridges across the river. The sign on the front of the lorry reads Engineer Bridge Priority. 111-SC-337112

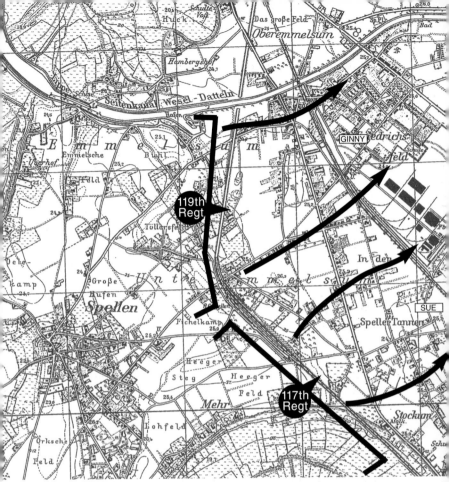

The battle for the underpasses along the Wesel-Dinslaken Railway.

The combined effect of planes, tanks, infantry and artillery stunned the Germans and the majority withdrew beyond the second railway embankment allowing 119th and 117th Regiments to take Objectives Ginny and Sue. The rapid advance made the village of Voorde in front untenable and 120th Regiment took Objective East Lana without a fight.

On 120th Regiment's front 1st Battalion had not been idle and had been pushing forward while Company K drove deep into the German rear. Lieutenant Colonel Williamson's men had moved forward across the railway alongside the rest of the division and at 18:00 hours Company B struck out towards Bruckhausen while Company K's tanks fired into the German rear from the top of the slope. The outcome was inevitable and although a few determined individuals put up a fight, most of the German soldiers caught in 120th Regiment's trap surrendered without firing a shot:

> The majority of prisoners taken were slovenly and apathetic. One group taken near Bruckhausen had no previous training and had seen no previous combat. Many surrendered easily and most were happy to be taken. One officer, typically stubborn, claimed he would not have surrendered if his gun had not jammed and claimed Germany would never give in. Others tried to maintain their dignity, but talked after small persuasion.

1st Battalion eventually rounded up 114 prisoners and captured three anti-tank guns, a halftrack and a *Panzer IV*; engineers also disarmed two 500-pound bombs set to blow craters at two vital road junctions.

79th Division's attack on Dinslaken

By mid afternoon 79th Division was in a position to renew the advance on its front. 313th Regiment had a firm hold along the Neue-Ernscher Canal on the division's right flank while 314th Regiment had moved up into line alongside 315th Regiment. However, as General Wyche prepared to attack Dinslaken, nature decided to play a part and brought the movement of tanks and tank destroyers across the river to an abrupt halt. At 14:00 hours the wind veered to the south-east, pushing the smokescreen away from the crossing site, revealing the activity along the river to German observers for the first time in the day. As the enemy artillery started to range in, the chemical mortars tried to re-register their targets to compensate for the wind but they soon found that the new target areas were either out of range or already occupied by friendly troops; General Wyche had to find another way of restoring the smokescreen, and he needed it as quickly as possible.

Smoke pots failed to produce enough smoke and while divisional headquarters put the call out for a smoke-generating unit the decision was taken to suspend certain activities along the river until the smokescreen could be re-established. Although the landing craft carrying men and supplies were too fast to become targets, the slow moving tank carrying rafts would be sitting ducks.

During the delay the tank companies sent advance parties across the river to reconnoitre routes and arrange guides so that

GIs move across a wrecked bridge towards 79th Division's final objective, the town of Dinslaken. 111-SC-272415

no time would be wasted when their vehicles eventually reached the east bank. After two hours' delay, smoke-generators were in action and as smoke filled the sky over the Rhine once more, the tanks and tank destroyers began to move down to the river and load onto the waiting rafts. But as the armour crossed, General Wyche decided he could wait no longer, Dinslaken had to be taken before it was dark and 314th Regiment moved out at 16:30 hours while the tanks were still moving forward to join the infantry.

Dinslaken, a maze of houses and industrial buildings surrounding a huge steel fabricating plant, was typical of the towns along the northern edge of the Ruhr; ugly to look at but perfect to defend. 1st Battalion came under fire first, drawing the attention of several *Stug III* assault guns near the factory while flak guns fired at 2nd Battalion from the outskirts of the town. As Colonel Robinson called for assistance, Ninth Army's artillery systematically targeted the German positions, turning the town into an inferno.

The arrival of 717th Tank Battalion on 314th Regiment's front quickly turned the tables against the Germans and although the light was fading fast, fires lit up the skyline as the Shermans moved in for the kill. The flak guns were destroyed one by one and the German assault guns withdrew to a safe distance as the GIs moved into the town. As 314th Regiment pushed into the burning ruins no one could fail to be impressed by the devastation wrought by Ninth Army's artillery, in particular the men of 717th Tank Battalion who were taking part in their first battle:

> *This town, centred around a large steel fabricating plant, was on fire most of the day, and Company C's 2nd Platoon received a heavy baptism of fire in more ways than one.*

By midnight Dinslaken was secure, increasing 79th Division's bridgehead to a depth of over three miles and while General Wyche's position was anchored to the south by 313th Regiment's line along the Neue-Ernscher Canal his men had contacted 30th Division to the north. German resistance had been ineffective and over 700 prisoners, mainly from the Hamburg Division's *588th Regiment,* had been taken; 79th Division's own casualties had been light (313th Infantry only suffered one fatality and eleven wounded). Although the smokescreen problems had delayed General Wyche's plans for several hours, it had made little difference to the outcome. At times many artillery batteries on the west bank of the Rhine had been silent due to a lack of targets and 79th Division had not had to call upon its assigned fighter-bomber group for assistance. Operation FLASHPOINT had been a total success and a tribute to Ninth Army's planning.

Alligators ferried ammunition to the front line units before returning to the river bank with wounded GIs.

Chapter 7

17TH AIRBORNE DIVISION SECURES ITS PERIMETER

Following the mayhem on the landing grounds the situation across 17th Airborne Division's landing zones had calmed down by the early afternoon and all three Regimental commanders were able to report that they had secured their perimeters and were waiting expectantly for the enemy reaction.

At 15:00 hours, Major General Miley was relieved to hear the news that Company F in 507th Parachute Regiment's area had

General Ridgway (second from left) listens to reports from American and British officers. 111-SC-264635

met Scottish troops south of Diersfordt Castle. They had crossed at Xanten the previous evening and had spent the morning driving the Germans out of Bislich before pushing forward to link up with the airborne troops. Half an hour later General Ridgway drove into 507th Regiment's area and located Colonel Raff's headquarters; Raff was pleased to report that his men had secured his sector of Diersfordt Forest and captured Diersfordt Castle, taking more than 800 prisoners, over half of them wounded. The paratroopers had also managed to take on the German armour with their new recoilless weapons, knocking out five tanks, including two Mark V Panther tanks. Although contact had not been made with the British paratroopers on the north side of the Regiment's perimeter, General Ridgway was able to confirm that 6th Airborne Division had also been successful and, despite heavy causalities on the drop zones, they were well on their way to securing all their objectives. After passing on the good news, the General's party motored off in their jeeps to find the divisional headquarters.

General Miley was acutely aware that the Germans could counter-attack at any time but he realised that his men would have to hold the Issel bridges until the British troops moving east from Bislich were able to bring tanks and artillery into his perimeter. It would take all night to build a suitable crossing over the Rhine and, in the meantime, his men would have to fend for themselves. As the news of the linkup spread, Miley's paratroopers dug in along the Issel Stream while patrols kept a look out for signs of enemy activity; it was going to be a long night. While a few paratroopers spent the afternoon processing prisoners, others continued to round up stragglers, some of them teenage Hitler *Jugend* fanatics. Meanwhile, the reserve companies spent the afternoon collecting equipment from the wrecked gliders and salvaging German equipment in the hope of finding spare arms and ammunition. As nightfall approached everyone was acutely aware that the Germans must counter-attack soon.

On 513th Regiment's front, in the north-east corner of 17th Airborne Division's area, German activity on the ground was virtually non-existent and 2nd Battalion dug in around its bridgeheads over the Issel. The situation along 194th Glider Regiment's front was similar and while troops consolidated their positions, supplies and ammunition recovered from

A paratrooper keeps guard over members of the Hitler *Jugend*, teenage soldiers who had volunteered to fight for the Führer.

B-24 Liberator bombers fly low over the Rhine carrying supplies for XVIII Airborne Corps.

The Liberators dropped essential supplies for General Miley's men.

Patrols search 17th Airborne Division's perimeter for German soldiers.

Gliders were searched for equipment and ammunition so it could be taken to the front line.

gliders and supply canisters were being distributed along the front line. Meanwhile, General Meindl was gathering the reserves of II Parachute Corps to strike back at the Issel and as the afternoon wore on the German artillery began to search for targets along 17th Airborne Division's perimeter.

On the western perimeter 507th Parachute Regiment contacted 513th Parachute Regiment in Diersfordt Forest during the evening and as it grew dark there were anxious moments in 507th Regiment's sector when Company I's patrols spotted figures moving through the trees. As the paratroopers waited with fingers on their triggers for the men to move closer, the message went the line along to hold fire, the enemy were wearing red berets; contact had finally been made with the 6th British Airborne Division. It meant that the whole of Diersfordt Forest had been secured and with his northern flank safe, Colonel Raff began to withdraw a large number of his men into reserve.

On the southern perimeter there had still been no contact with the British Commandos in Wesel by nightfall and the patrols sent out by Company K had been turned back by heavy

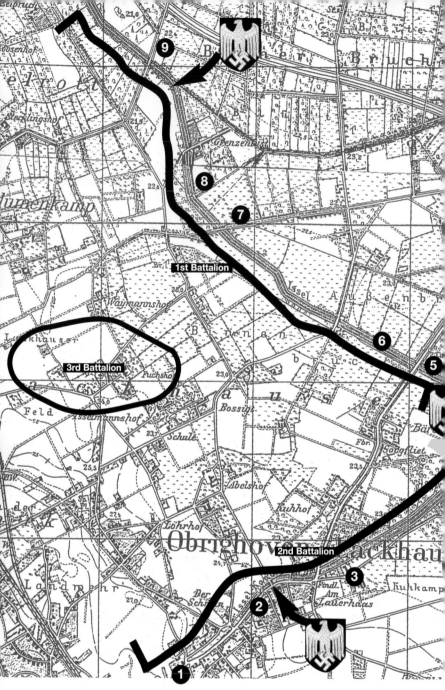

German counter-attacks against 194th Glider Regiment's perimeter.

fire; Company L's patrol had also run into trouble on the outskirts of the town. Contact was finally made at 03:00 hours on 25 March after a Commando patrol slipped through the German lines to link up with Company L.

The first attacks fell on 194th Glider Regiment's eastern perimeter where 1st Battalion covered a 4,700 yards front and seven of the Issel bridges. Casualties during the landing had been high and the Battalion commander had few local reserves to reinforce his thin line if the Germans broke through. The first infantry probe was made against Company A's position around Bridge 4 on the Battalion's right flank in the afternoon. As the hours passed further patrols probed all the bridges along 1st Battalion's sector, gauging the paratroopers' response at each position. Colonel Pierce waited anxiously to see where the main German effort would fall and each time the patrols were driven back, artillery searched for targets along the stream. The first blow fell late in the afternoon and threatened to break through Company A's sector before Company B's counter-attack restored the situation. A second company-sized attack struck the centre of 1st Battalion's line and had driven a wedge between the two front line companies before Company B came to the rescue for a second time. Time after time the Germans tried to find a way across the Issel and the Battalion After-Action report sums up the night along 17th Airborne Division's perimeter:

The attack was halted temporarily on several occasions during the night to repel enemy counter-attacks from the front, both flanks, and on one occasion from the rear. Elements of Company B were committed on both flanks of Company C at various times during the night to erase the counter attacking Germans. At or about 01:00 hours, rear security of Company C reported Germans in its rear, driven there by action of other friendly units nearer the river. This pressure was reduced by mortar fire and bayonet by Companies B and C. During the night, attacks varying from a squad to company strength continued. The artillery observers did an excellent job in getting massed artillery on the larger attacks as was evidenced by the large number of dead and wounded Germans found the next morning. At dawn only 300 yards separated Company C from the unit on the left and the entire area was filled with German dead. The 300 yards was effectively covered by fire.

On 194th Glider Regiment's southern flank, 2nd Battalion had taken all of its objectives except one by the middle of the afternoon. Company G suffered the heaviest losses during the landings and the survivors were delayed as they pushed south and rounded up large numbers of prisoners. The leading platoons crossed the Issel Stream at Bridges 2 and 3 but the first attempt to move along the south bank towards Bridge 1 was stopped by machine-gun and small-arms fire. Lieutenant Wittig's platoon only had nine men still standing when he volunteered to try to reach the bridge and his small party set off along the north bank of the canal in the afternoon. The first sign that something was wrong came later that evening when one of Wittig's men returned to the Battalion command post with bad news; the patrol had been ambushed and he did not know whether anyone else had survived. It was obvious that the Germans were intent on holding Bridge 1 as a base for launching attacks. The first attempt, by infantry and two *Panzer IVs*, threatened to overrun Company F's flank but they were dispersed with the help of accurate shellfire directed by Lieutenant Kehoe, the Battalion's artillery liaison officer. The bridge was the weak spot in 194th Glider Regiment's line and it had to be taken as soon as possible:

One platoon of Company E was to move forward to Bridge No 1 on the north side of the canal, push as far west as possible, relieve Wittig's platoon if possible, and at all costs hold and protect the west flank of the Battalion which at that time was looming more dangerous than the front. Lieutenant Robinson got the mission. No further word had been received from Wittig. Robinson moved his platoon at dark and within an hour and a half had moved to a point about 200 yards north of Bridge 1. Reporting on the last known location of Wittig's platoon, he reported finding one man dead, a member of the platoon, and no sign of the rest of it. Twice during the night Robinson's platoon was able to ambush enemy troops moving along the corridor between Wesel and the west flank of the battalion.

As Robinson secured the exposed flank, the rest of 2nd Battalion dug in along the 5,000-metre front, a front far too long for the men available to defend against a concerted attack. It was going to be a long night.

The commanding officer's concerns were raised when a light mist began to form along the canal during the evening and before long German infantry began to infiltrate between 2nd

Sporadic fighting continued as the paratroopers collected supply bundles from the drop zones.

Battalion's outposts. Lieutenant Anderson's platoon was ordered to search the Battalion's rear looking for enemy patrols but after rounding up three groups of German infantry, the main attack started. It appeared that the patrols had radioed many of 2nd Battalion's positions to the artillery and when the first shells began to fall around midnight, Company G and Company F were subjected to a devastating bombardment. As Company G began calling for artillery the barrage abruptly ended and German infantry swarmed towards their positions, overrunning the outposts. Moments later the radios and telephones went dead; and the only sign that members of Company G were still alive was the sound of gunfire and explosions around their positions.

An attempt to contact the lost Company ended in failure when the two man patrol was ambushed 500 metres from the Canal. It appeared that the Germans had penetrated deep into 2nd Battalion's lines and were threatening to unhinge the entire Regiment's line:

It looked bad. That Company G lines had been broken was considered a possibility. One platoon of heavy guns and two anti-tank guns in the Company G area could not be accounted for at that time. Heavy small-arms fire continued in the Company G area.

On the opposite flank Lieutenant Sheehy and Staff Sergeant Kovacs stumbled on sixty German infantry assembled around a *Panzer IV* near Bridge 2 rather than the anti-tank gun they had positioned to cover Company F's position. After a narrow escape the two men returned to Battalion headquarters to report the incident but with Company G out of contact and Company E covering the exits from Wesel, there were few reserves available to counter the enemy breakthrough. It appeared that 2nd Battalion's front was disintegrating.

With the help of Lieutenant Anderson's platoon in tow and a few spare bazookas, Lieutenant Sheehy returned to Company F's flank with a long list of objectives:

Their missions were to establish contact with Company G, locate any enemy forces within our lines and destroy or capture

With the help of their recoilless rifles and captured weaponry the paratroopers were able to deal with armour roaming across the drop zones; this man takes cover behind a wrecked German armoured car.
111-SC-253933

them if possible. The point where Lieutenant Sheehy had seen this group of enemy with the tank looked like a good rallying point for the infiltrating Krauts and the patrol made its way back to this point. The enemy tank at that time began laying high-explosive fire straight up the road towards the rear of the area. Going to the south side of the canal in the centre rear of Company G area, the patrol located the group that Sheehy had seen earlier although they had moved somewhat to the west. The size of the group was now about one hundred men with one tank. They were in position to force a crossing of the bridge near that point and penetrate the Battalion area north of the canal in some force. They radioed back the information and gave accurate coordinates. These were relayed to Lieutenant Kehoe and within five minutes he had the Corps artillery on the target; perfect shooting. Despite the fact that the group was within our lines, despite the fact that the fire was solely from the map, the fire was devastatingly accurate. Much credit here is due to Lieutenant Anderson who knew the ground and had studied his map so thoroughly that even on this dark night, being on this ground for the first time, he knew exactly where he was, making possible the accurate designation of the target. The enemy group scattered in confusion and the artillery began to fall and many casualties were suffered by the Germans as the next morning showed only too well.

Anderson and Sheehy ordered their men to hold their fire and as the artillery barrage came to an end, moved out in search of Company G.

They only encountered German infantry and during the early hours returned to Battalion Headquarters to report that their mission had only been partially successful. The news was extremely worrying and the only consolation was that machine guns and small arms could still be heard; even if Company G had been overrun, the survivors were still fighting for their lives along the canal.

Facing disaster, the Battalion commander sent his only remaining reserve, the Intelligence and Reconnaissance section, forwards to try to restore the left flank. The small group quickly ran into trouble and found itself embroiled in a German attack on Company G's command post. As the Intelligence section gave covering fire the company staff withdrew, firing everything from pistols to bazookas to keep the Germans at bay.

It had been a lucky escape but when Company G's commander reported to Battalion Headquarters, he was unable to shed any light on the situation along his sector of the Issel. Communications had been cut at the start of the attack and nobody had returned with news from the front line for several hours.

On Company F's front the artillery liaison officer had helped to disperse a second attack, directing shells on the gathering infantry and tanks across his front and, as the Glider troops ceased fire and waited for the next blow to fall, Captain Dukes noticed that the Germans had committed a fatal error. The infantry had failed to locate Company F's front line and had chosen to regroup only 300 metres from their foxholes. The opportunity was too good to miss and Dukes' men held their fire and watched as lorries brought German reinforcements to the assembly area (estimates put the final number at around 400 men). Timing his response to perfection, Captain Dukes gave the signal to open fire as the first salvo of shells landed on the German infantry. As the Glider troops' rifles and machine guns

A convoy of jeeps, horses and carts ferries men and equipment to the front line.

joined in the slaughter, panic set in and many Germans were shot down as they ran towards the American lines, bringing to an end the fighting on Company F's front for the time being.

As the long night came to an end and firing died down, the Germans withdrew to regroup, leaving the Glider men wondering when the next attack would begin. Although the situation at Bridge 1 was still precarious the Battalion Commander had no option but to move all of his reserves in the opposite direction to try to restore his right flank. However, at dawn a bedraggled soldier reached Battalion headquarters with good news; Company G, or what was left of it, was still holding its positions:

> *... the enemy made numerous attempts to infiltrate the lines and infantry, supported by tanks and self-propelled guns, and were able to penetrate the gaps... The Company had suffered heavy casualties but the two platoons had held the front and had inflicted heavy casualties on the enemy. Pushed back to some extent, especially on their left where the heaviest casualties were suffered... Most of the enemy were killed and the few remaining were captured within the battalion area. The tanks and self-propelled guns were knocked out. Not one man had given any inch of ground to the enemy. Counter-attacks were thrown back repeatedly during the night along the entire perimeter... Company G lashed out in attack at daylight and within half-an-hour had completely broken the enemy's will to fight and streams of prisoners began coming back... The woods, ditches, lanes and houses in front of Company G were littered with German corpses. Few escaped.*

As it began to grow light Lieutenant Robinson took advantage of the lull in the fighting and led his men towards Wesel to see if he could capture the troublesome Bridge 1. As it advanced, the platoon was surprised to see a small group of Glider men coming the opposite way along the canal; it was Lieutenant Wittig's party. Wittig's men had survived the night and slipped into Wesel under cover of darkness where they had contacted British troops. One of the Commandos had accompanied Wittig to formalise the contact with 194th Glider Regiment.

Robinson's platoon pushed on towards Bridge 1, rounding up dozens of Germans on the way; over 200 were collected over the next couple of hours.

The Germans were a spent force. Wesel was in British hands

and 30th Division was already driving along the opposite bank of the Lippe Canal behind their southern flank, threatening their rear. With daylight approaching the Allied Air Force was able to take to the skies once more; the Germans were trapped.

Throughout the morning 2nd Battalion searched its perimeter finding hundreds of German wounded and dead strewn all along the front, testament to the savage fighting. The haul of captured and destroyed equipment taken by 194th Regiment was staggering. Captured artillery and anti-tank guns, many of which had been used by the Glider men, totalled four 155mm guns, two 150mm guns, four 105mm guns, two 76mm anti-tank guns and nine 75mm guns. The number of anti-aircraft guns collected in the perimeter confirmed the power of the German air defences that had been waiting for the Regiment; eleven 88mm guns, ten 20mm anti-aircraft guns and two 20mm flak wagons. The anti-tank platoon had also been successful, making good use of their recoilless weapons as well as captured German equipment. They had accounted for five Panther tanks, five *Panzer IV*s and five self-propelled guns. The final tally of prisoners taken was 1,153 prisoners including most of 1052nd Regiment, half of another Regiment and the Elbe Artillery Regiment. However, the successful landing and subsequent defence of the Issel Bridges had come at a price, 194th Regiment's own losses had been high; 444 killed and wounded, over half of them on the landing grounds.

Paratroopers move out after destroying a German bunker.

Chapter 8

25 MARCH – ENTERING STAATSFORST WESEL

By the morning of 25 March, Ninth Army was firmly established on the east bank of the Rhine. Attempts to dislodge 17th Airborne Division had failed and at first light convoys of tanks, artillery and halftracks began to move into the bridgehead bringing welcome support to Major General Miley's beleaguered paratroops; his men would no longer have to rely on long range artillery from across the river. 155th Anti-Tank Battalion and the three-inch towed guns of 605th Tank Destroyer Battalion would be able to fend off armoured attacks while the halftracks of 387th Anti-Aircraft Automatic Weapons Battalion took the place of the captured German anti-aircraft guns. Artillery support supplied by the British 53rd Division, 25-pounder guns of the 692nd Field Artillery Battalion and a Company of 4.2 inch mortars, would also soon be on call. Plans were already being transmitted for the advance east and Shermans of the 771st Medium Tank Battalion were going to provide armoured support for Miley's paratroopers. The 6th

Paratroopers expand the bridgehead east of the Issel. 111-SC-206558

British Guards Armoured Brigade was also on its way forward to join the next phase of Montgomery's plan, the drive into northern Germany, codenamed Operation PLUNDER.

German activity had melted away on at first light on 513th Regiment's front allowing Colonel Coutts' men to move north and contact the British glider troops around Hamminkeln. While 513th Parachute and 194th Glider Regiments took advantage of the lull in the fighting, General Ridgway was explaining the next phase of the operation to General Miley. British troops were moving in force into 507th Regiment's area and Colonel Raff was moving to the east of Wesel, extending the division's right flank south of the Issel Canal. The first item on General Miley's agenda was to straighten 194th Regiment's line, removing the awkward salient east of Wesel. With 507th

Having reached the London Line, it was time to dig in and await the German response.

Parachute Regiment moving into position on the division's right flank, Colonel Pierce could move east to the London Line, expanding his hold on the east bank of the Issel Stream.

At 16:00 hours 3rd Battalion moved through 1st Battalion's positions, coming under rifle and machine-gun fire as they began to execute a turning manoeuvre across the Regiment's front. The glider infantry had run into 84th Division's final line of defences, a line of emplacements held by the 1052nd Infantry Regiment's cadre.

With no time to arrange effective artillery support 3rd Battalion's mortar teams and heavy machine-gun crews worked furiously, targeting each enemy dugout in turn as the glider troops advanced. Many German positions fought to the last round, or in some cases last man and dozens were killed. Eventually, 229, many of them wounded, were taken prisoner, wiping out 1052nd Infantry Regiment and the Elbe Artillery Regiment. With the London Line in 194th Regiment's hands, Major General Miley was ready for the next stage of the operation.

Despite the set back, General Strabe refused to withdraw and made one last attempt to break the paratroopers' line later that evening. The first attack fell on the boundary of 513th and 194th Regiments:

At darkness a German attack of about company strength, supported by tanks and other armoured vehicles was stopped by a massed artillery, mortar, machine-gun and rifle fire after it had penetrated Company B's front. All of the enemy were killed, captured or driven out. Immediately afterwards, Company C was hit on its left flank in the gap between Company B and the right of 513th Parachute Infantry Regiment. A platoon of Company C was immediately committed to extend the left flank of Company B and restore the position. This platoon was almost immediately enveloped and a second platoon of Company C was thrown in to further extend the left flank. The Germans also enveloped this platoon and the rest of Company C had to be committed. The position was restored and held for the rest of the night against continuous German attacks. Throughout the night troops were constantly shifted to meet threats that became increasingly more violent.

For the second night in a row the German attacks had been defeated, and with more tanks, halftracks and towed weapons moving into position alongside the paratroopers, General Miley's men knew that the time to strike was drawing near.

30th Division

In the centre of Ninth Army's front 30th Division's Major General Hobbs was looking to advance quickly through Staatsforst Wesel. Tanks were already moving forward to join the infantry and the divisional artillery had started to cross at first light; if he could strike quickly Hobbs could be through the forest by nightfall and into open country. With German reserves moving to block the division it was going to be a race against time; it was a race against time that Hobbs did not want to lose.

Fighter-bombers paved the way for 120th Regiment's advance onto the hills beyond Bruckhausen, codenamed Helen, and as 1st Battalion moved up the slopes in extended order, howitzers and mortars hammered the summit with white phosphorous shells to create a mile long smokescreen. Lieutenant Colonel Butch Williamson unleashed the second phase of his plan as the infantry advanced but as seven tanks and four tank destroyers carried Company A towards along the road towards the village, it looked as though the Germans were preparing to fight:

> As the troops were entering the woods which bordered the objective an enemy counterattack appeared to move forward to meet them; it proved to be separate groups, marching files and stray individuals, all with their hands raised and surrendering. In an hour and a half, the objective had fallen and 200 prisoners were being carried back.

Objective Helen was taken without a fight, allowing 1st Battalion to push east to the Autobahn; paving the way for the next stage of 120th Regiment's attack.

After following 1st Battalion to the Autobahn, 3rd Battalion turned south towards Objective Martha, moving quickly through the woods; Colonel Purdue was anxious to extend the Regiment's front along the west side of the Autobahn as quickly as possible.

> To keep the enemy pinned down in the assault, a rapid advance coupled with a steady volume of fire from the hip was employed successfully in the attack.

There was little opposition and 3rd Battalion had crossed the cutting to take Objective Martha within the hour. After hearing the news, Colonel Purdue ordered McCullough to push on and extend a protective flank for the final stage of 120th Regiment's drive on Kirchhellen:

> *Now move two-thirds of your unit east on Objective Rose, setting up your defense to face to the south, southeast and west. You should be prepared in the south and southeast part of Rose for a counterattack. Your mission is right-flank protection for our Task Force Hunt passing through you. One platoon of Tank Destroyers will be sent to you as quickly as possible.*

As 3rd Battalion moved through the trees, the tanks and support vehicles struggled along the single forest track and although there was no sign of the enemy, McCullough's men were over half a mile in front of the rest of the Regiment; Purdue was taking a chance.

Company I stumbled on a camouflaged machine gun on Objective Rose and as the GIs fanned out into the undergrowth, they directed two M10 tank destroyers forward to silence the outpost. It had been a valuable lesson. From now on the tank destroyers would lead, directed by three volunteers armed with a bazooka and sub-machine guns. For the next three hours

Armoured columns were restricted to a small number of forest tracks as they drove deep into German lines.

Company I inched their way through the quiet woods but their advance had not gone unnoticed; a German sentry had reported 3rd Battalion's position to the artillery.

The shells started to fall at 16:00 hours and while the GIs dug foxholes, shrapnel flayed the trees and incendiaries set fire to the undergrowth. With nowhere to hide, McCullough's men would have to 'sweat it out' and the queue of tanks and support vehicles behind the infantry found themselves confined to the forest trail by mines. 3rd Battalion faced a nerve-racking evening as it waited for the rest of the Regiment to draw up alongside.

The Germans had abandoned the woods in 117th Regiment's area and air strikes planned to hit Objectives Ann and Dot had to be rescheduled; Colonel Johnson's men were moving too fast. 3rd Battalion came under fire from AA guns covering the approaches to Buchholt but 1st Battalion came to the rescue, sending one company forward mounted on DD Sherman tanks. The flak crews surrendered as soon as the tanks approached and by mid afternoon 117th Regiment had reached the Autobahn taking 140 prisoners including 1221st Regiment's commanding officer.

119th Regiment had also made good progress along the south bank of the Lippe Canal, and although assault guns operating on the far bank continued to harass Colonel Baker's flank, 3rd Battalion swept the wooded hills overlooking the river, rounding up groups of Germans trying to reach Hunxe. Progress was slow but by mid-afternoon the GIs had captured 125 prisoners and seized a sizeable cache of weapons including seven 88s, eight 20mm AA guns, two radar stations and a searchlight; bazooka teams had also knocked out two *Panzer IV*s.

By midday on 25 March it was clear that German resistance was collapsing and General Hobbs had told Colonels Johnson and Purdue to arrange armoured columns in the hope of clearing Staatsforst Wesel by nightfall. The plan was to push GIs, mounted on tanks and tank destroyers, along the two forest roads while the rest of the infantry swept the woods. 120th Regiment would drive through the woods towards Kirchhellen on the division's south flank while 117th Regiment captured Hunxe on the Lippe Canal; 119th Regiment would then take over the advance along the canal, heading for Gahlen.

On 120th Regiment's front, 2nd Battalion joined 744th Light Tank Battalion and two Companies of the 823rd Tank Destroyer Battalion, forming Task Force Hunt led by the tank commander, Lieutenant Colonel Richard Hunt. The officers joined Colonel Purdue at his forward command post at noon as tanks pulled into position and the GIs of Company E climbed onboard. The tanks moved out at 15:15 hours.

The column was making good progress when a radio call from 3rd Battalion's command post at 17:00 hours changed the whole mood. A patrol had taken a prisoner belonging to the *60th Panzer Grenadier Regiment*; *116th Panzer Division* had reached Staatsforst Wesel – there would be no quick breakthrough.

As the Allies crossed the Rhine and began pushing east, General Blaskowitz had been considering how to deploy Army Group H's depleted reserve. *116th Panzer Division, XLVII Panzer Corps'* remaining division, was stationed on the Dutch border when Operation VARSITY began and 21 Army Group was threatening to break through at three points; on the British front

between Xanten and Rees, from XVIII Airborne Corps perimeter near Hamminkeln and south of the Lippe river on General Hobbs' front. Of the three, Blaskowitz considered that 30th Division's attack through Staatsforst Wesel posed the greatest threat.

At 14:00 hours on 24 March *Generalmajor der Panzertruppen* Siegfried von Waldenburg, *116th Panzer Division*'s commander, had been ordered to move in a huge arc around 21 Army Group's bridgehead to counter 30th Division's advance through the forest. But it took time to gather enough fuel for the move and the fear of Allied air attacks had delayed the division's move until nightfall and by the morning of 25 March von Waldenburg's *panzers* were closing in on the Lippe river.

Generalmajor von Waldenburg had to commit his troops piecemeal into the forest.

Allied air superiority meant that movement by daylight was extremely hazardous but risks had to be taken if he was to stop 30th Division breaking out into the open ground east of the Staatsforst Wesel. Throughout the morning small battle groups of tanks and halftracks ran the gauntlet of Allied fighter-bombers as they raced towards the bridges at Gahlen and Dorsten and although a few groups were attacked the leading elements crossed the river as Hobbs' three tasks forces prepared to advance.

General von Waldenburg was unaware that 30th Division had already crossed the Autobahn and sent his battle groups forward with orders to reinforce the beleaguered 180th Division; both Hobbs and von Waldenburg were about to receive an unpleasant shock.

The first German assault gun and halftracks to arrive caught Task Force Hunt in column as it headed towards Schwarze Heide, a large clearing on the road to Kirchhellen. Machine-gun and shell fire sent Lieutenant George Terry's men scrambling for cover as the tank crews struggled to manoeuvre off the narrow forest trail; three Chaffee tanks had been disabled before 744th Tank Battalion was able to respond.

120th Regiment runs into *60th Panzer Grenadier Regiment* on the Kirchhellen Road.

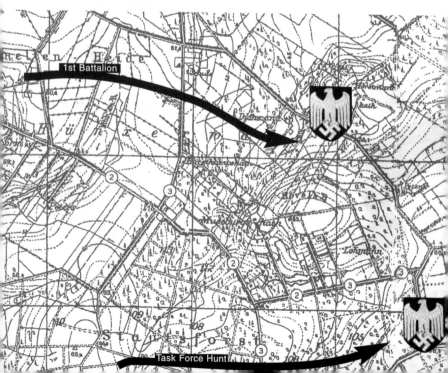

GIs hit the dirt as shrapnel from bursting shells rips through the trees.

Lieutenant Colonel Cantey was fortunate enough to have a considerable amount of artillery on call and as Company E fanned out into the woods, guns and howitzers began to target the German battle group, forcing it to withdraw. Hunt would later discover that his men had knocked out two tanks, four half tracks and a number of lorries; the retreating *Panzergrenadiers* had also left behind three 105mm field pieces and five anti-tank guns. Cantey's men found dozens of dead and injured men as they pushed forward and eventually rounded up forty prisoners, including the *Panzergrenadiers'* commanding officer.

By 19:00 hours the danger had passed and despite heavy casualties amongst men

After coming under fire GIs scramble for cover and try to spot their enemy.

and tanks, Task Force Hunt had held its ground. Colonel Purdue was anxious to follow up the success but as the German and American artillery pounded the woods, ammunition dumps and a truck loaded with shells exploded in sheets of flame, setting the trees either side of the only road on fire; Task Force Hunt would have to wait until dawn before it could resume the advance.

The rest of 120th Regiment had also encountered elements of *116th Panzer Division* as it moved towards Schwarze Heide and 3rd Battalion had been forced to withdraw a short distance after running into a prepared line of machine-gun posts. Meanwhile, 1st Battalion had also run into difficulties as it advanced across the steep wooded slopes of Bruckhauser Heide. Company A's scouts had seen men running through the trees as they approached Nottenbohm and Lieutenant Jack Henterly's platoon came under fire as it moved in extended order towards the hamlet. Running forward, the GIs formed a defensive perimeter around the first building only to find a large group of Germans, numbering around 100, assembling at the far end of the hamlet. Once again the artillery came to the rescue and a rapid salvo of 105mm shells from the Regiment's Cannon Company scattered the *Panzergrenadiers*, leaving Henterly's men in a precarious position out in front of the rest of 1st Battalion. As Company A's machine-gun platoon gave covering fire, Captain D'Amico ordered the rest of his men forward to rescue the trapped platoon:

> *Sergeant Dale Cline moved his squad down the road and took up positions around the burning house. Sergeant Trombley moved his squad one hundred yards past the burning house, but was stopped by another strongpoint, which consisted of two machine-gun squads and a rifle squad. Because cover was unavailable and the enemy had good observation and excellent fields of fire, the position became untenable. The platoon withdrew; but later that evening the company commander arranged for two light tanks from the 744th Light Tank Battalion to assist another platoon in knocking out the strongpoint. The tanks were late in arriving; so the company decided to attack without them and in a short time succeeded in capturing the strongpoint. With this point cleared the mission of Company A was complete.*

While 120th Regiment struggled to hold its own either side of the Kirchhellen road, 117th Regiment's transport had failed to arrive and as Brigadier General William Harrison, 30th Division's Assistant Commander, moved forward to take command of the Task Force, he was frustrated to hear that a number of the lorries carrying 2nd Battalion had become bogged down as they tried to push forward along the narrow forest road. Darkness was beginning to fall by the time the column rendezvoused with 743rd Tank Battalion and the elements of 843rd Tank Destroyer Battalion news of 120th Regiment's encounter with the *Panzergrenadiers* had begun to filter through. At 19:30 hours General Harrison confirmed the rumours by radio:

> *Plan of attack changed. 120th Infantry is up against* 116th Panzer Tiger *tanks. Button up your units in defensive positions for tonight, attack will be continued in morning.*

On 119th Regiment's front a prisoner had notified an interpreter that his patrol was expecting to meet *60th Panzergrenadier Regiment*. The information confirmed what General Hobbs had been afraid of; his men faced the entire weight of the *116th Panzer Division*. Veterans knew they faced a hard fight. The Old

A column of M-24 Chaffee tanks passes a burning Sdkfz 250/17, a three tonne German halftrack armed with a 20mm flak gun capable of being used in a ground or air support role. 111-SC-203439

Hickory Division had fought the 116th in the Normandy bocage nine months earlier during the bloody Battle for St Lô. The time for rapid advances had passed; 30th Division would have to fight for every square metre of Staatsforst Wesel.

The arrival of *116th Panzer Division* in the forest posed a serious problem for General Simpson for although he had superiority in men, tanks and artillery, the woods hemmed in 30th Division. The lack of suitable roads made it impossible to bring the full weight of XVI Corps to bear while the Germans were in an ideal position to keep Ninth Army's bridgehead bottled up. 8th Armoured Division had already crossed the Rhine but with no room to deploy, General Devine's tanks and halftracks would have to wait until the forest had been cleared.

79th Division was looking to extend XVI Corps flank towards

the Rhine-Herne Canal and the towns and villages along the northern outskirts of the Ruhr. Meanwhile General Hobbs would have to bludgeon his way through Staatsforst Wesel. There would be no respite for the Old Hickories until the forest had been cleared.

A few hours after the cancellation order was given, Brigadier General Harrison was notified that he should try a night advance to Meesenhof, a small hamlet on 117th Regiment's road, in the hope of gaining ground before the Germans dug in:

General Hobbs wants us to take Objective Sally tonight. Put your tanks in the lead followed by your foot troops. Follow the original plan without the trucks. Let me know where your foot troops are when you have them assembled.

The tanks moved along the forest track at 22:45 hours as the GIs searched the woods and apart from an occasional shot from German sentries and a lone anti-tank gun, Task Force Harrison's advance was unopposed. It reached its objective two hours later, capturing a huge 270mm artillery piece and two 150mm howitzers.

A platoon checks its weapons before moving out through the forest; the GI on the right is armed with a rifle grenade.

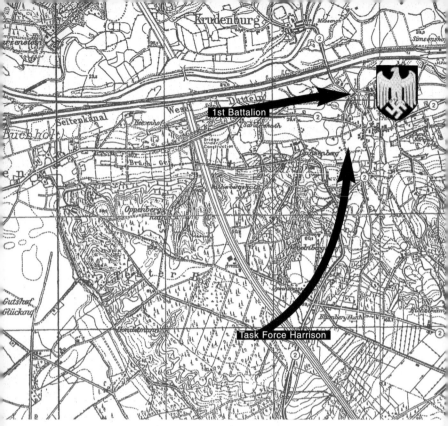

117th Regiment's battle for Hunxe.

Task Force Harrison's advance into the unknown allowed 1st Battalion to sweep the south bank of the Lippe Canal as far as Hunxe by the early hours, panicking the German engineers into blowing the river and canal bridges. One possible crossing for *156th Panzergrenadier Regiment* had been sealed off.

While 117th Regiment spent the night clearing Hunxe, Major General Hobbs ordered Colonel Baker to patrol the road towards Gahlen in the hope of securing two bridges either side of the village before the *Panzergrenadiers* arrived. Task Force McCown, 119th Regiment's 1st Battalion, advanced slowly through the night clearing a number of roadblocks before it reached the high ground overlooking the village. It was too late. Although the Germans had already destroyed the first bridge, the bridge on the far side of Gahlen was still intact but a rearguard of the 180th Division prevented McCown's men advancing any further. It was too late to bring up tanks and

Tank destroyers worked closely alongside the infantry during 79th Division's advance east of Dinslaken. 111-SC-335600

An infantry officer clings to the turret of a tank destroyer as he directs the crew towards a German strongpoint.

British Prime Minister Winston Churchill visited XVI Corps bridgehead on 25 March accompanied by General Anderson; General Simpson follows close behind.

while the GIs dug in they had to watch and listen while German tanks and halftracks crossed the Lippe Canal.

79th Division

On XVI Corps' right flank, 79th Division had to expand its bridgehead to make room for the 35th *Santa Fe* Division east of Dinslaken, allowing General Wyche to redirect his advance south towards to the Rhein-Herne Canal. On the German side, General Abraham had moved 2nd Parachute Division forward to support LXIII Corps' front in the hope of containing the bridgehead.

79th Division's attack began at first light on 25 March and tank destroyers from 813th Battalion worked closely alongside 315th Regiment, knocking out machine-gun nests and anti-aircraft guns en route to the high ground near Eppinghoven.

While 313th Regiment continued to hold positions along the Neue-Ernscher Canal, 314th Regiment advanced towards Hiesfeld. 40mm anti-aircraft guns on the outskirts of the village kept 1st Battalion at bay until noon when Company C found a way across the Rotbach Stream and moved into the houses. Company B followed and as the two worked a pincer move along the edges of the village, the German infantry withdrew beyond the Autobahn to the east; a strongpoint manned by a few fanatics was reduced to rubble by tank destroyers. Although Company E advanced quickly to the objective on 2nd Battalion's front, Company F came under heavy fire from a battery of six 88mm guns covering the roads into Eickhof from the Dinslaken rail embankment. After withdrawing to regroup, Company F followed the rest of the battalion and waited for nightfall in the hope that the gun crews would retire during the night.

Later that night Company F's commanding officer was ambushed leading a two-man patrol through Eickhof. Several hours passed before another, larger, patrol located and rescued the captain; it was a stern reminder that the German paratroopers had not given up the fight.

Chapter 9

26 MARCH – THE BATTLE FOR THE FOREST

17th Airborne Division strikes back

General Miley's opportunity to hit back at the Germans finally came on the morning of 26 March. Sherman tanks of 771st Tank Battalion and self-propelled anti-tank guns from 144th Battery had crossed the Issel Canal, joining the paratroopers during the night. As artillery batteries rolled onto the east bank of the Rhine and opened communications with the men at the front line, Miley's men knew that they could call on a devastating array of firepower.

A rolling artillery barrage started at 09:00 hours along the entire divisional front and all three Regiments advanced hugging the line of shell bursts, while the tanks and self-propelled guns followed at a close distance. Resistance was minimal. Although sporadic firefights broke out from time to time, the Germans were trying to withdraw; the counter-attacks over the past two nights had taken their toll on General Strabe's men.

507th Regiment overran strongpoints along the north bank of the Lippe river, taking dozens of prisoners, and 2nd Battalion had reached the Autobahn within an hour. 1st Battalion arrived two hours later after engaging a lone *Stug III* operating near Krudenburg; the *Panzergrenadiers* withdrew as soon as the paratroopers had knocked out the self-propelled gun. As the Regiment dug in along the Autobahn, Colonel Raff made himself comfortable in his new headquarters, the underground complex that had been the nerve centre for air defences stretching from Holland through to the heart of Germany. By nightfall patrols had managed to get across the Lippe river at Hunxe making contact with 30th Division and for the first time Ninth Army held a continuous line either side of the river.

German resistance along the rest of the divisional front was ineffectual. 194th Glider Regiment took 330 prisoners, wiping out 1221st Regiment from 180th Infantry Division, while 513th Regiment advanced steadily alongside 6th British Airborne

Division, capturing over 500 prisoners and the town of Brunen, over two miles east of the Issel Stream. It appeared that German morale was teetering on the edge. While 30th Division fought for every inch in Staatsforst Wesel, 17th Airborne Division appeared to have found a weak point in First Parachute Army's line. With 8th Armoured Division bottled up behind the centre of XVI Corps front, General Simpson wondered if it would be possible to break through north of the Lippe and, after discussions with General Dempsey, arranged for a British Armoured Brigade to move into the paratroopers perimeter. The time to unleash Operation PLUNDER was drawing near.

30th Division

During the night Major General Hobbs warned his regimental commanders to be on the guard against counter-attacks by armoured battle groups. Although *116th Panzer Division* was a mere shadow of its paper strength, the American tanks working alongside 30th Division were no match for the heavier German *panzers*. The Old Hickories faced a tough fight, one they could not afford to lose.

On 30th Division's southern flank 120th Regiment faced Schwarze Heide, a clearing in the forest codenamed Objective Hilda. The plan was for 2nd Battalion to conduct a pincer movement, sending two Companies along the north edge of the clearing while the third advanced south of the Kirchhellen road.

As Lieutenant Colonel Cantey's men prepared for an attack at dawn, patrols headed out into the darkness to check the line of departure for enemy activity. They found plenty. One of Company E's patrols made the first contact, finding a 105mm self-propelled gun waiting on the line of departure; the patrol quietly retired to report the worrying development. On Company F's front a patrol withdrew after hearing tanks moving across Schwarze Heide; a second patrol became embroiled in a firefight with German outposts and did not return until the early hours. It appeared that *116th Panzer Division* was preparing to make its own attack.

After hearing the reports, Colonel Purdue decided to bring 2nd Battalion's advance forward by an hour, looking to infiltrate the German lines before it was light, and Cantey passed on the new orders emphasising the need to move quickly to his subordinates:

Fox [Company F] *is going to the south; their job is to slip through, not to attack any tanks they meet. If they don't get through by bypassing, they won't get through at all.*

2nd Battalion's advance went to plan and while two companies pushed ahead on the flanks, a platoon remained behind to clear

Chaffee tanks move forward to support the infantry; the tank crews relied on the GIs to sweep the roads and ditches for mines. 111-SC-206437

the German outposts along the edge of Schwarze Heide. The early start had given Cantey's men the advantage but after advancing a mile the Germans struck as Company F was closing in on the far side of the clearing. Five tanks and a company of *Panzergrenadiers* roared out of the woods along the Kirchhellen road, catching Captain Jacobsen's men in the open. The first shell killed 1st Platoon's leader and sent his men scrambling for cover. Sergeant Javitch tried to rally them behind a farmhouse in the middle of the clearing as 3rd Platoon gave covering fire and Private Raymond Rottar ran ahead to the house clutching a handful of rifle grenades. The private's brave attempt to stop the tank ended as he crouched to take aim; a shell slammed into

German infantry attack with *Panzer Mk IV*s in support.

the building above his head, killing him instantly.

As shells rained down and the tanks advanced towards 2nd Battalion, Lieutenant Colonel Cantey's men were calling for their own armoured support but the Shermans were still held up some distance away by mines. 2nd Battalion would have to rely on close support from the artillery to stop the *Panzergrenadiers* crossing Schwarze Heide. Sergeant King's platoon was frantically trying to clear a route to the waiting Shermans when a German tank spotted them. Time and time again the tank fired but 2nd Platoon continued its work, dragging its wounded as it probed for mines; two men had been killed and another thirteen wounded by the time King cleared the road. 2nd Platoon's sacrifice allowed the Shermans to move forward to support the rest of the battalion.

The arrival of tanks behind 2nd Battalion's front forced the Germans to withdraw and as they resorted to shelling Schwarze Heide, Colonel Purdue had to admit that no one could cross the clearing during daylight hours; Cantey would have to wait until nightfall before he tried to advance again.

As the German main attack fell on 2nd Battalion, 1st Battalion had not gone unnoticed as it waited in reserve near Hovelsberg. A company of *Panzergrenadiers* had slipped through the American lines and caught Company A in the open; Lieutenant Walter Johnson later described the confusion when the Germans attacked:

> The men were stretched out on both sides of the road taking a break while I with a few other men checked some houses about 200 yards to the south of the road. It was about 10:00 hours in the morning. Suddenly all hell broke loose. Direct fire, artillery and mortars, hit us all at once, quickly killing one man and wounding eight others. Everyone was so stunned and scared that they could only think of hitting the ground and hoping they would get through somehow. With all this stuff coming in and everyone hugging the ground, Sergeant Alfred Bollengier, kept his wits about him, came up the road and got the men to fall back and bring the wounded men with them to a point farther to the rear about 400 yards where they could get enough cover to avoid further casualties.

Company A eventually repelled the German attack and Captain D'Amico reorganised his men in a defensive position below the summit of Hovelsberg in case the Germans returned.

One man has been hit while the rest of his platoon hugs the ground for cover during a German counter-attack. 111-SC-203437

While the rest of 120th Regiment battled with the *Panzergrenadiers*, 3rd Battalion had found a weak point in the German lines south of Schwarze Heide and advanced beyond Schlagers Heide. As Major McCullough pushed east towards Kirchhellen it soon became clear why the Germans had abandoned the area, the woods were littered with stacks of ammunition wired for detonation; 3rd Battalion was walking through a deathtrap. In spite of the dangers, Company I pushed on and while Lieutenant John Doyle's platoon spread out to try to disarm as many of the explosives as possible, McCullough's men froze every time a shell landed.

There were tense moments as 3rd Battalion closed in on its objective, when infantry were seen moving through the woods from the south. Although it appeared that the Germans were about to attack, the enemy turned out to be GIs from 35th Division; Major General Paul Baade's Division had moved into line earlier that morning on 30th Division's right flank. After tying in their positions with the newcomers, 3rd Battalion continued to move east and by mid afternoon Colonel Purdue was relieved to hear that McCullough could see the edge of the woods; after three long days the end of Staatsforst Wesel was in sight.

With his southern flank secure, Colonel Purdue's concern lay with his centre where the counter attack on 2nd Battalion's position had pushed Lieutenant Colonel Cantey's men to their limit; 1st Battalion would have to be committed if he was to clear Schwarze Heide that night. Company A was already heavily engaged at Hovelsberg hill, but the rest of the Battalion was available and at 13:40 hours Lieutenant Colonel Williamson received the order to move. Unfortunately, 2nd Battalion's support vehicles blocked the only way forward and the woods had been sown with wooden box mines that were impossible to detect. To drive off the single marked path invited disaster and it would take hours to probe the area by hand. The hours ticked by as Williamson's men crawled forward, prodding the ground with their bayonets, and by the time they had moved through 2nd Battalion's area the German bombardment had intensified to such an extent that Purdue called off the attack; he would have to wait until nightfall.

Despite the postponement, the capture of Objective June, Besten airfield at the far end of Schwarze Heide, was going to be

After coming under fire, these men warily crawl forward to try to identify the enemy position.

a difficult mission. 1st Battalion had to cross over a mile of open ground flanked by woods on either side while *Panzergrenadiers* and tanks waited to meet them at the far end. Aerial reconnaissance had also shown that a ring of concrete encasements armed with heavy calibre anti-aircraft guns protected the airfield. The attack needed to be carefully planned if Butch's Night Raiders were going to succeed; the after-action report details how Williamson intended to crack Objective June.

1st Battalion attack involved: <u>fire plan</u> to smoke the flanks with 81mm mortars, at the same time smoking the objective and firing successive concentrations by the artillery. (Some civilians later said the enemy was convinced there would be no attack with smoke at night.) It also involved an <u>armour plan</u> to use a platoon of tank destroyers along each flank protecting the infantry in the centre, with a section of tanks leading and a company following. It was, then, an extended armour box, moving within an extended smoke box. The infantry used two companies to lead.

There had been concerns that the woods were affecting the

reception of the SCR 300 radios and while Lieutenant Ernest Sharpe delivered short wave walkie-talkies to the Company Commanders, Sergeant Baler ran along the line giving out verbal orders to the platoon leaders. Nothing could be left to chance.

Throughout the afternoon German patrols had been probing 2nd Battalion's lines, reporting Cantey's positions to their artillery and by the time 1st Battalion was ready to move it was estimated that fifteen shells were hitting the assembly area every minute. Williamson knew that the artillery would target the line of departure as soon as the attack began and planned his

120th Regiment's battle for Schwarze Heide and Besten airfield.

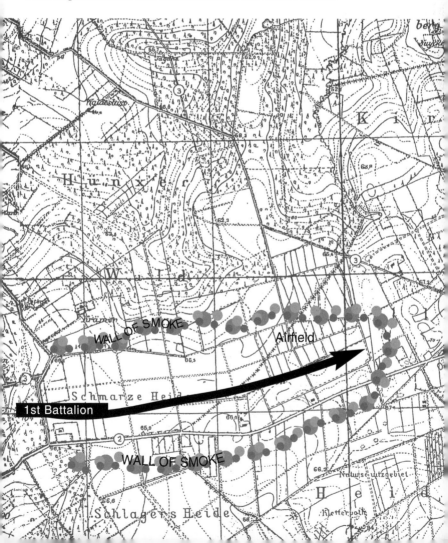

attack accordingly to avoid unnecessary casualties; his reserve company would wait at a safe distance until it was time to move forward.

As 1st Battalion assembled, artillery and howitzers fired smoke rounds across the objective and along the edges of Schwarze Heide, creating an impenetrable wall of smoke around the clearing, blinding any Germans waiting on the airfield at the far end. At zero hour a section of Sherman tanks roared across the open space while the two assault companies ran alongside. Tank destroyers followed, moving down the edges of the clearing with their guns aimed towards the woods while machine guns and mortars fired indiscriminately into the trees:

> *The tank destroyers were as ever effective; moving up close behind the attackers, they afforded a quick defence backing.*

The attack took the Germans completely by surprise and the

Trees and thick undergrowth confined vehicles to the forest tracks, leaving the infantry to secure large parts of the forest.

A large amount of ordnance was found abandoned in the woods around Besten airfield including this huge howitzer.

line of tanks and infantry came to a halt at the halfway point to allow the reserve company to catch up. As expected the German artillery had targeted the line of departure as soon as 1st Battalion advanced, missing Company A's assembly area some distance to the rear. Captain D'Amico gave the order to run forward as soon as the shelling slackened off and once they had caught up, the whole the Battalion advanced towards Besten airfield. The enemy reaction was subdued and as prisoners later explained, the smoke had lulled the Germans into a false sense of security; no one had ever attacked through smoke at night before. 1st Battalion pushed on relentlessly, overrunning the anti-aircraft positions surrounding the airfield and within the hour they had scattered the *Panzergrenadiers*, securing Objective June. The attack had been a complete success.

As Williamson's men dug in for the night, patrols uncovered an impressive array of weaponry and ammunition scattered around the airfield. Four huge 128mm anti-aircraft guns mounted in concrete emplacements were found on the perimeter and eight abandoned Sdkfz 250/17s, halftracks armed with 20mm flak guns were taken. The Battalion also found two rail wagons full of ammunition, two 75mm guns with halftracks, and stacks of abandoned equipment. As the three Companies formed a defensive perimeter around the edge of the airfield, Colonel Purdue was forced to send Lieutenant Colonel Williamson to the rear to receive medical attention for an injury to his hand. Williamson had been wounded at the start of the attack but had refused medical attention until he was sure his men had taken their objective. As Williamson left for the aid station he was proud of the fact that Butch's Night Raiders had broken through the enemy lines in a cloud of smoke.

120th Regiment's capture of Besten airfield secured 117th Regiment's southern flank and Colonel Johnson was anxious to renew his advance towards Objective Marie, in the hope of taking the hilltop anti-aircraft position before dawn.

3rd Battalion moved out at midnight and had soon overrun one flak position on the northern edge of Marie, however, 2nd Battalion had run into problems. German engineers had destroyed a bridge on the forest road heading towards the objective and the leading company lost its way looking for a way around. After two hours it appeared the problem had been solved when a company commander reported that he had reached the objective but he was quickly overruled by 743rd Tank Battalion's commanding officer; the company had taken a wrong turning and was nowhere near Objective Marie. 2nd Battalion was lost.

As patrols tried to locate the correct track, Colonel Johnson devised a plan to help his men. A gun crew from 118th Field Artillery Battalion fired white phosphorous shells onto Objective Marie at regular intervals and the explosions guided the lost battalion into position. By dawn 117th Regiment was firmly dug in along the edge of Staatsforst Wesel.

While the rest of the division battled their way through the southern half of Staatsforst Wesel, 119th Regiment was trying to advance along the Lippe Canal towards Gahlen. 1st Battalion had started to advance at 08:00 hours but once again the lack of roads and thick mud hampered the advance. Log roadblocks delayed the tanks following Company A along the only road and the Shermans with Company B were soon bogged down as they cut across country. One of 180th Division's rearguards protected the bridge and as 1st Battalion struggled forward, patrols could see vehicles crossing the canal and moving into

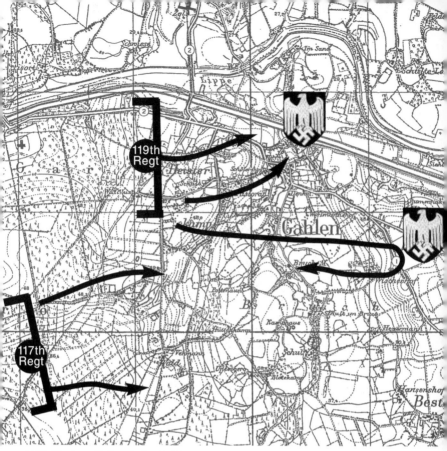

119th Regiment's battle for Gahlen.

Gahlen. 156th Panzer Grenadier Regiment had beaten 119th Regiment to the bridge. Frustrated by their lack of progress, Lieutenant Colonel Heslong's patrols had to stand by and watch as two Panthers moved into the village followed by trucks and motorbikes carrying *Panzergrenadiers*.

Gahlen had been codenamed Hubert after Sergeant Dick Wingate's popular cartoon character in *Stars and Stripes*, the front line newspaper. In a recent edition Hubert had been pictured eating K-Rations in a shell crater as a German sniper took shots at his group of cartoon comrades: the caption read 'Let's ignore the bastard, maybe he'll go away.' During a visit by Colonel Jesse Gibney, General Hobbs' Chief of Staff, Colonel Baker wryly commented that this Hubert could not be ignored; the *Panzergrenadiers* intended to stay and worry 30th Division's flank for as long as possible.

151

The light American Chaffee tanks were no match for the larger German tanks with their thick armour and heavy guns.

While the engineers removed the roadblocks, 1st Battalion had to watch as the rest of *156th Panzergrenadier Regiment* crossed over the canal and over the hours that followed five tanks, five self-propelled guns and trucks moved into Gahlen, bringing the number of men defending the town to around 350. Objective Hubert was going to be a tough nut to crack.

As the final roadblock was dragged to one side, Company A began to move across the fields towards Gahlen as the tanks rolled down the road. The advance was short lived. Machine-gun fire brought the infantry to a halt and a hidden German tank disabled one of the M24 Chaffees, blocking the only route forward. With his men pinned down and the rest of the tanks stuck behind the blazing tank; in Heslong's words, Company A was in a 'pretty hot spot'. As the Germans focussed their attentions on Company A, Company B worked its way across the fields, infiltrating the outskirts of Gahlen by nightfall.

While 1st Battalion battled for Gahlen, Colonel Baker received orders to push east towards Dorsten (codename Objective Scott) at the first opportunity to block the next bridge along the division's flank. 3rd Battalion made the advance that night but as the tank destroyers were unable to follow, the attack on the town quickly ran into trouble. Company L was met by a tank and heavily armed *Panzergrenadiers* and as Lieutenant Colonel Stewart's men fell back, two platoons were cut off in the outskirts of the town; Stewart's men faced a long night in the flaming ruins of Objective Scott.

79th Division

As 30th Division advanced through Staatsforst Wesel, General Anderson was anxious to protect XVI Corps' southern flank and with the help of Task Force M from 35th Division, Wyche was expected to elongate his flank at the same rate. For the second day running, 313th Regiment was to hold its line along the Neue-Ernscher Canal while patrolling towards the Rhine-Herne Canal. Colonel Bibber was pleased to hear that the Hamburg

What the Americans lacked in armour, they more than made up for with their artillery and time after time they dispersed German attacks before they reached 30th Division's lines. These 25-pdr howitzers are deployed along the incomplete Autobahn cutting.

Division had abandoned the area. 79th Division's chemical mortars had saturated the area with over 10,000 white phosphorous shells on 24 March as they maintained the smoke-screen across the river and the bombardment had forced the Germans to evacuate the area; they had never returned.

As 315th Regiment withdrew into reserve ready to join the advance to the Rhine-Herne Canal, 1st Battalion led 314th Regiment towards Zurforst Wesel, a large wooded area. After clearing 2nd Parachute Division's outposts along the Autobahn, Company A infiltrated the woods but Company B found its way forward blocked by two tanks and a line of infantry emplacements. While 2nd Battalion engaged strongpoints along the southern edge of the forest, 3rd Battalion followed Company A into Zurforst Wesel and by nightfall the woods had been cleared. After a frustrating day Colonel Robinson was pleased to report that an important objective had been taken.

While 314th Regiment dug in along the eastern edge of Zurforst Wesel, 315th Regiment had moved across to the division's southern flank and during the course of the night Colonel Schriner took up positions alongside 313th Regiment on the Neue-Ernscher Canal. With 30th Division close to breaking out of Staatsforst Wesel, General Anderson had decided it was time to widen his grip on the east bank of the Rhine. At first light 79th Division would attack south heading for the Rhine-Herne Canal.

Chapter 10

27 MARCH – BREAKING FREE FROM THE WOODS

By 27 March Operation VARSITY was coming to an end paving the way for the next phase of Montgomery's plan, Operation PLUNDER. The German troops facing 17th Airborne Division were at breaking point and as more tanks and artillery moved onto the east bank of the Rhine, it was only a matter of time before General Miley broke free into open country. 30th Division was still making steady progress in Staatsforst Wesel and while one of its Regiments had already broken free from the northern corner, another had reached the south-east perimeter. To the south 79th Division was preparing to expand the bridgehead towards the Rhine-Herne Canal to make room for 35th Division to enter the line. It was only a matter of time before First Parachute Army's line snapped.

17th Airborne Division
6th British Guards Armoured Brigade had joined 513th Regiment in reserve during the night and after the trials of the past few days Colonel Coutts' paratroopers were looking forward to acting as mounted infantry. However, before the advance to Dorsten could begin, the rest of the division had to push beyond the Paris and Detroit lines and clear the road through Schermbeck.

Yet again the German rearguards were unable to stop the 507th Regiment's coordinated attacks and before long Colonel Coutts instructed 2nd Battalion to mount up and lead the rest of the Regiment towards Schermbeck. The column of Shermans and Hellcats reached the Paris Line at the far side of the town by mid morning and as 1st Battalion followed behind, they found that the Germans had abandoned the ruins. By nightfall 507th Regiment had reached the Detroit Line and after four days of hard fighting it appeared that the paratroopers had finally broken First Parachute Army's line; the armoured column could attack at dawn.

30th Division

As it began to grow light groups of *Panzergrenadiers*, bypassed during the night, were rounded up in Staatsforst Wesel and in 117th Regiment's sector bazooka teams had to hunt down a *Stug III* still operating behind its lines.

As General Hobbs' men consolidated their positions and prepared to advance out of the forest, *116th Panzer Division* struck back at 117th Regiment's sector. At 10:00 hours two tanks and a company of *Panzergrenadiers* emerged from Besten village (Objective Jo-Jo) and attacked 2nd Battalion. An hour later the main body of tanks and halftracks broke free from Gahlen and headed for 3rd Battalion's positions. Overcast skies meant that the *Panzers* could operate in the open without having to worry about air attacks and Colonel Johnson was left hoping that 118th Field Artillery Battalion could keep the Germans at bay. 117th Regiment's Signal Journal records the tense moments as *116th Panzer Division* made its final attempt to contain 30th Division in Staatsforst Wesel:

12:05   *3rd Battalion says they are receiving heavy small-arms fire and direct fire in their area.*

12:10   *Enemy infantry approaching Objective Jo-Jo; have placed artillery in their path. Also, there are tanks in position blocking that approach in case of any enemy armour.*

12:15   *Enemy infantry and tanks approaching from the northeast, between Objective Jo-Jo and Objective Marie; they are keeping us busy now.*

12:45   *One enemy Mark V tank withdrawing north out of Marie.*

13:00   *One enemy tank between Jo-Jo and Checkpoint 5, situation clearing up some but still having trouble in northeast sector of Marie.*

13:25   *Enemy infantry moving northwest out of Jo-Jo on Highway 1.*

13:40   *Things clearing up in northeast sector of Marie and enemy making withdrawal to northeast.*

The American howitzers and mortars had dispersed the *Panzergrenadiers*, leaving the tanks vulnerable to bazooka teams; they soon withdrew to safety. Company G's commanding officer later recalled that the barrage had been the heaviest he had ever witnessed and his men agreed with the following statement:

> *I'll give the artillery credit for keeping the remainder of the enemy from attacking.*

116th Panzer Division's final counter-attacks against 117th Regiment. **Inset**: Half-track with the *Windhunde* (Greyhound) emblem of the *116th Panzer Division* on the front.

As the attack on 3rd Battalion subsided, a second column of *Panzers* and halftracks headed for 2nd Battalion's sector. Following a warning from the Piper Cub artillery observer plane circling overhead, Colonel Johnson had sent three Sherman tanks to the danger point but the crews missed 2nd Battalion's guides and drove straight through the American lines towards the approaching Germans. Two tanks managed to return to 1st Battalion's lines but the third was captured and turned against the GIs. Yet again it was down to 118th Field Artillery Battalion to keep the Germans at bay and by nightfall the danger had passed; 117th Regiment had weathered the storm.

On 120th Regiment's front 3rd Battalion expanded its perimeter along the edge of the forest, contacting 1st Battalion, and by mid morning another section of Staatsforst Wesel had been cleared, however, it had not gone unnoticed. Shelling intensified as the GIs dug in and a lone *Stug III* moved close to threaten 3rd Battalion. Private Leake took the initiative and ran forward, using rifle grenades to force the assault gun to withdraw; eventually he struck lucky when a grenade penetrated the machine's engine and forced the crew to bail out as it burst into flames.

As the GIs consolidated their perimeter and looked forward to moving into reserve, General Hobbs sent through new orders to 120th Regiment. Although the men had been in action for four days without a break, Colonel Purdue had to take one more objective before turning his sector over to the 8th Armoured Division. He wanted three hamlets covering the approaches to Kirchhellen clearing before the tanks moved forward and the attack was planned for later that night. In the meantime Purdue instructed Major McCullough to cut the Besten road on the Regiment's north flank to guard against German counter-attacks from the direction of Gahlen.

Lieutenant Shaw's platoon from Company I climbed on board a platoon of tanks and two tank destroyers and at 10:00 hours the small armoured column raced across the fields drawing fire from all directions as it reached the Kirchhellen road. Realising what Shaw was trying to achieve, the *Panzergrenadiers* counter-attacked from every direction, destroying the tank destroyers, two of the tanks and killed or wounded twenty-four of Shaw's men. The survivors held on until nightfall, severly restricting the *Panzers'* movements.

Company K tried to come to the aid of the beleaguered platoon but a damaged bridge and mines prevented the tank moving forward leaving the infantry exposed to heavy fire from Besten village. Once again low mist prevented McCullough calling for air support and as his men withdrew General Hobbs realised that the capture of Besten could wait until 119th Regiment had moved up behind the village.

On the north flank of 30th Division's front 119th Regiment was heavily engaged along the south bank of the Lippe Canal as

Sherman tanks roll forward once again after defeating another counter-attack.

This Sherman had to be pushed off the road into a shell crater after it had been disabled, to make way for other vehicles.

60th Panzergrenadier Regiment tried to breakout from Gahlen. Colonel Baker's men had spent the night fighting for their lives in the village but the arrival of tanks and tank destroyers at first light turned the tide in 1st and 3rd Battalions' favour. The GIs and Shermans battled the *Panzergrenadiers* and their *Panzers* throughout the morning but as the hours passed, one street after another fell into American hands.

With the 17th Airborne Division closing in on Schermbeck north of the Lippe, there was no chance of retiring north of the river, and the way into the woods blocked by 119th Regiment, the Germans were only left with one option, a break out to the east. The *Panzers* withdrew first, taking up positions on high ground overlooking Gahlen to the east, and gave covering fire as the *Panzergrenadiers* withdrew towards Dorsten. By midday on 27 March, Objective Hubert was safely in 119th Regiment's hands.

On 120th Regiment's front Colonel Purdue had spent the day preparing to capture Objective July, the three hamlets along the ridge overlooking the approaches to Kirchhellen. 2nd Battalion had been chosen to make the attack and Lieutenant Colonel Cantey's three Companies were detailed to seize Ekamp, Janinhof and Holthausen in turn, while Company K from 3rd Battalion secured the main crossroads to their rear. After the success the previous evening on Besten airfield, Purdue had arranged for a mile wide smokescreen box to protect the troops. Once again the GIs were to break through the German lines in a cloud of smoke.

As it began to grow dark, artillery and mortars started to shell the hamlets. Company G moved into position facing Ekamp on the left, while Company F deployed opposite Janinhof and Company E prepared to advance against Holthausen on the right. Columns of tanks and tank destroyers moved up ready but, as they were confined to the roads by the poor ground conditions, the infantry would probe the German defences on their own. The tanks would wait until the roads were clear. As the final preparations were made and zero hour approached, the artillery switched to smoke creating a huge 'U' shaped wall of smoke around Objective July.

The signal to move out was given at 21:00 hours and as Lieutenant Colonel Cantey's men advanced down the slopes towards Kirchhellen, German artillery fired blindly into the

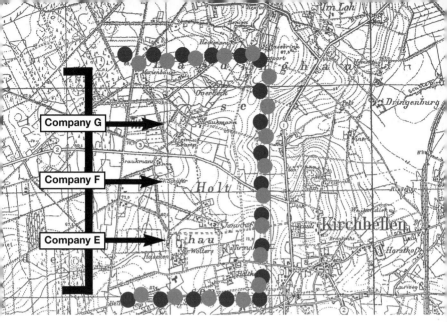

120th Regiment clears the road to Kirchhellen.

smoke. Company G came under machine-gun fire as it approached Ekamp but while the rest of Captain Montcrieff's men hit the dirt, Private Cashion ran ahead with his machine gun and fired on the Germans' flank. Cashion's actions distracted the enemy long enough for the squad leaders to kick their men into action and thirty prisoners were taken in the charge that followed. Ekamp was taken soon afterwards and the tanks and tank destroyers rumbled forward to join Montcrieff's men on the slopes overlooking Kirchhellen.

A mobile flak gun engaged Company F as it moved towards Janinhof but the vehicle withdrew as Captain Jacobsen's men moved closer to the hamlet. Company E also came under fire from flak guns as it approached Janinhof and the new commander, Lieutenant Guy E Hogle, was forced to rally his men several times. After knocking out one halftrack, Company E encountered a *Panzer IV* covering the approaches to the village. It was time to call up the armour but as the radio failed at the critical moment, Lieutenant Hogle decided to take on the *Panzer* with rifle grenades while Lieutenant William Barenkamp went to the rear to contact the tanks.

Hogle began to stalk the tank as the rest of the Company gave covering fire and before long he hit the *Panzer's* engine with a smoke grenade, blinding the crew inside. A bazooka team came

161

Brigadier General John Devine and the 8th Armoured Division had to wait in reserve until 30th Division had broken free of the forest.
111-SC-197518

forward, firing two rounds into the *Panzer's* tracks to disable it, and forced the crew to bail out; it had been a sharp lesson in anti-tank warfare. Soon afterwards the American armour pulled up alongside Company E and followed Lieutenant Hogle's GIs into Holthausen; by 03:00 hours the road forward lay open.

As 120th Regiment cleared the ridge overlooking Kirchhellen, 117th Regiment moved into Besten, finding it clear of German troops, *116th Panzer Division* had withdrawn from the outskirts of Staatsforst Wesel. The time to unleash 8th Armoured Division had arrived and the *Thundering Herd* was on the move.

79th Division

27 March marked the start of the second phase in General Anderson's plan for expansion on his southern flank. With 30th

162

Division on the verge of clearing Staatsforst Wesel, XVI Corps needed more space to deploy 35th Division on the east bank of the Rhine and General Wyche received the order he had been waiting for during the early hours; he could advance south to the Rhine-Herne Canal.

The advance started before dawn and 313th Regiment moved quickly towards the canal, through drab villages surrounding huge factories and refineries. 2nd Parachute Division had abandoned the area between the two canals but Colonel Bibber's men soon found to their cost that the paratroopers had been digging in on the south bank of the Rhine-Herne Canal for the past forty-eight hours.

Outposts spotted 2nd Battalion as it approached the canal and as the GIs regrouped, German engineers blew the bridges and the infantry opened fire from the embankment beyond. The way forward was blocked but on 1st Battalion's front Colonel Bibber had more luck. GIs rushed one bridge before the German engineers realised they were under attack, and set up a defensive cordon on the far side of the canal. General Wyche was delighted to hear that he had a bridgehead and as 315th Regiment moved up alongside 313th Regiment his staff began to plan how to exploit the coup.

314th Regiment faced stiff opposition as it attacked Holten and Wehofen (codenamed waffle-iron town due to the regular criss-cross plan of its streets) on the left of 79th Division's front for although organised resistance had collapsed, groups of

Teams armed with anti-tank weapons, the *Panzerfaust* and the *Panzerschreck*, (German version of the bazooka), hunted down the American tanks as they cleared Wehofen and Holten.

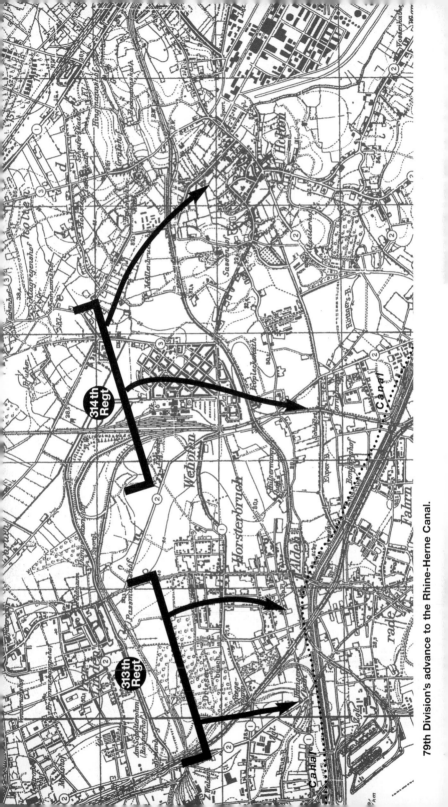

79th Division's advance to the Rhine-Herne Canal.

The highly effective, one shot *Panzerfaust*.

fanatical soldiers and civilians continued to fight on. Snipers fired at unwary GIs while *Panzerfaust* teams crept through the ruins in the hope of catching a Sherman tank unawares. Progress was slow and from time to time the alarm was raised

A Sherman edges forward after firing shells into a German held house.

when a lone German tank was spotted lurking around one of the factories.

2nd Battalion's patrols found machine-gun posts covering the Dinslaken railway on the Regiment's left flank and 717th Battalion's tanks found it difficult to manoeuvre through the ruined villages and industrial plants. *Panzerfaust* teams knocked out two of Company B's Shermans and two others were bogged down as they tried to find a way forward to support the infantry. Meanwhile, an early breakthrough on 3rd Battalion's front turned out to be a trap. German troops held their fire until Company G had crossed the railway and were advancing across the open ground beyond before opening fire from the oil refinery east of Holten. It took several hours to recall the company but by moving through 315th Regiment's sector, Colonel Robinson's men managed to attack and capture the refinery before nightfall. By the end of 27 March 79th Division had taken many of its objectives and 35th Division was starting to take over, the *Cross of Lorraine* men could look forward to a long rest.

Chapter 11

28 MARCH – OPERATION PLUNDER BEGINS

By nightfall on 27 March it was clear that *116th Panzer Division* had been broken and at first light 8th Armoured Division began to move through Staatsforst Wesel as General Hobbs' weary GIs waited for dawn in their foxholes. They had fought continuously against the *Panzergrenadiers* and their tanks since crossing the Rhine four days earlier. The firing had died down once 120th Regiment had cleared the outskirts of Kirchhellen

8th Armoured Division used the treadway bridge connecting Wallach and Ork, in the centre of 30th Division's sector, to cross the Rhine.

YOU ARE NOW
CROSSING THE
RHINE RIVER
THROUGH COURTESY
OF E CO. 17 ARMD
ENGR BN. AND
C CO. 202
ENGR. C. BN.

An American paratrooper and a British tank commander share a smoke before heading off towards Holsterhausen.

but the men's nerves were still shredded after the hardships of the past few days. At first light the sounds of tracked vehicles in the woods behind the GIs' front lines momentarily alarmed a few but their fears quickly subsided as the tanks and halftracks came into view; they were American.

If 30th Division had acted as the anvil to draw the German reinforcements into battle, General Devine's tanks would act as Ninth Army's hammer. 8th Armoured Division had started to cross the Rhine on 26 March and hour after hour columns of tanks, halftracks, armoured cars, howitzers and supply trucks had filed onto the east bank and lined up along the forest roads behind 30th Division. Three tank battalions, the 18th, 30th and 80th, three armoured infantry battalions, the 7th, 49th and 58th and three armoured field artillery battalions as well as reconnaissance troops, engineers and logistics vehicles, had waited in Staatsforst Wesel for the past forty-eight hours and, at long last, the moment had arrived; Montgomery's planned breakout across northern Germany was about to begin.

On the left flank Combat Command A (CCA) led by Brigadier General Charles P Colson had orders to pass through 30th Division and pass south of Dorsten while Combat Command Reserve (CCR) pushed through Kirchhellen to attack Zweckel in front of 120th Regiment. However, if Brigadier General Devine thought the Germans were beaten after their trials in Staatsforst Wesel, he was mistaken. Heavy fighting broke out all across 8th Armoured Division's front and the advance party of the 80th Tank Battalion soon found themselves surrounded by elements of the *116th Panzer Division* in Kirchhellen. Although Brigadier General Colson managed to outflank the German positions in the town, rescuing the trapped tank crews, mines stopped Colonel Robert Wallace advancing any further.

Pershing tanks head deep into German territory as Ninth Army begins the breakout into northern Germany.

When it seemed as though General Simpson would have to rethink his plans for a rapid breakout along the Lippe river, a second armoured thrust was well underway in 17th Airborne Division's sector, north of the river. Colonel Coutts had welcomed Brigadier Greenacre, 6th Guards Armoured Brigade's commanding officer, into his headquarters during the night and the two had worked out how to mount 513th Parachute Regiment on the British tanks with the intention of advancing past Holsterhausen on the northern outskirts of Dorsten.

While the *Thundering Herd* wrestled with the *116th Panzer Division's* cadre, the makeshift armoured column began passing through 17th Airborne Division's lines at 08:00 hours with 507th

The end of the war is in sight as these GIs begin the long march into the heart of Germany.

GIs pass through German civilian refugees in a shattered town.
111-SC204735

Regiment following behind, sweeping the fields and farms either side of the road for stragglers. There was little sign of enemy activity and as the tanks crossed the Boston and Tampa phase lines, before bypassing Holsterhausen, the paratroopers could reflect on the past few days' fighting as they struck out into open country.

The column kept pushing east, capturing a huge ammunition dump mined with time fuses set to blow at midnight, 29 March; Colonel Coutts' men had beat the deadline by over twenty-four hours. German resistance was limited to rearguards left behind to protect demolition teams and at one bridge, an officer braved machine-gun fire to deactivate eight demolition charges; his actions allowed the tanks to push on towards Haltern. By midnight 513th Combat Team and 6th Guards Armoured had driven eighteen miles into German held territory – the breakout had been made; Operation PLUNDER was underway.

By the end of March the Allied Armies were streaming across Germany on all fronts. Operation PLUNDER marked the beginning of the end for *Generalfeldmarschall* Albert Kesselring's troops. As 21 Army Group raced past the northern outskirts of the Ruhr, First US Army continued to capitalise on the Remagen bridgehead. Having shaken himself free from the Westerwald, General Courtney Hodges was given the order to drive across the plains north of Frankfurt, turning north to link up with Ninth Army east of the Ruhr. General Patton had not been idle either and was expanding his small bridgehead across the Rhine, heading towards Frankfurt from the south. More attempts to cross the Rhine followed and although a few were stopped, it was only a matter of time before all of Eisenhower's Armies were driving into the heart of Germany.

After five and a half long years the end of the Second World War was in sight. With the Americans, British, Canadians and French pushing from the west and the Russians from the east, the end of Hitler's thousand year Third Reich was only a few weeks away.

German prisoners being marched to the 'cage'.

Chapter 12

TOURING THE BATTLEFIELD

The starting point
Wesel is the starting point for the two car tours; it is five miles west of Junction 6 of the E35 Autobahn. Pedestrian precincts and one-way systems cover large areas of Wesel and you are advised to make use of the on street parking in the surrounding areas if you wish to walk around the town. The Allied bombing on the night before the crossing devastated the town centre and it had to be cleared and rebuilt in the post war years. The few buildings to survive were the town's churches and the tourist information centre can be found in front of the main church in Grosser Markt, at the western end of the main shopping precinct, Hohn Strasse. The contact details are:

> Stadtinformation
> Grosser Markt 11
> 46483 Wesel
> Telephone: 0281 24498
> Fax 0281 1053

It is open from 09:00 until 12:00 from Monday to Saturday and 14:30 to 17:00 from Monday to Friday.

Cycles are available from 2 Rad Hetkamp Cycle Shop at 19 Korbmarcherstrasse, on the north side of Hohn Strasse, a short distance east of the Tourist Information Centre. They cost around £4 (six euros) per day to hire; a passport is needed for identification.

Staying in Wesel
There are a large selection of hotels in and around Wesel, catering for all tastes and budgets; green tourist signs give directions to them.

Hotel	Address
HAUS POOTH	Dorfstrasse 3
HOHE MARK	Am Reitplatz 9
HOTEL GALLAND	Reeser Landstrasse 2
WACHT AM RHEIN	Rheinallee 30
CITY-HOTEL	Doelenstrasse 8
HAUS DUDEN	Konrad-Duden-Strasse 99
ZUR AUE	Reeser Landstrasse 14
KAISERHOF	Kaiserring 1
RHEINTERRASSEN	Rheinpromenade 7
WELCOME HOTEL	Am Tannenhäuschen 7

There is a full range of facilities in the town and a short walk along

173

Hohe Strasse provides a good insight into the range of shops, restaurants and bars available.

Usually only people who come into regular contact with tourists during their course of work, for example at the tourist information centre and in hotels, have a good understanding of English, so be prepared to speak German and have a phrasebook to hand.

The Kaiser's Gate opposite the railway station is one of the few surviving relics of the fortifications protecting Wesel.

Touring the Area

Although there are maps in this book, it would be wise to purchase touring maps of the area. Two Kompass 1:50,000 scale maps cover the area. Map Number 752, Niederrhein Nord – Reichswald and Gocher Heide, covers Tour 1 to the west and north of Wesel; Map Number 753, Naturpark – Hohe Mark, covers Tour 2 to the south and east of the town.

Two car tours follow and both start at the railway station (Bahnhof in German) alongside the ring road on the eastern outskirts of the town. Kaiser Tor, the Kaiser's Gate, is a short walk to the west of the station; it is the last surviving part of the town wall and now houses a restaurant in the old guardhouse on the upper floors.

Tour 1 – 17th Airborne Division's Perimeter

From the railway station head north along Kaiserring and follow Wesel's ring road as it follows a tree-lined avenue around the northern edge of the town. Following signs for Rees, go straight on at five sets of traffic lights and at the T-Junction at the sixth set of lights, turn right into Reeser Landstrasse, again signposted for Rees. Head out of the suburbs of Wesel, known as Feldmark, keeping straight on and after 1.5 miles, where there is a turning for Rees to the right, keep in the left hand lane, signposted for Flüren, and drive straight ahead at the traffic lights. Turn left at the roundabout after one mile and drive through the centre of Flüren. The road swings to the right and enters open countryside at the far end of the small shopping centre; the start of 17th Airborne Division's landing grounds. ❶

507th Parachute Regiment's drop zone, codenamed Drop Zone W, was Flürener Feld, a small area of open ground at the south-east tip of Diersfordt Forest. The first group of Dakotas misjudged their bearings and dropped 1st Battalion over a mile to the west (right of the road), on the opposite side of the forest, however, the rest of the Regiment landed where Colonel Raff expected astride the Bislich road. 2nd Battalion landed in the fields to the left of the road, where part of the

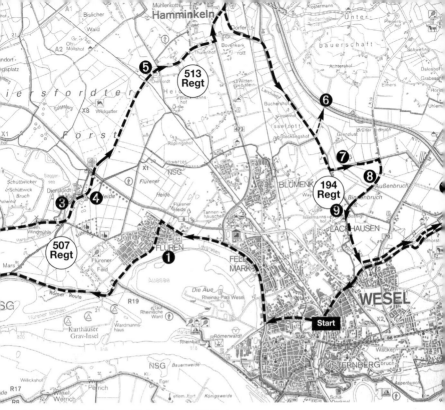

Tour 1: 17th Airborne Division's perimeter.

landing ground has now disappeared beneath the Auesee, one of the many lakes alongside the Rhine. 3rd Battalion hit the ground to the right of the road where the modern suburbs of Flüren are. After capturing the German anti-aircraft guns in the area, the two battalions headed west into Diersfordt Forest.

Continue along the road past Flürener Feld and after a mile the road bends to the right in front of the huge flood bank protecting the Rhine. The forest appears ahead as the road heads west towards Bislich, cutting through the trees after 1.5 miles. 2nd Battalion secured this area, and the paratroopers cleared the thick woods and undergrowth as they moved west towards the British bridgehead. Beyond the woods, the road bends to the right and heads north and after one mile turn right at the crossroads, signposted for Diersfordt. ❷

Part of Drop Zone W where only part of 507th Parachute Regiment landed; one battalion landed on the far side of Diersfordt Forest in the distance.

Operation TORCHLIGHT had begun at 02:00 hours on 24 March and troops of the 15th (Scottish) Division had crossed the Rhine 1.5 miles west of the crossroads. After securing the riverbank and seizing Bislich village, the Scots began to move east and at 15:00 hours contacted Company F near here. Half an hour later General Ridgway and his staff group drove through 507th Regiment's area and headed for General Miley's headquarters.

Heading east, passing a quarry entrance to the left after half a mile, part of 1st Battalion was dropped in the fields to the right of the road. After gathering the men together, Major Paul Smith led them towards their objective, Diersfordt Castle which can be seen beyond the lake (a reclaimed quarry) to the left. Park at the large restaurant, called Haus Constanze, to the right after half a mile. The original driveway leading up to the castle is across the busy road; take a short walk along the overgrown tree-lined avenue to visit the castle.❸

A large number of high-ranking German officers were captured in Diersfordt Castle.

The 'castle' comprises a gatehouse, two large château buildings, a chapel, stables and a disused moat and although the grounds are private it is possible to view the area from the perimeter. As Smith's group approached from the south and Colonel Raff gathered the rest of 1st Battalion to the north, it became obvious that the complex was strongly held. Machine guns, mortars and anti-aircraft guns increased their fire as the paratroopers worked their way towards the castle. Anti-tank grenades and a 57mm recoilless gun disabled two Panther tanks as they drove down the driveway but the final assault was left to 3rd Battalion, which joined Colonel Raff after moving through the woods to the east. The paratroopers had soon cornered the Germans in the main building and by nightfall a group of senior officers of 84th Division surrendered in the main tower.

Return to your car and continue to head north, parking to the right after a quarter of a mile, at the signpost for Kriegsgräberstätte;❹a German military cemetery. During the battle the area was chosen as a casualty station for Allied troops and several hundred were buried in the large grassy area beyond the parking area. After the war Allied war graves were concentrated into large cemeteries to aid future maintenance and 7,647 British and Canadian graves were moved to Reichswald Military Cemetery and another 3,310 soldiers were re-interred

Diersfordt Forest German Cemetery; the Allied graves were relocated to cemeteries in Holland and Belgium after the war.

at Rheinberg Military Cemetery. Three thousand three hundred and one US casualties were taken to Margraten Military Cemetery in Holland. Only the German graves remain, a sombre burial ground in the woods beyond. Memorials to men from Diersfordt who died in the war flank a large wooden cross at the top of a flight of steps at the far end of the cemetery; the majority were killed on the Russian front.

Return to your car and turn right out of the parking area, heading north through the woods and continue straight on at the crossroads signposted for Hamminkeln. Leaving the forest, passing the level crossing after half a mile, ❺ the fields open up either side of the road; the site of 513th Parachute Regiment's landing zone. Drop Zone E was to the south (right) of the road but, yet again, the pilots of the Dakotas misjudged their target as they flew through the wall of German anti-aircraft fire around Diersfordt Forest.

Colonel Coutts' men were dropped to the left of the road on the drop zone of the 6th British Airborne Division, in places over 1.5 miles north of where they expected. All three battalions suffered heavy casualties, either from flak in the air or as they gathered on the ground, but before long German resistance faded away. Groups of men soon gathered together and although some headed north, the twin spires of Hamminkeln's churches helped the officers to correct their error. By mid afternoon 2nd Battalion was heading into Diersfordt Forest to meet 507th Regiment while 3rd Battalion moved east towards the Issel river; 1st Battalion remained in reserve south of the road after clearing Drop Zone E. During the battles on the ground Coutts' men destroyed two *Panzer IV*s and a self propelled gun as they drove across the drop zone; they also captured batteries of 88mm guns and turned them against the Germans.

Turn left at the T-junction, one mile from the railway, signposted for Bocholt. Keep straight on past the turning to the left into Hamminkeln

177

Hamminkeln

513th Parachute Regiment was supposed to land south of the Diersfordt – Hamminkeln road but the majority landed in the British sector to the north; Hamminkeln's twin church towers in the distance were useful for redirecting the paratroopers to their objectives.

and turn right for Brünen after 600m. Cross over a level crossing and turn right into Bruchweg, 250m beyond the entrance for Hamminkeln-Ost 2 factory. Bruchweg heads south, running parallel to the Issel Stream. The river, or rather a canalised stream (protected by two metre high flood banks) is 200m to the left. This area was the northern edge of 513th Regiment's perimeter and after clearing German troops from the woods, 2nd Battalion met British paratroopers moving south from Hamminkeln on 25 March. After two miles turn left at the crossroads with Vierwinden to visit Bridge 10, stopping in the small parking area alongside the bridge after 300 metres.❻

The Issel Stream was an ideal defensive position for the lightly armed paratroopers with its high embankments and deep watercourse. Bridge 10 was on the left of 194th Glider Regiment's sector. Company C held the area and although enemy activity on the afternoon of 24 March was limited, German reserves attacked in force

later that night. Infantry drove a wedge between the Glider Battalion and the paratroopers, crossing the river at Bridge 10, but counter-attacks by Company B stopped them and after hand-to-hand fighting the perimeter was restored:

At dawn only 300 yards separated Company C from the unit on the left and the entire area was filled with German dead. The 300 yards was effectively covered by fire.

The Issel Stream was a perfect defensive position for the lightly armed paratroopers.

Tanks and infantry mounted on halftracks tried to rush the bridge several times the following night but a combination of artillery and mortar fire broke up each column. The attacks eventually came to an end the following morning.

Turning around in the parking space, retrace your route along Vierwinden and turn left back onto Bruchweg. Turn left at the T-junction signposted Bruchweg after 750m and cross the Issel at Bridge

7 after 200m. ❼ Turn right onto Molkereiweg at the T-Junction and re-cross the Issel at Bridge 6.❽ German attacks continued throughout the night of the 24th but the heaviest blow fell on this part of 194th Glider Regiment's line twenty-four hours later.

Heading south-west, the fields either side of the road are lined with ditches, fences and trees, with farmhouses and outbuildings at regular intervals; hardly the ideal place to land over 300 cumbersome gliders. The area was scattered with flak positions and there were pitched battles between their crews and Colonel Pierce's men for several hours across this area on the morning of 24 March. Gliders fell burning from the sky as others hit the ground and skidded across the grass and obstacles, spilling their contents onto the ground. Despite the mayhem men gathered into small groups, engaging any German soldiers in sight as more gliders landed.

After ¼ mile take the second turning on the right signposted for Lackhausen; park in the car park after a few metres, outside Hotel Hausdinger.❾ The hotel was 1052nd Regiment's headquarters and a field gun positioned in front of the building hit eight of 2nd Battalion's gliders, one after the other, as they came into land. Enough glider troops survived to overwhelm the garrison and captured 145 prisoners, including the Regiment's commanding officer. Colonel Pierce set up his headquarters in the building soon afterwards.

Colonel Pierce's command post. A field gun hit glider after glider with high explosive shells as they came skidding across the fields surrounding the château.

Returning to the main road, turn right and continue to head south, turning left at the T-Junction in ¼ mile signposted for Borken and Brünen. Turn right at the 30mph speed limit after 300 yards, turning left after 50 metres in front of the supermarket and make an immediate right turning into Wurmflakstrasse and head through an estate. The canal once ran parallel to this road, in the trees to the left, and the awkward junction is at the site of Bridge 3.

Continue east out of the houses. Company G's perimeter ran through the woods to the left, where an embankment marks the line of the abandoned canal, and throughout the afternoon and night after the landing German armour and infantry tried time after time to break through the American lines. The Company was cut off for most of the night and for several hours Colonel Pierce was convinced that it had been overrun; only the sounds of firing in the woods gave him cause to believe that some men were still fighting on. The Germans eventually withdrew at dawn leaving hundreds of dead and wounded

Bridge 4 at the apex of 194th Glider Regiment's perimeter was overrun by German attacks several times.

behind; the survivors of Company G, although battered, had survived to hold their perimeter.

Keep to the narrow road as it turns sharp right and sharp left, followed by a second sharp left after another ¹/₂ mile and park in the parking area to the left where the road ends. Take a short walk to the bridge, Bridge 4 where some of the fiercest fighting took place on 194th Regiment's front.⑩

The Bridge stood at the eastern apex of Colonel Pierce's perimeter, in an awkward salient. Bridge 5 can be seen to the north-west along the Issel Stream, 1st Battalion's line. The Issel Canal ran through the trees to the west, 2nd Battalion's line. If time permits and you want to stretch your legs, it is possible to walk in either direction along 194th Regiment's perimeter. German troops attacked the bridge time after time, infiltrating the American lines on a number of occasions but by dawn on 25 March the Germans had been beaten. The Regiment had captured over 1,100 prisoners and around forty field and flak guns and they had accounted for fifteen German tanks and SP guns and hundreds of killed or wounded.

Return to your car and retrace your route back to the awkward junction at Bridge 3. Turn right at the end and immediately left onto the main road, heading for the centre of Wesel, or Stadt Mitte. Heading through the suburbs, the road climbs over a huge railway bridge (American paratroopers and British commandos met in the vicinity of the bridge for the first time), turn left signposted for Rhienbrücke onto Wesel Ring Road. The railway station is on the left after a short distance and several sets of traffic lights.

Tour 2 – Crossing the Rhine and the Battle for Staatsforst Wesel
Travelling south from the railway station go straight on at the traffic lights and after half a mile turn left at the T-Junction, signposted for Dinslaken and Voerde, where there is a second set of lights (still heading south). The road crosses the Lippe river, a fast moving watercourse that is much wider than the stream on the Airborne perimeter; turn right 200 metres beyond the bridge, heading for Spellen. This marshy strip of land between the Lippe river and the

Wesel – Datteln Canal,  which is now home to several factories, was not included in XVI Corps plan. While 17th Airborne Division secured the area east of Wesel, 30th Division cleared the area to the south using the canal as a protective flank. Although flak guns and self-propelled guns continued to operate for some time on the north bank as 119th Regiment pushed east, 1052nd Infantry Regiment was forced to withdraw from the exposed salient.

The canal is one mile south of the river. Entering Friedrichsfeld, turn right into Böskenstrasse 300 yards beyond the canal bridge, following

Tour 2 – Part 1: Crossing the Rhine.

Joy

The German view of Objective Joy, an underpass on 119th Regiment's front. Artillery fire and fighter-bombers scattered the infantry and anti-aircraft crews waiting for the Americans.

the sign for Spellen. The road passes beneath the railway after 500 yards, ❷ one of the three bridges on the 119th Regiment's front; this one was code-named Joy. The 2nd Battalion was closing in on the bridges and the embankment by dawn on 24 March and aerial observers noted considerable enemy activity on the east side of the railway. Infantry, flak guns and tanks were waiting and targeted the American engineers as they bulldozed through the obstacles beneath the bridge. By mid afternoon the road was clear and after fighter-bombers and artillery had paved the way, tanks passed beneath the bridge while the GIs crossed the embankment. Friedrichsfeld was in American hands by nightfall.

Continue straight on towards Spellen. 119th Regiment crossed the Rhine to the east of the road and while 2nd Battalion moved towards the railway, 3rd Battalion assembled in woods north of the village. As the spire of Spellen's church and the north end of the village, codenamed Patty, appears on the horizon, the woods can be seen to the right of the road.❸ Delays on 117th Regiment's front meant that 3rd Battalion had to take on the 200 strong garrison alone. Resistance collapsed following 117th Regiment's advance into the southern end of the village supported by Sherman DD tanks two hours later.

Entering Spellen, the road turns sharply to the left in front of the church and right afterwards; turn right into Auf der Gest, a narrow side road, 100 yards beyond the church. Then as the road meanders down towards the

119th Regiment faced a long fight in the northern outskirts of Spellen, Objective Patty, until 117th Regiment approached from the south.

Rhine, it is possible to see the enormous embankment stretching from left to right in the distance. As 119th Regiment crossed the dyke to the right, moving towards the northern end of Spellen, 117th Regiment advanced over the fields to the left to seize Ork, a small hamlet. Park at the junction end of the single track road before the no entry sign where Talackerstrasse turns to the left. ❹ Take care parking your vehicle (not suitable for anything larger than a car), the road is quite narrow and farmers use it for their tractors.

119th Regiment's crossing point in front of Spellen.

Walking straight on beyond two farms, the road rises onto the top of the embankment overlooking the Rhine.

117th Regiment's crossing point in front of Ork.

Incredible scenes unfolded along the river on the morning of 24 March 1945 as Ninth Army unleashed its firepower against the Germans holding the east bank. For an hour, 1,000 shells a minute pounded the riverbank and villages beyond, demoralising the men of 180th Infantry Division. 119th Regiment moved down to the river 500 metres to the north while 117th Regiment crossed 500 metres to the south. As the barrage moved east, dozens of assault boats roared across the fast-flowing river, depositing GIs on the shoreline. Next came the armour and while amphibious Sherman tanks, Alligators and DUKWs swam across, rafts ferried light tanks to the east bank. At first light engineers started work and by the end of 25 March lorries and tanks were able to drive across a treadway bridge, one of the longest ever built.

After taking a short walk along the riverbank, return to your car and follow Talackerstrasse into Ork. 117th Regiment quickly cleared Ork ❺, the 150 strong garrison was still sheltering from the barrage when 1st Battalion moved into the hamlet, but two hours passed while 2nd Battalion waited to be transported across the river. As dawn broke the exhausted GIs advanced alongside Sherman DD tanks into Objective Polly, the southern edge of Spellen. Go straight on at the minor

The Rhine as it swings south to 79th Division's crossing sites.

crossroads, turning right onto Mehrumstrasse at the crossroads beyond the hamlet. 2nd Battalion advanced towards Spellen on the horizon straight ahead.

Head south towards Mehrum and into 120th Regiment's sector. The dyke to the right is the winter levee, ❻ built to protect the village when the river level rises, and Company G crossed the embankment to cut the road. After passing through the centre of Mehrum the road curves to the left at the foot of the river embankment; park in the lay-by on the right and walk to the top of the slope to view the river. ❼ From the top of the dyke it is possible to see where the rest of 120th Regiment crossed the river, 500 metres to the right, before entering the village. After 2nd Battalion had taken Mehrum, Company K moved east along the embankment heading for Gotterswickerhamm while the rest of 3rd Battalion waited to be transported across the river.

Return to your car and turn right, following the road along the foot of the embankment towards Gotterswickerhamm and after one mile stop in a second parking place on the right at the outskirts of the village ❽. Looking south, 79th Division crossed the Rhine south of the power station an hour after 30th Division had entered the river. Although the division's exploits are covered in the book, the tours do not extend as far south as General Wyche's crossing because industry and nature have successfully conspired to change the area beyond all recognition. A wooded nature reserve, with no access for cars, covers a mile wide strip along the riverbank while the villages captured by 79th Division have expanded into one large conurbation centred on Dinslaken.

Heavy fighting ensued along Gotterswickerhamm's main street but as soon as the SS leader in the village had been killed, the rest of the garrison surrendered, leaving the way open for 120th Regiment. Entering the village, turn right at the small roundabout and the road bypasses the church before hugging the riverbank as it heads east. Turn right at the T-Junction just beyond the village and take an immediate left in front of the power station, heading through Möllen.

Part 2 Map
After leaving the outskirts of Möllen, head straight on at the crossroads into the woods, signposted for Tenderingssee and after one mile turn right into Schwarzerweg. The thick woods hid Task Force Plummer as it rolled forward, taking the Germans covering the road by surprise. Turn left at the T-Junction after half a mile heading into Bruckhausen noting the high wooded ridge, known locally as Bruckhauser Heide, dominating the skyline; a formidable obstacle to 30th Division's advance and one that General Hobbs wanted to clear before the Germans reorganised. ❾

Follow Dinslakenstrasse through the centre of Bruckhausen, where the task force paused for the night having made a six-mile penetration

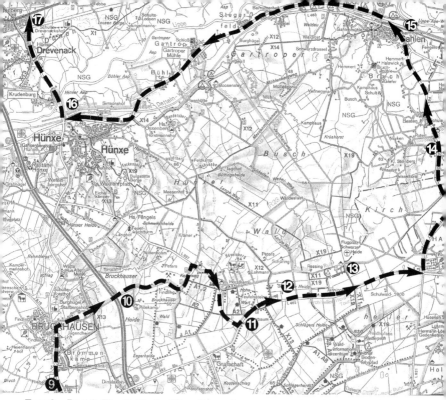

Tour 2 – Part 2: The Battle for Wesel Forest.

into the German lines; on a clear day it is possible to see the power station cooling tower on the east bank of the Rhine away to the left. As Plummer fired into the backs of the enemy positions across the fields, the rest of 120th Regiment pushed forward rounding up dozens of prisoners and by nightfall a large hole had been ripped in 180th Infantry Division's line.

Slow down to turn right at the far end of the village into Bergschlagweg, a minor road (it is just before the large yellow road sign directing traffic left to Bucholt). The narrow road was the only available route for 120th Regiment's tanks as the GIs advanced up the slopes onto Bruckhauser Heide. The road crosses the Autobahn at the top of the ridge, which was nothing more than a cutting through the forest in 1945, as the war stopped construction ❿. It was a useful staging area for 120th Regiment's Task Force Hunt on the afternoon of

30th Division used the Autobahn (incomplete in March 1945) to assemble Task Force Hunt and Task Force Harrison.

Wesel Forest is a tangle of trees, undergrowth and marsh; ideal defensive terrain.

Three Chaffee tanks at the head of Task Force Hunt were knocked out on this stretch of road when they ran into *116th Panzer Division's* advanced elements.

Besten Airfield

Butch's Night Raiders crossed Schwarze Heide in a cloud of smoke.

25 March. 2nd Battalion mounted Chaffee tanks and Hellcat tank destroyers as 3rd Battalion pushed through the woods to the south and east of here, unaware that the advanced elements of *116th Panzer Division* had entered the forest.

Follow the road as it winds through the forest flanked on both sides by ditches and a tangle of trees and undergrowth, while the few open spaces are waterlogged for most of the year round. Wesel Forest was perfect defensive territory where a few roadblocks could easily bring 30th Division's advance to a grinding halt.

One mile beyond the Autobahn, turn right at the crossroads onto Wilhelmstrasse and left at the T-Junction after another mile, signposted for Kirchhellen. Task Force Hunt came from the right heading towards Schwarze Heide clearing.

The road was narrower in 1945 but on the afternoon of 25 March, General Hobbs was still hopeful that his men could reach the eastern edge of the forest by nightfall. Everything changed when patrols captured an advanced party of *116th Panzer Division* and as it grew dark the task force ran headlong into a group of German assault guns and halftracks heading in the opposite direction. ⑪ Three Chaffee tanks were disabled before the American artillery scattered the German battle group, setting vehicles and ammunition dumps on fire, blocking the road until dawn. The edge of the clearings known as Scharwz Heide and Schlägers Heide are only half a mile from the T-Junction but it took 120th Regiment two days of hard fighting to reach the open ground as tanks and *Panzergrenadiers* fought to block the road.

Head east across the clearing in the

forest. ⑫   The first attempt to cross ran headlong into a German counter-attack by tanks on the morning of 26 March and as the GIs fell back in disarray, they had to rely on their artillery to disperse the German battlegroup. By nightfall 120th Regiment had reached the western edge of the clearing and Colonel Purdue had devised a complicated plan to capture Besten airfield at the far side.

Under cover of darkness 1st Battalion, known as Butch's Night Raiders, sent its leading company forward supported by tanks while the artillery created a U-shaped wall of smoke around the edges of the clearing. Tank destroyers used the roads to cover the flanks while the rest of the battalion hung back in the woods; they ran forward when German artillery had subsided. The advance was a complete success and Lieutenant Colonel Williamson's men overran the German positions covering the Besten Airfield in a cloud of smoke.

The airfield is signposted on the left after half a mile as Flugplatz Schwarze Heide; turn in the side road and stop in the parking area. ⑬   There is a raised viewing area to survey the airfield where fixed anti-aircraft positions and halftracks mounted with 20mm flak guns were captured along with huge stores of ammunition. 1st Battalion's advance secured 117th Regiment's position in the woods to the north where the leading battalion lost its way as it advanced in the dark and had to be guided in by white phosphorous shells. With the airfield safely in 120th Regiment's hands, the end of Wesel Forest was in sight.

There is a café and restaurant at the airfield, and it is a useful stopping place for refreshments. Return to your car, go back to the main road and turn left for Kirchhellen; the edge of the woods is half a mile away and the skyline is dominated by the town's heavy industry.

120th Regiment's final objective was to clear the hamlets on the slopes overlooking the town on the night of 27 March. Another smoke box, extending to over a mile wide, was used to cover the infantry, while the armour kept to the roads in close support. There was little resistance as *116th Panzer Division* was fully engaged around Besten and Gahlen to the north and the advance opened the way for the tanks

The end of Wesel Forest; chimneys and cooling towers dominate the skyline over Kirchhellen.

and halftracks of the 8th Armoured Division.

Turn left at the crossroads for Gahlen, skirting the forest where 120th Regiment dug in to weather the German counter-attack. Take another left at the crossroads in half a mile, again heading for Gahlen

Gahlen

Gahlen seen from the Besten road, site of the German counter-attacks on 27 March.

and pass through Besten village, **⑭** codenamed Jo-Jo. A single platoon under Lieutenant Shaw mounted a handful of tanks and tank destroyers and raced towards the village to stop the German tanks reaching Kirchhellen. Four Shermans and M18s were knocked out and many of Shaw's men were killed or injured holding the road but their sacrifice severely restricted *60th Panzergrenadier Regiment* and its tanks.

Continuing past Besten, 119th Regiment was struggling to contain *156th Panzergrenadier Regiment* in Gahlen, the village in the valley in the distance. **⑮** Some tanks and halftracks managed to break free on 27 March and, taking advantage of the overcast skies that had grounded the Americans' air cover, used this road to counter-attack

Gahlen Church. Heavy fighting took place in the village as 119th Regiment tried in vain to stop *156th Panzergrenadier Regiment* crossing the Lippe Canal.

117th Regiment's positions along the outskirts of the wood to the left. Intense artillery fire directed by the American observation planes scattered the infantry, leaving the tanks exposed to bazooka teams waiting in the trees.

Turn left, signposted for Gahlen, after half a mile and follow the road as it winds its way through the centre of the village past the church and watermill. 119th Regiment had hoped that German engineers would blow the bridge over the Lippe Canal if they bypassed the village codenamed Hubert. However, Colonel Baker's men arrived too late and were pinned down or cut off as they tried to move into the village; the American tanks were easily picked off as they followed along the single road.

At the far end of the village turn left onto the main road and head west, signposted for Hunxe. 119th Regiment was forced to advance on a very narrow front and while log barriers blocked the road, thick woods to the south and the canal to the north hemmed in the infantry. After a mile the road makes a sharp turn to the right and then left as it swings over the canal bridge; the retreating engineers demolished the original bridge as 119th Regiment approached.

Follow the road west along the north side of the canal.

119th Regiment had to push along the narrow forest tracks across the canal to the left while German assault guns roamed along this road looking for targets.

30th Division raced *116th Panzer Division* along the banks of the Lippe Canal to try stop the *Panzers* reaching the forest.

The road crosses the canal after two miles and bypasses Hunxe, which is to the left. Task Force Harrison reached the village on the evening of 25 March as 180th Infantry Division's resistance collapsed. New development and rebuilding has changed Hunxe completely so keep to the main road, bypassing it. Turn right at the traffic lights and cross the canal signposted for Borken and Bocholt.

The abutments of the original bridge destroyed by the German engineers as Task Force Harrison approached, are to the right of the new bridge. ⑯ Bypassing Drevenack after one mile, turn left onto the A58 signposted for Wesel. ⑰ 6th British Guards Armoured Brigade, with American paratroopers onboard, drove east along this road heading for Holsterhausen on the morning of 28 March. While 8th Armoured Division was fighting *116th Panzer Division*'s cadre in Kirchhellen, the armoured task force on 17th Airborne Division's front had found a weak spot in the German line. It had reached Haltern by nightfall, an advance of eighteen miles; Operation PLUNDER was underway.

Head back into Wesel five miles to the west. If you want to head onto another destination you may wish to join the E35 Autobahn; there is an intersection half a mile from Drevenack. Head north for Arnhem and Rotterdam or south towards Düsseldorf.

6th Guards Armoured Brigade broke out along the Holsterhausen road on 28 March with 513th Parachute Regiment perched on top of their tanks.

CHRISTIAN CELEBRATION

Understanding the Prayer of the Church

J. D. Crichton

GEOFFREY
CHAPMAN

Geoffrey Chapman
An imprint of Cassell Publishers Limited
Villiers House, 41–47 Strand, London WC2N 5JE
387 Park Avenue South, New York, NY 10016–8810

First published 1976 as *Christian Celebration: The Prayer of the Church*
Reissued as part of 1-volume *Christian Celebration* 1982
Second edition first published 1993

British Library Cataloguing-in-Publication Data
A catalogue record for this book is available from the British Library.

Library of Congress Cataloging-in-Publication Data
Available from the Library of Congress.

ISBN 0–225–66671–5

Typeset by Colset Pte Ltd, Singapore
Printed and bound in Great Britain by
Biddles Ltd, Guildford and King's Lynn

Contents

Preface

~~~~~~

THIS BOOK has occupied me for many months. The material to be handled is very considerable; the office, whether that of the diocesan clergy or that of monks and nuns, is a complicated form of prayer that has grown over many centuries. The *Divine Office* of 1971 has indeed simplified matters but the fact that its contents fill three bulky volumes shows that the simplification has been somewhat relative. Again, in all this multiplicity of texts it is not always easy to see the meaning that underlies them. At a practical level, it cannot be said that the office has been a prayer that the clergy have found easy to use, much less the people who until recent years, when it was freed from the obscurity of a dead language, hardly knew what was to be found inside a 'breviary'. For these and other reasons it has seemed necessary to write at some length about certain aspects of the office. There is the question of what *sort* of prayer the office is. I have tried to say something about this. The General Introduction states that the Divine Office is the prayer of Christ in his church (3–9) but it seemed important to examine this statement and to attempt to support it with other New Testament material not found there. One long chapter is devoted to the history of the Divine Office, a difficult and complicated matter not yet fully elucidated, which is necessary for an understanding of the new form of the office. Without that understanding the work of the revisers might seem merely capricious and the history shows us that the important distinction between the 'cathedral' office and the monastic office is valid. The observations of the revisers on the crucial importance of Lauds and Vespers rest on that understanding. Other matters that seemed to call for attention are the use of the psalms, the nature of the lectionaries and the meaning of intercession now represented in the office by the 'prayers'. The first two call for expert knowledge to which I do not pretend. It is to be hoped that the efforts of a general practitioner are not hopelessly inadequate. The hymns and the collects called for a more extended treatment than I was able to give them. Books, especially nowadays, have to be confined within certain limits.

~

I have kept certain traditional terms. Thus, except in the historical part, I have used *Lauds* and *Vespers* for morning and evening prayer. That they are Latinized words seems to me no reason for dropping them. The Latin contribution to the English language is being jettisoned so rapidly that there is a danger that we shall soon be talking some kind of neo-Anglo-Americano-Saxon. Likewise, I have continued to call the two principal New Testament canticles by their Latin names, the *Benedictus* and the *Magnificat*. Since the office uses the Septuagint–Vulgate numeration of the psalms I have kept it almost throughout. When discussing the scripture lectionary I have used the term Apocalypse, used by all the old lectionaries, for the Book of Revelation.

This book completes the trilogy to which I set my hand some five years ago. The three books, with the *Ministry of Reconciliation*, complete what I have to say on the revised liturgy. Not that it is all there is to be done. There is the vast corpus of the Mass-lectionary which deserves commentary, not simply of a scriptural-exegetical kind but one that would take account of the liturgical context in which the various pericopes appear. Another need is a commentary on the liturgical year as it now appears in the texts of the official books. Both call for a high degree of scriptural and liturgical knowledge. It is to be hoped that younger liturgical scholars will turn their attention to them. Meanwhile I am glad to have been able to do the work I have done and it is no small thing in these days that it has been published. I hope it will be useful to others.

Memoria of St Charles Lwanga and Companions
3 June 1975

J.D.C.

Abbreviations

~~~~~~

CL = The Constitution on the Liturgy (1963) translated by Rev. Clifford Howell, SJ (Whitegate Publications, Cirencester, 1963).

GILH = *The General Instruction on the Liturgy of the Hours*, translated by Peter Coughlan and Peter Purdue (Geoffrey Chapman, 1971). Referred to in the text as 'The General Introduction'. It is to be found also in the *Divine Office*, 1; in Latin in *Liturgia Horarum*, 1.

DACL = *Dictionnaire d'Archéologie Chrétienne et de Liturgie*, ed. F. Cabrol and H. Leclercq.

F. X. Funk = *Didascalia Constitutiones Apostolorum* (Paderborn, 1905; ed. anastatica, two volumes in one, Turin, 1964).

JBC = *The Jerome Biblical Commentary*, ed. R. E. Brown, J. A. Fitzmyer, R. E. Murphy (Prentice-Hall, Englewood Cliffs, NJ/Geoffrey Chapman, 1968).

LHEW = Robert Taft, SJ, *The Liturgy of the Hours in East and West* (Liturgical Press, Collegeville, MN, 1986).

LMD = *La Maison-Dieu* (Paris, 1945); given with number of fascicle and year.

LQF = *Liturgiewissenschaftliche Quellen und Forschungen* (Münster).

NJBC = *The New Jerome Biblical Commentary*, ed. R. E. Brown, J. A. Fitzmyer, R. E. Murphy (Prentice Hall, Englewood Cliffs, NJ/ Geoffrey Chapman, 1989).

ODCC = *Oxford Dictionary of the Christian Church* (1974 ed.).

QLP = *Questions Liturgiques et Paroissiales* (Mont-César, Louvain).

The works of Bishop Pierre Salmon present a particular difficulty for reference purposes. He has written several times on the office in different places.

OD = *L'Office Divin* (Paris, 1959; American trans.: *The Breviary through the Centuries*, Liturgical Press, Collegeville, MN, 1962).

EP = 'La Prière des Heures' in *L'Eglise en Prière*, ed. A. G. Martimort (Paris, Tournai, etc., 1961).

ODMA = *L'Office Divin au Moyen Age* (Paris, 1967).

Other works by the same author are given with the necessary details.

STL = *The Study of Liturgy*, ed. Cheslyn Jones, Geoffrey Wainwright, Edward Yarnold, SJ, Paul Bradshaw (SPCK, London/OUP, New York, 1992).

~

Texts

~~~~~~~

The Latin text of the office is:
Officium Divinum . . . LITURGIA HORARUM iuxta Ritum Romanum, 4
volumes (Vatican Press, 1971–72).
  The English translation is:
The Divine Office. The Liturgy of the Hours according to the Roman Rite, 3
volumes (Collins, London, Glasgow/Dwyer, Sydney, Australia/Talbot,
Dublin), 1974.
  For the New Testament I have used the Jerusalem Bible version (Dar-
ton, Longman and Todd, 1966) though with occasional reference to the
Revised Standard Version and the New American Bible. For the psalms
I have used the Grail Psalter as found in the *Divine Office* where it is
slightly revised. I have also occasionally referred to *The Psalms: A New
Translation* (Collins, Fontana, 1963) which is also the copyright of The
Grail (England).

ONE

~

The Problem of
Liturgical Prayer

~~~~~~

W HAT IS THE PROBLEM of public prayer whether we call it
the Liturgy of the Hours, the Divine Office or Mattins and
Evensong or by any other title? It seems to be a comparatively new problem. For more than two millennia Jews, Christians and
Muslims have prayed at least twice daily according to fixed forms and
traditional patterns. Up to and including the first decades of this century
devout Catholics attended Vespers on Sunday evenings and, even though
the office was in Latin, seemed to find satisfaction in it. Some at least
attended the long office of *Tenebrae* sung in the evening of the last three
days of Holy Week and it is improbable that the later medieval 'decora-
tions', the gradual extinguishing of the brown candles after each psalm
or the *strepitus* at the end (which in some choirs and places where they
sang became a mini-battle of books) were what attracted them. No doubt
the haunting plainsong of the responsories and the solemn polyphony
had something to do with it but these could only be heard in very few
churches. Again, for generations of Anglicans the offices of Mattins and
Evensong have provided a vehicle for true worship and devotion.

Much of this has gone. The offices, it is true, remain, now revised,
reformed and reshaped, but the people are absent. No doubt social and
sociological changes in society have had much to do with this. Evening
services were a nineteenth-century invention and reflected the social patterns of the time. The gentry and the well-to-do went to Mass or Mattins
in the morning and (on the whole) the servants in the evening. Hence
the cold Sunday supper. Since then the patterns of social life have
changed radically. There is no longer a leisured class and those who
are well-to-do for the most part do not go to church at all. People are
intensely mobile. Even if they are at home for the week-end they will be
out in their cars most Sundays and for most of the day. Entertaining,
visiting, recreation of various kinds fill up their day and even if they are
Christians one church service a day is as much as is possible or desired.
There is little hope of a second liturgical assembly on Sundays.

~

1

But not only has there been an abandonment of public prayer, but prayer of any kind has come to be severely questioned. Many, it is said, who formerly prayed do so no longer, though one wonders how those who say this know. For many public prayer seems to be too remote, too formal for them to find it helpful for their life. What is sought is a sense of immediacy, of intimate contact with God which can be experienced in less formal contexts, in the familiar atmosphere of the house group or the charismatic gathering. Then again, people are so *busy*, not merely about household chores or the earning of a living, but often enough about the service of others whether their immediate neighbours or the poor and deprived at home or in places far away. If it is true that there is less praying, it is also true that Christians are far more concerned and active about the welfare of others than they used to be in former times.

However, that is not the whole picture. If people nowadays do not observe the traditional times and occasions, if they do not pray regularly morning and night (though it is surprising how many admit to doing so – and not only the old either), many pray in ways that are more consonant with the rhythm of modern life. Apart from the routine (slavery, if you like) that factory and shop and office impose on people, modern life is largely unpatterned. People are forced for a variety of reasons to move about a great deal, they have to do things when they can and not always when they want to. It is into this sort of life that many fit their prayer. They will attend day or week-end recollections, they will make retreats (which even the devout did not do in the nineteenth century), they will attend conferences where there is nearly always some kind of group-prayer or they will join groups, sometimes of the pentecostal kind, where they will be drawn into prayer. It is significant too that right in the heart of the industrial racket there exist small and humble communities who pray in quiet and silence. A moving description of such a group, the Little Brothers of Charles de Foucauld, is given by Father Mark Gibbard: 'There was incessant noise outside but oddly enough this seemed to drive you to prayer rather than distract you from prayer'.[1] The well-spring of prayer has not dried up.

All this may seem to have little enough to do with liturgical prayer but not necessarily. Even small groups who take life seriously and try to live some form of community life, however loosely organized, discover empirically the need for an ordered, structured prayer. One such group was the Taena Community, who began without any formal Christian attachment, and who discovered the need for organized prayer with a predictable pattern to be said at stated times. In due course they came to the divine office or a form of it which was used every day at the appropriate hours.[2]

This experience—and it is not singular—points to an important truth. Communities discover the need for a *structured* prayer that will go beyond the needs or insights of individuals and will be the means to express the worship of the group. It is indeed surprising that so many religious congregations in the last four centuries have been able to sustain some sort of community life without a structured prayer, except the highly repetitive 'Little Office of Our Lady'. There was indeed the daily meditation but this was completely individualistic, a factor that was not mitigated by the miscellaneous 'devotions' that also formed part of the community's prayer. It is perhaps not surprising that communities of this kind have run into crisis in recent years[3] or that on the rebound, as it were, they have taken up with enthusiasm the morning and evening prayer of the new office.

Even so, the objection is pressed that formal offices and the like restrict the movement of the Spirit. The quick answer to this is: are we always certain that it is the Spirit who is moving us? But I think that we must look at the matter in another way. Most of us are pretty self-centred, not so much in the sense that we are selfish (though that too may be true) as that we are restricted by personal experience and mental capacity. The mind and heart need to be opened to wider horizons than are normally given by our grasp of reality or by a prayer that is purely individual. We need, in other words, to be opened *out* to the reality and presence of God, of the God who transcends us and who is made known in all the breadth and length of his redeeming work in his Son, Jesus Christ. Our very desire needs to be extended for we may desire too little. For St Augustine the object of our desire is nothing other than God himself, in all the fullness of his being, and in all the blessedness he has prepared for us. This beatitude is very great, he says, and we are small and limited.[4]

But if we are to desire we must first know and this immediately suggests that the content of common prayer, or indeed prayer of any kind, must be the self-disclosure of God, in a word the Bible. But knowing is obviously not sufficient and, to continue St Augustine's thought, prayer is the expression of the desire for God who has revealed himself and that desire can continue without ceasing. It is as it were the ground-base of the Christian's life. But at certain hours and on certain occasions we use words to express that desire and these are signs that remind us how much progress we have yet to make in desiring as we should. The *words* serve to expand the desire and without them our desire would die. Not that a great many words are necessary or not always: to use many words is one thing, but a continuing desire is another (*aliud est sermo multus, aliud diuturnus affectus*).[5] But words are necessary, he goes on, and he gives a miniature commentary on the Lord's prayer with liberal quotations from the psalms. Anticipating what is to be said lower down about the words, the prayers, i.e. the psalms which the church has elected to use, let us see why St Augustine thought the prayer of the psalms was so important: 'God could give us no greater gift than that he should make the Word, through whom he created all things, our head. . . . The Saviour of the body, he prays for us and in us and we make our prayer to him. He prays for us as priest, he prays in us as head and we pray to him as our God. *Let us then discern our words in him and his in us.*'[6] For St Augustine, as for all Christian antiquity, Christ was in one way or another present in the psalms and this is the principal reason why the church has made them the substance of her prayer.

But when we have said that the Bible as revealing the object of our desire and the psalter as the means by which we may express that desire are understandably the content of Christian prayer, we have still to see how most appropriately they may be used. Is the continuous reading of the Bible from cover to cover in a given space of time the right way to use it for *prayer*? Does the prayer of the psalms consist of the recitation of them in considerable numbers one after another? Both of these ways have been practised at one time or another. In Cluniac monasteries at one time all 66 chapters of Isaiah were 'dismissed' in a week and there were parallels elsewhere. The desert monks recited great numbers of psalms at once, 36 in some places and eighteen in others. But this was the monastic tradition and in other circumstances a different pattern was adopted.

As we shall see in greater detail later,[7] in Spain and southern Gaul in the fifth–sixth century, the number of psalms used for morning and evening prayer, which were intended for both the clergy and the laity, was small. But there was always a reading from the Bible and in addition intercessions and the Lord's prayer. These may be said to be the essential elements of public prayer. From the Roman tradition we can gather a different but still very balanced pattern. In the somewhat fossilized Masses of Ember days in the former Roman missal we find six lessons divided by graduals, which were no doubt originally psalms, intended as meditations on the preceding reading, and collects. The scheme at its best can be seen in the existing Vigil Service of Easter Eve where there is the same pattern but where also reading and psalm (i.e. canticle) and collect are identical in theme and deliver therefore the same message in different ways. A similar scheme can be seen in the brief and informal services that accompanied Egeria's visits to the Holy Places in the fourth century:

> Prayer
> (appropriate) lesson
> (appropriate) psalm
> Prayer (and a blessing if a bishop is present)[8]

It is one of her most constant observations that the texts whether readings or psalms were always appropriate to the occasion and while this seems to have struck her as something new, she evidently did not find the *pattern* new.

From these traditions we can gather another fact about Christian prayer. As we see with particular clarity in the Easter Vigil, these forms reflect and convey a particular view of salvation history which is so much more than the recounting of facts. In these ancient forms of prayer there is in the readings the proclamation of God's approach to man offering his love and inviting man's response. What therefore is proclaimed in the readings is reflected on in the following psalm which, in the tradition recorded by Cassian, is followed by a silence. The collect sums up the prayer of the whole unit. This, as far as we can see, is the oldest form of Christian public prayer. Mere antiquity does not of course prove that it is the right way of prayer but the fact that countless generations found it satisfactory is an indication that it is so. But there is another reason for thinking that this is the right way and this reason is to be found in the answer to the question: what is prayer?

Here of course we are thinking of Christian prayer and on reflection it is odd that sometimes it has been thought of as a straining upwards or outwards to a God who was very far away. It was very much *our* effort and because it was, the pressure had to be put on. There was tension, we screwed ourselves up, it was all so very difficult.[9] This sense of tension was, I think, greatly increased by the forms of prayer that have been common in post-Reformation times. They were a curious combination of the mental ('mental prayer') and the voluntarist. A considerable power of reflection on self was required which had to issue into constant 'resolutions' which had to be made, varied no doubt, day after day. It is not surprising that people felt discouraged. In the same period there was too an emphasis on the human individual who, often unwittingly, was the real centre of concern, and the theology of grace (Molinism and its derivatives) that emerged in the late sixteenth century did much to foster the notion that he was.[10]

This is not to say that all in that tradition was bad. Far from it. It sanctified innumerable souls – the record of sanctity, both official and unofficial, since the sixteenth century is impressive. But it is not merely a matter of totting up 'saints'. What is clear is that this tradition did something that was of the highest importance. It can be described as the interiorization of religion. In the Middle Ages, especially before the fourteenth century, one gets the impression that the recitation of formulas was too often mistaken for prayer. There were all those additions to the office that was already long: the fifteen psalms that preceded 'mattins' in monastic houses, the seven penitential psalms that were said on certain days, and the inclusion of the 'little offices' of the Blessed Virgin and the Dead in the daily course. Furthermore, the medieval Christian, including the priest and often the monk, seems to have found reflection on self very difficult and the official prayer of the church was not seen to have an essential reference to the living of the Christian life. The post-Tridentine Christian realized that prayer must engage the mind and the heart and must have an issue in daily living if it was not to be hypocritical though the notion of daily living was not always, or as often as it should have been, extended to social life. By a roundabout route these Christians had come back to the teaching of St Benedict that in singing the psalms mind and voice should be in harmony, a phrase that was inserted into the Constitution on the Liturgy (11).[11] Unhappily the Christians of this tradition were for the most part indifferent to the public prayer of the church which in any case had become very formal and which was hardly accessible as prayer to the multitudes of religious who did not know Latin.

In the older tradition, represented by the Rule of St Benedict, the prayer of the office went forward in an atmosphere of tranquillity and private prayer was a prolongation of public prayer. As Benedict said, the prayer of the brethren 'ought to be short and pure, unless it chance to be prolonged by the impulse of divine grace'.[12] He was not indifferent to the movement of the Spirit and saw the office with its tranquillity as providing the *kairos*, the privileged moment, for the reception of the Spirit. Moreover, in the Benedictine tradition the spiritual life is the matter of a life-time – hence enclosure – and the monk and nun have time to grow spiritually.[13]

These considerations have their importance but they do not answer the question: what is prayer? The central Christian insight in this matter of prayer is, I think, that it is primarily a response to God who has revealed and given himself. In Christ he has revealed himself and through Christ we are able to learn something of the breadth and height and depths of the love of God towards us and of God who *is* love. Through Christ and in the church, he becomes accessible to us. In the liturgy 'God speaks to his people'[14] for if revelation was a once-for-all event, it has to be actualized for us here and now, it has to make its impact on us in this twentieth century. Only then can we respond to the revealing word and to the ever-present love that enfolds us in itself. Although he did not use this language of response, that great prayerful soul, Baron von Hügel, was saying the same thing in the more conventional terms of his time when he spoke, as he did so often, of 'the grand prevenience of God'. God is there, God is before us, offering himself to us – in the traditional language, prompting our thoughts and our desires (Romans 8:15, 16, 23). Again, in wholly traditional language, in the proclamation of his word in the liturgy God is offering us his grace, inviting us to open our minds and hearts to him so that in faith and love we can take his word to ourselves. This is the fundamental reason why in the liturgy, in all liturgy and especially in liturgical prayer, there must be a reading of holy scripture. It may be that it was not always so. It may be that Christians in the early centuries like the desert fathers were so God-possessed that they could recite the whole of the psalter at once or needed only phrases of psalms to sustain their contemplation though we do not know how well the system worked. At a fairly early stage Pachomius felt the need to put some order into it. In any case, these were rather special Christians, very different from those of the twentieth century. It may be too that at times in the past the scripture-reading content of the office was non-existent (as was the case in Jerusalem) or very small. But this cannot be regarded as a typical or a desirable situation.

It does not matter which aspect of prayer we take, response remains central to it. In the prayer of praise and thanksgiving, generally regarded as less self-interested, the individual Christian or the community is responding to God's revelation of himself. In the psalms, as indeed in the eucharistic prayer, there is a regular pattern: we praise God for what he is and what he has done. Thus 'Sing a new song to the Lord . . . Let Israel rejoice in its maker/let Zion's sons exult in their king . . . *For* the Lord takes delight in his people . . .' (Psalm 149). Again, in Psalm 117, which is composite, the goodness of God without further definition seems to be the motive of praise: 'Give thanks to the Lord for he is good' but the text immediately goes on to say 'for his love endures for ever' and the psalm then details how that love has been expressed towards the psalmist and the community. And even when, as in Psalm 8, the opening seems to be a burst of pure praise 'How great is your name, O Lord our God, through all the earth' the psalm lower down spells out in detail what the greatness of God implies: 'When I see the heavens, the work of your hands/the moon and the stars which you arranged/what is man that you should keep him in mind. . . . You have made him little less than a god. . . .'[15] The response that issues in prayer comes from the contemplation of God who has revealed himself. It is an exulting in the greatness, the glory, the love and beauty of God and is expressed perhaps most succinctly in the phrase of the *Gloria in excelsis*: 'We give you thanks *for your great glory*'.

Evidently the response is a going out from ourselves to God and this is why some have regarded it as a 'purer' form of prayer than any other. But in fact our response will be conditioned by a number of factors. It will be conditioned by what we know of God, or more exactly by the authenticity of our knowledge of God. If we think of him as some kind of primitive, tribal deity, the inexhaustible dispenser of favours, or one who requires constant placation, the praise and thanksgiving will be coloured by self-interest. For good or for ill, prayer always raises the question of God, of who and what he is. This is one reason why we should always be praying consciously in Christ who is the revelation of the Father. But our response will also be conditioned by our own state, by our feelings of inadequacy, by our sense of sin, by our sheer need. If a sense of personal inadequacy is dominant, we shall want, in the phrase of St Augustine, to appear 'as beggars before God', displaying our moral wretchedness, the rags and tatters of our lives. If we have sinned, we shall want to 'answer' with repentance, to respond to the invitation to repentance of the gospel. If we have reason to be grateful, we shall respond with prayers of thanksgiving which merge into the prayer of praise for here the two seem to fuse and then we are at the heart of the worship that is given to God by the prayer of the church. Since all these themes of prayer weave in and out of the psalter, perhaps it becomes easier for us to understand why the church has made use of the psalms from the beginning.

We shall have to consider the psalms elsewhere in this book but meanwhile there are certain truths about prayer we can learn from them. The psalter, heavily conditioned as it is by the religious culture from which it emerged, can be seen as the Prayer Book of Mankind. The psalms range over the whole gamut of human experience, from intense physical and spiritual suffering, from loneliness and a sense of helplessness, to the most exultant praise. If there are some psalms where the speaker seems to be repulsively self-righteous ('I have done everything the Law, or you, God, have asked for and yet you treat me like this . . .'), he is speaking very consciously in the presence of God. This perhaps brings us to the very heart of prayer. The psalmists had a vivid sense of the reality of God, they were extraordinarily God-conscious and even if they complain at times that he is remote, they had a sense of the immediacy of his presence. This is why on the one hand they could pour out their hearts in petition, in anguished cries and even rebukes. But on the other hand, it was this sense of the presence of God and of his holiness, power and beauty that drew from them those almost ecstatic songs of which the group 148–150 are the best known.

For a recent writer the psalms provide an answer to the anguished question of man's destiny: what is the meaning of life? And he shows how the ultimate extremity of despair can in the psalms issue into the celebration of God's glory:

> Reduced to the ultimate extremity of despair we go beyond in a hymn of praise. When the Jewish editors of the Old Testament called what we now call the Psalter or Book of Psalms, *tehillim*, 'praises', they may not have been much concerned about literary genres, but they were aware of the ultimate point of liturgical

celebration and the celebration of life: the praise of God's glory, even in the abject desolation of abandonment by God. When Jesus cries out on the Cross (Mt. 27:46), 'My God, why have you forsaken me?', he is using the opening words of Ps. 22(21), addressed to the holy one 'enthroned on the praises of Israel' (v. 3) and which concludes with a song of praise. The desolation, the ultimate extremity of the why-question is the way of its overcoming in praise, in resurrection, in glory.[16]

It is perhaps a surprising conclusion which some may think paradoxical. But it does not seem to be entirely new. The truth it expresses in the terms of modern existential *Angst* and which I think deepens our insight into the matter, is found in another register of reference in St Thomas. Working within the austere categories of a rational ethic – *religio* (worship) is a sub-division of justice – he sees man as achieving the fulfilment of his human personality through the relationship that is established by worship. Submitting himself to God his last end or, we may say, the purpose of his existence, he is united to God and thus achieves beatitude.[17] Where the modern theologian speaks of explanation, a revealing of the meaning of life or a light thrown on the human predicament, St Thomas speaks of fulfilment (*perfectio*), the fulfilment of man's destiny through union with God. His account is calm and objective and seemingly untouched by experience though we cannot forget his exclamation after his vision of God towards the end of his life: *omnia ut palea*. All he had thought and written was but straw compared with the vision he had seen. But the modern theologian has brought all this teaching to a new level of consciousness and sees man immersed in the tragedy of life, reaching out for light, explanation, the dividing of the veil through which he hopes to see the meaning of his life.

We cannot go further into this matter here but it is worth remembering that when we are engaged in prayer and the praise of God, we are not performing a merely ritual act. We are moving towards God who has called us to himself and as we express ourselves, our desire for him, in petition and praise, we are celebrating him and we are celebrating life, our life which will achieve fulfilment in him, the source of beatitude, and the resolution of the problem of human existence.

There is another aspect of the matter. As we catch some glimpse of God's wonder, greatness and holiness, like the psalmist we feel impelled to adore, to bow down before this greatness and to acknowledge our littleness before his face. But with this comes also a longing, a desire to be united with the God who is love and who has poured out his love on ourselves. Adoration moves into love and is indeed a mode of loving. Somewhat as the lover is 'caught' by the beauty of the beloved and breathes out names that add nothing to that beauty, names that are in a sense useless and yet are necessary to sustain the love, so the Christian who has caught a glimpse of the glory and beauty and love that is God, utters his praise and adoration in 'useless' words which in fact reach the Lover through Jesus Christ, our advocate and mediator. For St Augustine we worship God by faith, hope and love. We respond to him first in faith, we trust in his goodness and the whole of our praise, thanksgiving and petition is suffused with the love that is poured into our hearts by the Holy Spirit. It is this that lifts prayer out of the category of 'duty' or obligation, out of the sphere of mere moralism ('it is good for you') and ultimately out of that sort of spiritual self-seeking which a former Bishop of Oxford called 'a self-regarding soul-culture'.[18]

It is here too that, I think, we can see a point of convergence between contemplation and public prayer. In principle they are not, as is sometimes supposed, in conflict with one another though certain temperaments may be more given to the one than the other. If we are to profit from liturgical prayer, we need times and occasions when we can stand back from it and from the ordinary tasks of life. We need time for reflection on what God is, we need to recall at greater leisure his saving works through which he has revealed himself, revealed his 'faithful love' throughout the millennia. For, to repeat, it is only this sense of God and of his presence to us and to the world that can turn our 'sayings', our words, into prayer. But at the same time, the psalms, the readings and other texts of the office are a vehicle of contemplation. They are uniquely centred upon God, they reveal a myriad of aspects of his saving love and through them the worshipper is, or can be, drawn towards him who is the source of their being and its ultimate meaning.

Obviously, if this is to happen the two kinds of prayer, contemplative and private, and official and public, must not be kept apart. If private prayer is done in abstraction from liturgical prayer, it is likely to become thin in content and will move in a very narrow circle of ideas that may become obsessive. If it is done in abstraction from community, whether the local one or that of the universal church, it tends to become unduly self-regarding and self-centred. It can be readily admitted that the balance is not always easy to maintain but if there is a deliberate exclusion of the liturgical and the communal, the results are not likely to be happy. In fact, the two kinds of prayer will enrich each other and it is one of the best features of the new office that it has made possible a contemplative prayer of the hours.

To that extent, the problem is at least in principle overcome. But there is another. In modern times we have forgotten the necessary link between the interior and the exterior, between what we think, experience and desire and what we do. In the matter of prayer, there has been the tendency to think that the more interior it was, the more genuine. Indeed, in the past some spiritual writers have had difficulty in finding a convincing justification for vocal prayer which they thought was a lower species. It is obviously true that vocal prayer which does not engage the mind and the heart is senseless but it has not always been understood that it is natural, i.e. in accord with the exigencies of the human person, that we should express in exterior ways, by words and music and gestures, what we think and feel. If the lover never tells his love, its very existence is doubted. Vocal prayer is then not so much a lower form of prayer as a necessary part of it and if with St Augustine we see it as the expression of our desire for God, if in particular we see the prayer of praise and adoration as a manner of loving God, we shall also see that it is natural to want to express our love, our praise, our adoration in words. There is in fact a double movement in prayer: the words of liturgical prayer penetrate our minds and hearts and feed them. On the other hand, our interior prayer sooner or later demands expression and this it finds both in liturgical prayer, which is a channel for so much we cannot express adequately, and also in the prayers, however inadequate, we make up ourselves. In any case, it is difficult to conceive of a prayer that never expressed itself exteriorly.

This of course is for our own sake and not for God's and it is part of the whole strange business of worship and prayer that though it is centred upon God, it ultimately turns back on ourselves. This is true, whatever kind it may be, praise, adoration, thanksgiving, repentance or petition; it is for *our* good for of course God does not need our praise and thanksgiving.[19] We do not pray to do good to God and the odd notion of giving 'external glory to God' – the grander the ceremonial, the greater the glory given – has disappeared from religious talk and writing since Vatican II showed that the glory given to God is to be found in the life and conduct of the worshippers. To quote once again the phrase of Irenaeus, *Gloria Dei, vivens homo*, it is the Christian responding to God not only in worship and prayer but also in his life who is a showing forth of the loving action of God upon us. Once this has happened, others are drawn to respond to God in like manner and in their turn witness to the presence of God in the affairs of men.

There is then a basic human need to express our prayer in words, not to mention song and gesture. We are body–soul creatures and because we are we need to offer a two-fold worship to God, interior and exterior,[20] and once you say vocal prayer and external worship, you say community. The impression has sometimes been given that the 'purest' prayer was that of the 'alone with the Alone' or the flight of the self to the One. But this is the language of Plotinus and his circle who were not Christians and were indeed hostile to Christianity. There is no doubt, as we have said, that we need private prayer and we recall Matthew 5:5–6, though this passage does not set private prayer in opposition to public prayer. It is thinking rather of motive.[21] Christian prayer is radically communal. It is the prayer of the *ecclesia*, the assembly that is the body of Christ, and all Christian prayer is prayer in Christ and through Christ. Even the most solitary mystic is praying in Christ and if he is not, his prayer is no more than a psychological exercise. He may be more or less conscious of the fact in the time of his prayer which, it would seem, is anyway without concepts. He may during prayer not be conscious of the community of which he is a member but he none the less remains one and on return to the normal duties of life gladly accepts that he is. Nor is it accidental that so many of the mystics have felt impelled to utter in writings what they are the first to say is unutterable. They are driven by a sense of service to their fellow Christians with whom they wish to share the vision of the divine glory they have seen. Nor is it without importance that most of the mystics were members of religious orders who celebrated the liturgy day by day in community. The really solitary mystic seems to have been a rarity in the history of the church.

Vocal prayer then is a human necessity and, as I have said elsewhere, implies community which again is a fundamentally human need.[22] But perhaps it needs to be emphasized that it is as necessary to prayer as it is to sacramental worship. Sartre's 'Hell is others' is not only the complete antithesis of the Christian gospel, it is also totally inhuman. Human beings are united with each other by a whole network of relationships that extend from the closest and most intimate in the family to all the inter-connecting forces that make social life possible. For Christians these relationships are deepened and enhanced by the grace of Christ but they remain human and we do not lose the need for them just because we are Christians. It is not without significance that as it has become more and more difficult to establish and maintain these face-to-face relationships which the sociologists tell us are of the essence of community, smaller groups, whether charismatic or not, have felt the need to meet both to foster personal relationships and to express them in prayer. In another context it has been said often enough that the very position of monks in choir expresses in concrete form the truth that they are brothers and that *together* they are turned to God by and in their prayer. But when we are considering Christian prayer, once you say 'community' you are saying 'church' and thus we come to the prayer of the church. But this is a vast subject which will be broached in the next chapter.

But one thing that follows from these notions is that as soon as you have community you discover the need for a structured prayer, one that can be shared by 'others'. If there is no recognizable pattern, a community simply cannot pray together. Hence the need of a form of prayer in which the various parts follow each other in ordered fashion to form a whole that has a discernible meaning. Mere strings of prayers and other texts that follow one another in a haphazard way simply baffle the mind and the emotions and leave the worshipper in a state of disarray. On the other hand, the very content of the prayer must be such that it can meet the varying temperaments and needs of a community. If the content is individualistic and even idiosyncratic, it is obviously unfitted for community prayer.[23] In the Bible, and particularly in the psalter, the church has found the texts that in differing arrangements at different times have provided the forms of prayer that can express the life of Christian communities. Other texts like responsories whose content is almost wholly biblical, hymns at least to some extent, and collects which are more heavily dependent on the biblical texts than is always realized, are simply extensions of the principle that the church prays out of the Bible. There is no need to repeat that it is because of this that the divine office can be and is the response of the community to God who has disclosed himself in the word of the Bible. Nor it is necessary to emphasize that that self-disclosure was made to a community, first the people of Israel and then to the new Israel which through the saving work of Christ continues while transcending the existence of the old. Further, as the proclamation of the word and salvation itself came first to the community, so it follows that community as community must respond to the saving initiative of God. This it does largely in the words in which that salvation was made available.

But if the words of the church's prayer are those of a community, it does not follow that they are impersonal and say nothing to individual members of the community. The Bible is supremely personal. It is the word of God to his people seeking their response and their commitment. As we know from an experience that stretches back from our own times to that of the desert fathers the words, the phrases of the church's prayer, can be appropriated and become our own so that they become the very breath of our prayer. As in all liturgical worship there is a nice and sometimes difficult balance to be maintained between the communal and the personal. If the first is over-emphasized, worship can become formal and even hypocritical, if the latter is given free rein it can turn to sheer idiosyncrasy. Given a right understanding of the forms and patterns of the office both extremes can be avoided and it may be said at this point that the new *Liturgy of the Hours* has done much to restore a balance that was not to be found in its predecessor.

Briefly, the case for common prayer seems to be exactly parallel with that for a communal rite of the eucharist. Just as the community needs a rite in which it can express itself and lift itself up in offering to God, so it needs a rite of prayer through which as community it can respond to God in praise, adoration, thanksgiving, repentance and petition.

All the foregoing is one way of putting the matter. There is another that was in vogue for a very long time and since it played an important part in the system of obligation that affected clerics for centuries, it will be useful to look at it. The line of argument ran like this. Worship, including of course public prayer, is an act of the virtue of 'religion' which regulates the activities of man in worship.[24] Further since God is the supreme being and creator and since we are totally dependent upon him, we owe him a *debt* of homage, reverence and an acknowledgement of his sovereignty. This debt we pay by 'the acts of religion' which include prayer. But since in the not very alluring phrase of Aristotle we are 'social animals' and since in as much we form society, the whole of society has a debt to pay as the community of mankind. This prayer has been organized according to times and occasions and in certain patterns so that mankind can render the debt. It is out of this thinking that emerges the notion of *obligation*. All Christians have an obligation to pray and this they should do morning and night. But this is not sufficient. The prayer should ideally go on all the time and since obviously ordinary people engaged in the necessary tasks of their daily living cannot do this, certain persons are 'deputed' (by the church) to do it for them and thus throughout the world the daily round of prayer and praise is kept up.

This view, though it cannot be said to be erroneous, is a somewhat bleak philosophy which seems to make little appeal to people today. It is more ethical or even deontological than religious and since the obligation was backed up by centuries of customary law and legal injunctions of a more formal kind, common prayer acquired a strongly juridical flavour. If for instance a priest (and the obligation bore on the clergy quite heavily) 'said his office' for the day, even without attending very much to its content, and even if it did not engage his mind and heart (as often it did not), he had satisfied his obligation and all was well.[25] The man clothed in severe black reading out of the little black book was in some mysterious fashion giving glory to God.

The trouble with this philosophy is that it not only stressed obligation but insisted on an obligation based on juridical notions which have played so large a part in the Christian thinking and practice of the Western Catholic church. In the last analysis, this juridical theory turns the whole Christian order upside down. It is, as we have seen, in the nature of things that we should respond to God in prayer and worship and if we see the meaning of life and something of the reality of God, we cannot but respond to him whether or not there are any laws telling us to do so. Obligation then arises out of that situation and is only justifiable on the assumption that that is the situation. Too often in the past the divine office has been seen as simply obedience to a positive law of the church with the consequence that there seems to have been current the notion that if the law were abrogated, there would be no need for common prayer. Since in recent years not only legalism but law itself has fallen into disrepute, there are those who in former years recited the office out of a sense of duty, but have now abandoned it, sometimes, it would seem, without putting anything else in its place. Since most of us are not geniuses at prayer, there may well be the danger that there is no prayer-life at all for such people. Even a daily celebration of the eucharist, if unsupported by prayer, can easily become a formality.

It is another matter what may be demanded by law and basically what is in question is not so much law as education. But that apart, every right-thinking Christian, every right-thinking Jew (for the prayer of the church was almost certainly conditioned by and based on Jewish prayer forms) and for that matter every Muslim, recognizes the duty to approach God in prayer morning and evening and even if there were no 'office' for these times we should be obliged to pray to God. In this sense the prayer of morning and evening, organized into offices, is no more, but *no less*, than the recognition of the church that such prayer is in the nature of things and at the same time the means of fulfilling the obligation.[26]

This era now seems to have passed. Apart from urgent recommendations to say at least Lauds and Vespers and of course at the appropriate times, the Introduction to the *Liturgy of the Hours* has little to say about obligation. Perhaps it was not the business of the Congregation for Worship to do so but it is none the less the great merit of that document that it has attempted to formulate a theology of common prayer and it is on this that it has based its recommendations. The era seems to be past in another sense. The revised office seems to have met the needs of vast numbers of the clergy who have taken it up very readily. The reason may well be that the new office is by its structure and content visibly *prayer*, the prayer of Christ. His presence is made clear throughout the hours and this gives the user of the office a sense of praying in Christ. But this matter too must be explored in the next chapter.[27]

Notes

~

[1] *Why Pray?* (London, 1970), pp. 12–13.

[2] See George Ineson, **Community Journey** (London, 1956).

[3] Though of course there are other reasons.

[4] *Ep*. 130, 7; PL 33, c. 500. In the background here lurks the question of disinterested love of God which gave Fénelon so much trouble. It is a complex matter but if the above seems to suggest that for St Augustine love was always self-interested there are two phrases that show he did not hold that view and they will serve to provide the solution to the problem: if we love God, he says, we at the same time love ourselves: 'we love God for himself and we love ourselves and our neighbour for his sake': *ibid.*, c. 499. The two loves, if they are two, coincide. When we love God we are loving the end and purpose of our existence **even if we never think of it**.

[5] *Ibid.*, c. 501.

[6] *Enarr. in Psalm.* 85, i; PL 36, c. 1081. The passage is quoted in part in *Mediator Dei*, n. 152 (Eng. trans.).

[7] See Chapter 3 and Caesarius of Arles: *Césaire d'Arles: Sermons aux peuples*, 1, introduction p. 152: readings from scriptures in morning prayer and sometimes at least a sermon. Sources Chrétiennes, 175 (Paris, 1971).

[8] See J. Wilkinson (trans.), *Egeria's Travels* (London, 1971), p. 64.

[9] This is not to deny that prayer *is* difficult or that we do have to make an effort, but as it seems to me, a wrong notion of prayer produces unnecessary tension that we should be glad to be rid of.

[10] In the theology of grace, it has been said, 'The Tridentine teaching hardened into a position which seemed to divorce the gift of grace from Giver'. See Cornelius Ernst, *The Theology of Grace* (Dublin, Cork, 1974), p. 6.

[11] The Rule, ch. 19 and cf. ch. 20 'Let us be sure that we shall not be heard for much speaking, but for purity of heart and tears of compunction' (translation of Justin McCann, *The Rule of St Benedict*, London, 1951 and 1972, p. 69).

[12] See Rule, ch. 20, *ed. cit.*, p. 69.

[13] As an abbot said to me years ago, 'It is the *life* that finds you out. If you can live it, you will find yourself being formed. We do not need special techniques.' This last may be questioned. Some modern monks have profited from the tradition of Zen Buddhism though they may be finding there what is already implicit in the Rule.

[14] CL 33.

[15] Surely an enormous statement for an Old Testament poet.

[16] See Ernst, *The Theology of Grace*, pp. 70-1.

[17] See ST II-II, 81, vii, 84, i, 2. In this St Thomas is saying in rather different language the same as St Augustine in his letter to Proba, Ep. 130 (see above).

[18] Dr K. Kirk in his book *The Vision of God* (London, 1931).

[19] ST 81, vii, 2.

[20] John Damascene in ST 84, ii.

[21] See JBC, II, p. 73, J. L. McKenzie on Mt 6:5-15: 'Prayer said when one is not being observed is surely prompted by the proper motive. The saying does not refer to public common prayer in the temple or the synagogue.'

[22] See *Christian Celebration: Understanding the Mass*, p. 38.

[23] On reflection it is odd that so many modern religious communities were able to survive for so long on the public recitation of prayers that were obviously meant for private use.

[24] Thus St Thomas. See references above. He had much more to say of course and his question on 'Devotion' is particularly interesting.

[25] Of course the spiritual writers and various devices like the prayer *Aperi, Domine* attempted to induce the notion that the priest was engaged in prayer and should do his best to make it such, but it cannot be said that these efforts were highly successful. The instrument, the office, was faulty, and the language, Latin, was for many a real barrier.

[26] Significant of a whole mentality was the practice of some clerics who, when for perfectly legitimate reasons they were unable to say the whole office on a particular day, in fact said none of it. It did not occur to them that it would have been wholly fitting to say Lauds and Vespers.

[27] On the *Liturgy of the Hours* see canons 1173-1175. Still mostly a clerical exercise. For obligation, canon 276, #2, no. 3. The legislation is however much less legalistic than that in the former Code. Canon 1173 speaks of the *church* listening to God speaking to his people and through the office actualizing the memory of the mystery of salvation.

~

18

The Prayer of the Church

~~~~~~

*I*T HAS BEEN STATED in the previous chapter that public prayer is an exigency of community and if we are to understand what this means in the Christian context we have to explore the relationship between prayer and the church, the assembly (*ecclesia*) of God's people. But since the church is the sacrament-sign of Christ we have to examine, however briefly, his prayer which according to the Constitution on the Liturgy (83) is prolonged or continued by the church.

The prayer of Christ

It is manifestly impossible here to deal with the whole vast question of the prayer of Christ in the gospels.[1] All we can do is select one or two points that are particularly significant for our purposes.

If we examine the three occasions in the synoptic gospels where indications are given of the content of Christ's prayer we find that they are marked by the use of the word 'Father' (Abba): 'I bless you, Father, Lord of heaven and earth . . .' (Matthew 11:25; cf. Luke 10:21); in Gethsemane with the addition of 'my': 'My Father, if it is possible let this cup pass me by . . .' (Matthew 26:39, 42; Mark 14:36 ('Abba'); Luke 22:42); and on the cross in a passage peculiar to Luke: 'Father, into your hands . . .' (Luke 23:46). 'Abba', we are told, is a familiar form of address used by children to their father and though it could be thought of as 'Daddy' it conveyed a nuance of respect that is not found in the English expression. As we can see from the texts, it is this expression that Jesus always used in his prayer to his Father. There is no doubt that it is proper to Jesus for 'there is no single instance of God being addressed as Abba in the literature of Jewish prayer'.[2] Furthermore as Matthew 11:25 shows, the word is a revelation of the unique relationship between Jesus and his Father. This was the invariable undertow of his life, and the doing of his Father's will was the very meaning of his existence and mission (cf. John 5:30; 6:38–40, etc.).

~

This relationship was *revealed* on certain occasions such as his baptism (Mark 1:9–11) and his Transfiguration and in Luke on both these occasions we note that the revelation comes, as it would seem, as the result of Jesus' prayer (Luke 3:21, 22 and 9:29). At other times it was *expressed* and, it would seem, with great emotion. The utterance in Matthew 11:25–27 seems to be almost ecstatic, expressing both the depth of the relationship and the longing of Jesus, so frequently expressed in the Fourth Gospel, to be with his Father. Something of the same sort may be said of the Transfiguration. Apart from other aspects of the event, it may be seen as the breaking through into the order of this world of the sublime and intimate union that Jesus had with his Father.

Perhaps no incident reveals so clearly that this relationship was real, personal and not merely 'theological', as that of Gethsemane. In Mark the word 'Abba' is actually used (14:36), and the total dependence and submission of the Son to the Father is revealed precisely in the work of salvation that he was bringing about. Finally and more important than all else, the reality of the relationship is revealed by the struggle, in traditional language the *agony*, that submission to the will of the Father demanded of him.[3] Jesus was always Son and he realized this existentially in the experience of his life. He was *conscious* of his Sonship and it was the most precious thing in his life. Nothing must be allowed to interfere with it and when Jesus so ruthlessly repelled Peter ('Get behind me, Satan', Matthew 16:23) it was because Peter was in danger of running against the will of the Father for the salvation of mankind to be effected by his Son through suffering.

An exploration of the use of 'Father' in the Fourth Gospel would take us very far. All we can do is to note one or two passages. John 11:41 seems particularly significant for the calm assurance of Jesus and for the unaffected simplicity with which he speaks to his Father. There is nothing of the ecstatic quality of Matthew 11:25 or of the excitement of the Transfiguration. Here indeed is a revelation of the constant prayer or interior dialogue that went on all the time: 'Father, I thank you for hearing my prayer [a prayer that has been made in silence]. *I knew indeed that you always hear me.*' Of this he was sure but he uttered his prayer and revealed his assurance for the benefit of those standing by.

With John 17 we move into a different world. The prayer is solemn, hieratic, and we must suppose that it bears the marks of editing and minor changes that had occurred in the process of transmission. For our purposes we may note that the prayer speaks of community, of love and unity. Jesus is addressing the apostolic body whom he envisages as being sent as his witnesses, as the men through whom others will believe in Jesus himself. The union he prays for is the reflection and consequence of the deep and intimate union that exists between himself and his Father, a union that it is his will should continue into the future. Finally, this union is the fruit of love and through it Jesus will be in them and they in him. However wary we should be in reading later notions back into first-century documents, it seems clear enough that Jesus is here speaking of the church and promising that he will be present to it, that its members will be united with him and that there will be dialogue at the level of faith and love between them and himself. If this dialogue is to be apparent it will have to be voiced in prayer and it will be a prayer 'in Christ': 'Father, may they be one in us, as you are in me and I am you' (17:21).

From this brief consideration of the prayer of Jesus in the gospels we can conclude that his was essentially a filial prayer, the prayer of Son to Father, and that it was the expression of the intimate union that exists between them. If Jesus is the model of the Christian, he is the model in this matter too, not merely in the sense of giving us 'a good example' but rather in the sense that our prayer is to be of the same kind. It is the plain teaching of the New Testament that Christians are by baptism the sons or children of God – in the phrase of a well-known theologian, we are *filii in Filio*;[4] we are sons in the Son and through his saving work that is mediated to us through the sacraments. This relationship which is established by Christ is nourished and strengthened by all the practices of the Christian life but especially by prayer and when we say the Lord's prayer we are putting ourselves in the posture of Christ who made and makes it possible for us to pray the prayer of the children of God. Nowhere is this teaching so clear as in St Paul (Romans 8:15, 16; Galatians 4:6) who using the old Aramaic word shows that we are praying as *filii in Filio*: 'The proof that you are sons is that God has sent the Spirit of his Son into our hearts: the Spirit that cries "Abba, Father" and it is this that makes you a son . . . and if God has made you son, then he has made you heir', with Christ, as Paul adds in the Letter to the Romans. The passage also shows that when we pray the Lord's prayer we are praying 'in the Spirit', who prompts us to do so, and thus it suggests the basic Trinitarian form of prayer: to the Father, through the Son, in the Holy Spirit.

~

The Lord's prayer

But the Lord's prayer has another importance. It is the first prayer of the community that is the church and itself the supreme community prayer. That this was the intention of Christ and the understanding of the disciples is the conviction of Professor Jeremias: 'The request at Luke 11:1 therefore shows that Jesus' disciples recognized themselves as a community, or more exactly as the community of the age of salvation, and that they requested of Jesus a prayer which would bind them together and identify them, in that it would bring to expression their chief concern . . . *When the Lord's Prayer was given to the disciples, prayer in Jesus' name began* (John 14:13f.; 15:16; 16:23).'[5] The Lord's prayer is then not simply the model prayer in the sense that it tells us what words to say or even in what order to use them–though that is true–it is the basic prayer of the Christian community because in it we are praying as the community of Christ to the Father, through the Son, who brought it into existence and holds it together in unity, and *in* the Holy Spirit who prompts our prayer and returns it to the Father. Prayer at its deepest is thus shown to be not merely a saying of words but a kind of living in God. The ultimate model of it is the Trinity itself, which is supremely life, where the Three Persons perpetually live in each other and communicate their love to each other.

But the Lord's prayer also provides the pattern of the church's prayer. It is the response of the Christian community ('our') to the Father, a response which, to repeat, is prompted by the Holy Spirit. Its members are praying consciously through the Son who has made them children of the Father. They seek first the glory of God and in total submission to the Father desire only that his reign (kingdom) may come and envelop the earth, for this is his will. Turning now as it seems to their own needs but still mindful of the coming reign, they ask for the bread that will indeed support them day by day but which is an anticipation of the eschatological banquet when God's saving will shall have been accomplished.[6] They then turn towards each other to seek forgiveness for they know, as the Lord has told them, that they must be a community of reconciliation and love. Finally, they ask that they may remain faithful to God who is always faithful so that they may withstand the final eschatological test as well as the trials of daily life which anticipate it.

At the risk of underlining the obvious, let us say that the Lord's prayer is God-centred and not man-centred and the same is true of the Divine Office especially through its use of the psalms. It is the prayer of a community that seeks to do God's will, the accomplishment of which is its sole reason for existence. In the Divine Office through the scripture readings and in the terms of the history of salvation, God's saving purpose is unfolded year by year. As in the Lord's prayer, there is petition for every kind of human need the satisfaction of which is one way or another of bringing the reign of God into the lives of ordinary men and women. At certain times of the year, notably Advent, the Divine Office puts before us the biblical teachings on the consummation and in prayer and hymn we pray that we may be delivered from destruction in the Final Test.

The prayer of the church

Our brief commentary on the Lord's prayer has anticipated a little the question of how the prayer of Christ is related to the prayer of the church and it must be said to contain the answer in germ. We have now to tease out the argument and exploit other evidence.

The documents of the church state that the prayer of the church is the prayer of Christ, as we see from the Constitution on the Liturgy (83) where it deals with the Divine Office: 'Christ Jesus, high priest of the new and eternal covenant, taking human nature, introduced into this earthly exile that hymn which is sung throughout all ages in the halls of heaven. *He joins the entire community to himself*, associating it with his own singing of this canticle of divine praise. *For he continues his priestly work through the agency of his church* which is ceaselessly engaged in praising the Lord and interceding for the salvation of the whole world. She does this, not only by celebrating the eucharist, but also in other ways, especially by the Divine Office.' To this we may add the statement of article 7: 'He is present, lastly, when the church prays and sings'. Since the same passage goes on to say that the liturgy, all the liturgy, is an exercise of the priesthood of Christ, the statement obviously means that the presence of Christ in the church's prayer is a priestly presence.[7]

The view is cosmic. It embraces the perpetual praise of heaven and sees the prayer of the church as a participation in it and as the anticipation of the eschatological fulfilment when all the redeemed in the company of Mary and the saints will sing: 'Blessing and honour and glory and power, through endless ages, to him who sits on the throne, and to the

Lamb'.[8] What seems to underlie the statement of the Constitution is Hebrews 1:1–2 which speaks of the coming of the Son into the world and in particular verses 8–9, a quotation from Psalm 44(45), which the Christian tradition has interpreted as the anointing of Jesus for the priesthood. It is the priestly Christ who brings into the world the eternal praise of heaven and by joining the community of the church to himself makes it possible for it to take part in the same heavenly song. Behind this we catch a reference to Hebrews 12:22–24: 'But what you have come to is Mount Zion and the city of the living God, the heavenly Jerusalem where the millions of angels have gathered for a festival *with the whole church* in which everyone is a "first-born son" and citizen of heaven. You have come to God himself, the supreme Judge, and been placed with the spirits of the saints who have been made perfect and to Jesus, the mediator who brings a new covenant and a blood for purification which pleads more eloquently than Abel's.' Jesus is the mediator, supremely the priest, who by his covenant of love has joined the earthly church to the heavenly church so that, the suggestion is, the worship of both is one.

We may draw the same inference from the book of Revelation where, as will be remembered, we find several vivid pictures of heavenly worship at the centre of which is the sacrificed Lamb ('between the throne . . . and the circle of elders'). The texts of the worship are given, 'Holy, holy, holy . . .' and the voices sing of the Lamb who has 'bought men for God, from every race, language, people and nation and made them *a line of kings and priests*, to serve our God and to rule the world'.[9] To the heavenly court are joined in chapter 7:9–17 the countless multitudes of the redeemed, 'a line of kings and priests', who worship God and the Lamb: 'Victory to our God, who sits on the throne and to the Lamb!' Further on we read that the prayers 'of all the saints' are offered with incense by an archangel before the throne of God (Revelation 8:2–5).

If the mediation of Christ precisely in prayer is not mentioned, he is present as the Lamb that was slain who is *Redeemer*. He has loved his chosen ones and washed away their sins with his blood and made them a line of kings and priests and *therefore* they are able to give praise to God: 'To God be glory and power for ever and ever' (Revelation 1:5, 6). He is *Mediator* in the eschatological events that are unfolded throughout the book. With him are associated the vast numbers of the redeemed, those who have washed their robes white in the blood of the Lamb and who 'stand in front of God's throne and serve him (*latreuousin* – i.e. worship) day and night' (Revelation 7:15). Whatever else heaven is, according to Revelation it is a liturgical community in which the saved are united with Christ and give continual praise and thanks to the Father.

If we are to evaluate these texts aright for our purpose here, we must understand that the writer is attempting to express as best he could what he had experienced in a mystical encounter with God. It is not a photographic record of actual happenings but, as in all such experiences, the mystic brings to his descriptions of them something of his own mentality and ideas derived from his ordinary living. Without, I think, straining the evidence we may conclude that in the writer's descriptions of heavenly worship there is reflected something of what he and his fellow-Christians experienced in their ordinary assemblies. The scenario is unimportant but we may say that they experienced *as a community* union with the Redeemer, they expressed their sense of union in praise and petition, and above all they were conscious of the interpenetration of the two kinds of worship. Through their humble weekly worship with its 'spiritual songs' and its simple eucharist they were aware of the vast cosmic worship of the celestial community in which they, through their worship, took part.

If we now go to other parts of the New Testament we can, I think, find a closer relationship with the statement of the Constitution. St Matthew's gospel, which has often been described as the most ecclesial of the gospels, has some relevant material in what is the most ecclesial of its chapters (18). There we find the well-known passage, which is in fact cited in the Constitution at the end of the statement given above: 'Where two or three are gathered together in my name, I shall be there with them'. If we add to it the sentence that immediately precedes it we see at once that the text has to do with *prayer*: 'I tell you solemnly once again, if two of you on earth *agree to ask* anything at all, it will be granted to you by my Father in heaven'. Clearly here we have prayer of the community, however small it may be, and the members of the community must be 'agreed', in harmony with one another.[10] We are reminded of the descriptions of the first Christian community in the Acts of the Apostles where the believers are said to be of 'one mind and heart' and showed that they were in the eucharist, in 'the prayers' and in the common sharing of all they possessed.[11] But this harmony was something more than likemindedness: the union that they have is rooted in

~

their union in Christ for they must meet *in his name*, for that is the meaning of that phrase.[12] The meeting then in Matthew is a meeting for prayer and for a prayer that is communal; its members are united in Christ and *because of that union*, all that they ask will be granted by the Father. In one sentence we have the basis and indeed the essential meaning of the public prayer of the church which has come to be called the Divine Office.

Nor does the teaching of the Fourth Gospel go beyond that of Matthew. It is richer and its implications are spelt out at length but it is the same: 'If you remain in me and my words remain in you, you may ask what you will and get it'; or again, 'The Father will give you anything you ask in my name' (John 15:7, 16; cf. 14:13). In both the Matthew and the John passages what is insisted on is union, the union of Christians through Christ with the Father and union through love with each other. Here indeed is the heart of Christian prayer. Just as in the eucharist we are able to offer because our offering is enfolded in Christ's, so we are able to pray and 'have access to the Father' because our prayer is incorporated into the prayer of Christ and becomes his. This, according to St Augustine, is why union with Christ in prayer, a union of *life* on which is based the union of mind and heart, is fundamental and essential to Christian prayer.[13] Finally, and to return to the Constitution, it is because of this union that Christ can be said to be present in the prayer of the church.

It may be said that these passages come rather late in the composition of the New Testament, Greek Matthew generally being regarded as late as AD 80 and John, as we know, is of the last decade of the first century. This however strengthens rather than weakens our case for it means that the church was now experiencing in life what Jesus had taught. The church, which had now broken away from the Temple worship, had for some time been finding its own way in the matter of prayer, perhaps precisely in the process of prayer, coming to a deeper realization of its union with Christ. However that may be, the texts are to be seen as indications of what the first Christians found there.

What is not explicit in these texts is that the prayer of the church is precisely the prayer of Christ the priest. For this we have to go elsewhere. Although the notion of Christ's priesthood is said to be 'absent from the Pauline corpus',[14] we note that his 'intercession' in Romans 8:34 is set in a paschal context: 'He not only died for us—he rose from the dead and there at God's right hand he stands and *pleads* for us'. This seems to be the theme of the heavenly sacrifice, that is, one offered by a priest, and we note that the word for intercession here is the same as that used in the well-known passage of Hebrews, 'He is living forever to make intercession for all who come to God through him' (7:25): *entugchanein.* Whatever may be the truth of the Romans text[15] (and if the *notion* of priesthood is not there the *reality* is, for Christ's redeeming work was for St Paul a sacrifice; cf. 1 Corinthians 5:7), the one from Hebrews is certainly priestly.

In the Letter to the Hebrews we have the fullest exposition of the priesthood of Christ in the New Testament though we cannot recount it here. We note that the above passage occurs in a priestly context; the priesthood of Christ brings into existence a new covenant, his priesthood is 'for ever', replacing and transcending the old one and because of this his 'power to save is utterly certain, since he is living . . .'. This covenant he brings into existence as *mediator* (9:15) for he is 'the high priest of the blessings to come, through the redemption, wrought by the shedding of his blood and the perfect sacrifice which he offered, namely himself'. Priest, mediator, sacrifice all come together. But as in Revelation the interpenetration of the earthly and the heavenly worship is always in the background: this high priest who offered the once-for-all sacrifice is now exalted to the right hand of the Father and is now the *leitourgos*, the 'minister' of the sanctuary presiding as it were at the heavenly liturgy and offering the worship and the prayers of the 'saints' (8:1, 2).

It might seem that all this is connected with sacrifice alone but we recall that as priest (though not in the order of Aaron) during his lifetime he 'offered up prayer and entreaty, aloud and in silent tears'[16] and because he submitted so humbly to the Father's will, his prayer was heard and he became the source of salvation to all who obey him (5:7–10). Then at the end of the letter there is the curious passage (13:15) where the writer prays that we may offer a *sacrifice of praise* to God, the fruit of lips that acknowledge his name.[17] The first phrase comes from Psalm 49(50) which is precisely about interior, genuine worship and the second from Hosea 14:3 which delivers a similar message. This is the main emphasis but, as one commentator says, Christian worship, disentangled from the material conditions of Old Testament worship, consists of 'the praise of God, the homage of faith and adoration given to God which is happily described as "the fruit of lips"'.[18] But the phrase should not, I think, be taken merely in the sense of interior worship if by that is meant wordless worship. The ancients whether Jews or Christians felt a need to express their worship and for the writer we may safely assume (does he not quote a psalm?) that he had vocal prayers in mind also and perhaps primarily. Moreover the 'sacrifice of praise' is said to be ceaseless, which reminds one of the injunctions of the gospel and other parts of the New Testament to pray always, and sacrifice at any rate took place at fixed times. Although Bonsirven's viewpoint is a little different from ours, he ends his commentary with an enthusiastic description of the virtues of Christian prayer: 'Not only can this spiritual sacrifice [which he seems to take as wholly interior] be offered ceaselessly but it has a supreme value: presented by Jesus Christ, to whom we are intimately united and who has made himself our mediator and as it were the expression (of our prayer), our prayer becomes the prayer of the Son of God and shares in the efficacy of his intercession.'[19]

This is perhaps sufficient to show that the prayer of the church, whether it is praise or thanksgiving or petition, is the prayer of Christ and that when the Christian is engaged in public prayer, he is united in an especially intimate way with Christ the priest and the intercessor. This may explain the expressions we find in the tradition that the office is the *Vox ecclesiae* (the Voice of the Church) or more significantly still *Vox Sponsae* (the Voice of the Bride) though the origin of these terms is to be found in the Christian use of the psalms. But whatever the origin, these phrases express very briefly the pregnant truth that the prayer of the church is the prayer of Christ. Another term, also found in the tradition, points in the same direction: *Chorēgos*,[20] leader of the choir, or in Latin *Magister chori*. The head and leader of the choir is Christ himself who joins their prayer to his own and offers it to the Father.

If the teaching of Hebrews is thought to be a little eccentric and perhaps without any very wide circulation in the early church, we can turn to the prayer of Christ in John 17. If it may not be properly called Christ's 'Priestly Prayer',[21] it was a prayer that in the Johannine tradition was put on the lips of Christ the evening before his death. It may indeed be said to be the paradigm of the prayer of the church. It is strongly ecclesial in character: Jesus is praying in the midst of his apostles (even if they are never called such in the whole chapter). He is praying for them and for the unity that will always be the mark of the Christian community – a theme that is found almost invariably in the liturgical

prayer of the early church. His vision goes out to the future, to all who
will believe in him through his disciples. He will be in them and they in
him and the bonds of unity will be faith, love and prayer. Finally, he is
dedicating himself to his sacrifice the next day (17:19) and if priestly
language is not the language of John (and it has often been said that John
saw the 'robe without seam' as the priestly robe), Jesus seems to have his
sacrifice in mind as he prays to be 'dedicated' or 'consecrated' for it. The
implication of the passage is that when the Christian community prays
it does so through Christ who is saviour and priest. This is but to echo
the Constitution on the Liturgy which sees Christ present in the prayer
of the church exercising his priestly office (7). Priesthood and sacrifice
have been so closely associated (especially when sacrifice, as in the
(corrupt) practice of the Old Testament, is seen as simply a ritual action)
that it may seem a little odd to think of prayer as a priestly act. It will
then be useful to recall that all liturgical prayer (with some exceptions
in East and West) is 'through Christ our Lord'.[22] That is in prayer, as in
all his redeeming work, Jesus is *mediator*, he is exercising his mediatorial
function[23] and as the Letter to the Hebrews has shown us, mediation
was effected through the exercise of his priesthood. What perhaps we
need to do is to extend our notions of sacrifice which even for the Old
Testament, as prophet and psalm reiterate, was a pleading from the heart,
accompanied by prayers, without which the ritual act was regarded as
not merely useless but pernicious. And if we ask how the effects of
Christ's redeeming work are made available to us now the answer given
by the Letter to the Hebrews is that it is through the 'intercession' of
Christ, as it were presenting and pleading his sacrifice before the throne
of his Father. No doubt we are conscious of metaphors here but the
range of expression at our command in these mysterious matters is
limited. As far as Christ and his Father are concerned we cannot suppose
that there is any doubt about the issue of the intercession. Christ does
not intercede 'in the hope that' or 'with an expectation that' he will be
heard. He intercedes in the certainty that his redeeming sacrifice and the
prayer that goes with it will be efficacious for the salvation of mankind.[24]
And it is on this that the efficacy of the church's prayer is based.

It looks then as if for us too prayer and sacrifice must go together
and it is at this level that the prayer of the Divine Office must be seen
as related to the eucharist and as a celebration of the paschal mystery.
The Divine Office has often been described as the 'setting' for the

eucharist or as 'a round of prayer'. But this is not sufficient if it is thought to be merely a verbal or psychological extension in the sense that it 'reminds' us of the saving events of the paschal mystery. The Divine Office is related existentially to the eucharist, it is its prolongation at the level of *life*, in its own particular manner it makes present the redeeming work of Christ throughout the day.

This is made clear by the texts of the office itself. At the climax of the two key hours of the day, Lauds and Vespers, are the songs of redemption, the *Benedictus* and the *Magnificat*. Lauds is a celebration of the Risen Christ and Vespers explicitly the 'evening sacrifice', as so many of the psalms, especially the Sunday psalms, show. And in the other day-hours various phases of Christ's redeeming work are pointed up especially by the collects. The church has been conscious of this from the earliest days, before the organization of the Divine Office, when the themes of Christian prayer can be discerned.

A further element of the prayer of the church that must not be forgotten is that it is prayer 'in the Spirit'. The church is the Spirit-filled body of Jesus Christ and prays not only through Christ but also in the Spirit. For St Paul, the Spirit is at the very heart of that prayer, one might almost say, the Spirit is the breath of prayer for it is the Spirit who voices the desires, the longings, the needs of the church even when its members are less than half aware of what they are asking for: 'The Spirit too comes to help us in our weakness. For when we cannot choose words in order to pray properly, the Spirit himself expresses our plea in a way that could never be put into words, and God who knows everything in our hearts knows perfectly well what he means and that the pleas of the saints are according to the mind of God' (Romans 8:26).[25] The 'pleas of the saints' are the prayers of the members of the church—so we have the ecclesial note again—and in these prayers the Holy Spirit is present, prompting them, inspiring them and the other Advocate[26] carries them to the throne of God. Secondly, because the Spirit is supporting and breathing out the pleas of the saints, the prayer that results is 'according to the mind of God'. Here again we have the note of union: the church united with Christ and praying in the Spirit is able to approach God with the conviction that the prayers will be heard. Thirdly, the text suggests that what we ask for is often beyond our knowledge. For St Augustine this is precisely 'the unknown reality' of God and it is the Holy Spirit who inspires in us the desire for the indescribable greatness and beauty of

God, an interpretation that seems to be close to the meaning of the text. But we may also think of it as something that goes beyond our expectations *because* our petitions are 'according to the mind of God' and the church in the course of history has had this experience as have individual Christians. In our own time this was the way of it with the prayer the church made before and during the Second Vatican Council. Few if any can have had any notion of what was to happen and many in the course of it felt it ought to be taking another way. But the Spirit intervened and guided the Council 'according to the mind of God' and not according to the designs of men. When then the Christian community prays, the Holy Spirit is actively present in its prayer which is taken up by Christ, priest and mediator, and becomes his own. It is here that we find the dignity and power of the church's prayer and if it must always be a fully human operation on our side, the Spirit will come to help us in our weakness and enable us to unite our prayer with Christ's and give acceptable praise and thanksgiving to God.

Such then is the prayer of the church. There is little need to elaborate the theme further though it needs to be applied to particular situations. According to Matthew 18 the 'church' can consist of as few as two or three but the prayer is always the prayer of a community. It is essentially communal prayer and this conditions its structure and forms. It must be of such sort that it can be used by a body of people. As in the eucharist, there must be dialogue, distribution of parts and hence a certain 'hierarchy'. In the course of centuries the church has evolved certain structures and forms and it is not unimportant to realize that all of them, whatever their differences, have been devised to enable a community to worship God through Christ in the Holy Spirit. The Divine Office is just as much a liturgy as the eucharist and as the latter expresses and manifests the church in its celebration, so does or should the Divine Office. It can be described as the voice of the community or, if you like, simply as the praying church with all the depth and width that the word 'prayer' implies.

If this is so, we are naturally led to enquire a little more closely into the make-up of this community. The Divine Office has been imposed on the clergy as an obligation for so many centuries that it has come to be regarded as an almost purely clerical exercise. 'Father' had to say *his* office and if it was dimly glimpsed as a peculiar form of prayer, it was one with which the laity had nothing to do. The situation was somewhat similar to that which prevailed with the eucharist about seventy years ago. The 'saying of Mass' was a clerical perquisite which the 'faithful' were allowed, indeed obliged, to witness. But whereas the Catholic world now realizes that the Mass is the action of the whole community, it has not yet come to accept that the same is true of the Divine Office. Yet the principles that underlie the communal celebration of the eucharist are exactly the same for the office. The celebration of the Divine Office is not a private function and all who take part in it are exercising liturgical ministries whether it be of singing, reading or serving.[27] The theological basis for this is again the same as that for the Mass: all share in the priestly office of Christ and because this is so, all can and should exercise that priesthood in prayer and so be united with the eternal intercession of Christ. The priestly community of prayer is the correlative of the priestly Christ who is ever living to make intercession for us.

Whether and how the people can be persuaded to take their part in the prayer of the church is another matter to which we shall return.

Notes

[1] For which see A. Hamman, **La Prière** (Desclée, Tournai, 1959), pp. 78–94 and pp. 385–412 for the Fourth Gospel.

[2] See J. Jeremias, **The Prayers of Jesus** (SCM, London, 1967), p. 57. Other scholars have since contested the truth of this statement.

[3] Cf. also John 12:27, 29.

[4] See E. Mersch in his posthumous work, **La Théologie du Corps Mystique** (Desclée, Paris, 1949).

[5] See Jeremias, **op. cit.**, p. 94.

[6] See **ibid.**, pp. 101–2, for a very rich and full commentary on this petition: e.g. 'it entreats God for the bread of life', and he goes on 'For Jesus earthly bread and the bread of life are not antithetical. In the realm of God's kingship he viewed all earthly things as hallowed.'

[7] It may be remarked that the first passage (83) is practically a verbatim quotation from **Mediator Dei** (Eng. trans., CTS, no. 152) which mentions simply the incarnate Word. The Constitution has added the teaching on Christ's priesthood thus considerably strengthening the statement of **Mediator Dei**.

[8] **Mediator Dei**, Eng. trans., no. 222. It is the conclusion of the whole Letter.

[9] Cf. Rev 4:1–10; 5:9, 10 (the translation of JB is rather free) and also 1:6.

[10] The Greek word **sumphōnēsōsin** = 'are in symphony'.

[11] Acts 2:42–47; 4:32–35.

[12] See JBC, II, on John 14:13, p. 453: '"In the name of Jesus" implies a communion of persons'.

[13] **In Ioannem, Tract.** 102, PL 34, 1896.

[14] JBC, II, on Rom 8:34, p. 318; NJBC, p. 855.

[15] We should note that in Rom 8:26 the same Greek word with **huper** is used of the action of the Holy Spirit.

[16] Presumably a reference to the agony in the garden.

[17] 'Acknowledge' ('confess', **homologountōn**) is a worship word, used frequently in the psalms.

[18] J. Bonsirven, **Epître aux Hébreux** (Verbum Salutis series; 2nd ed., 1943), p. 529.

[19] **Op. cit.**, p. 530. He refers to Heb 7:25, 1 John 2:1 (Jesus the advocate), John 14:13, 15:7, which we have used above. He accepts that the word 'intercede' in Heb 7:25 (and presumably in Rom 8:34) has the meaning of 'advocate' though he thinks its meaning can be legitimately extended (see p. 340).

[20] Cf. for example, Clement of Alexandria. For a eucharistic interpretation see Cheslyn Jones, **The Study of Liturgy** (2nd ed., rev., SPCK, London/OUP, New York, 1992), pp. 202–3, and C. J. A. Hickling's reservations in n. 41, p. 208.

[21] Cf. Christopher Evans, **Lumen Vitae**, vol. 24, no. 2 (1969), p. 582. The writer states that there is no mention in it of 'sin or sacrifice'. Perhaps not of sin but 17:19 seems to refer to the sacrifice of the cross.

[22] See J. A. Jungmann, **The Place of Christ in Liturgical Prayer** (Eng. trans., Geoffrey Chapman, 1965; reissued 1989), **passim**.

[23] Cf. St Thomas, III, 22, 4, ad lum.

[24] Only human beings can prevent its effect.

[25] The translation of this passage is not without its difficulties and the JB version (above) may be said to be a maximalizing one. In RSV and the New American Bible it is the **Spirit's** intercessions 'for the saints' that the Father understands and the phrase 'in a way that could not be put into words' (the 'unutterable groanings' or 'sighs') is more closely related to the Spirit. In the Greek 'the wordless groanings' are directly related to the Spirit who however is said to 'hyper-intercede', i.e. to 'intercede over and above' our pleas (cf. JBC, **in loc.**, p. 317; NJBC, p. 855). **Both** Spirit and 'saints' then are pleading and this may be a sufficient basis for the view we have taken in the text.

[26] Cf. 1 John 2:1.

[27] Cf. CL 26, 28.

THREE

An Historical Sketch of the Divine Office

~~~~~~

*I*T MIGHT BE THOUGHT that the theology of the Divine Office which we have tried to construct in the previous chapter would be reflected in the prayer of the early church. The matter is not so simple as that and as we have learnt in the theology and liturgy of the sacraments there is not always a straight line of development as older scholars sometimes thought. Furthermore, no department of liturgical studies is so complex and in some matters so obscure as the history of the Divine Office. Studies like those of Batiffol and Bäumer–Biron of some ninety years ago are now known to be seriously defective. Yet for an understanding of the Divine Office or the *Liturgy of the Hours* which is now the official prayer of the Roman church, some knowledge of its previous history is necessary. *How* did this new office come about? Was it thought up by some academic liturgists in Rome? What were the criteria they adopted for its construction? Until the proceedings of the Congregation for Worship are made known, it may not be possible to answer all these questions but a consideration of the history of the office from the beginning until now will throw light on the matter.[1]

Origins

That the first Christian communities, whether at Jerusalem, Antioch, Corinth or elsewhere, were praying communities is clear from even a superficial acquaintance with the New Testament and there is no need to multiply references some of which have been given in the previous chapter. It is altogether another matter to discover non-eucharistic, regular and organized prayer. In the Acts of the Apostles there are, according to my count, twenty-six references to prayer but nowhere is it possible to discover a daily 'order' or course of prayer. Of these references ten are concerned with special occasions, such as prayer for Peter when he was in prison (12:5) or the sending of Paul and Barnabas on a

~
34

mission (13:3) or the appointment of elders (14:23). Two other references call for comment.

1. Acts 4:21–31 records the prayer of the community on the release of Peter and John from imprisonment by the Jewish leaders. This too then is a special occasion and has no eucharistic content. It is however an instance of some interest because something of the content of the prayer is indicated. It is strongly Jewish and we find the Christians using a psalm (2), interpreted in a Christian sense, as the theme and framework of the prayer. Evidently it would seem that the Christians had already discovered how to use the psalms not only for preaching but also for prayer.[2] Finally, it may be worth noting that it was a charismatic form of prayer-service. The community was filled with the Holy Spirit, the house is described as rocking and all began boldly to proclaim the word of God. The account gives us some indication of what an early prayer-meeting could be like.

2. In Acts 2:42 we read that the newly converted Christians 'remained faithful to the teaching of the apostles, to the brotherhood (koinōnia), to the breaking of bread and to the prayers (hai proseuchai)'. What were these 'prayers'? You can read the text as the description of four activities, teaching or rather listening to the teaching, being faithful to the koinōnia by associating with it, by celebrating the eucharist, and by prayers, understood in the sense of a prayer service. This however does not seem probable. As Professor Jeremias has pointed out the four phrases are governed by the one verbal participle: proskarterountes ('persevering in' or 'devoting themselves to' or 'being faithful to'). What is envisaged then is one action in four movements: to use modern terms, the ministry of the word, the celebration of the eucharist by the koinōnia (and we remember Ignatius of Antioch's emphasis on being faithful to the one eucharist) and 'the prayers' which may have been psalms or intercessions during the eucharist.[3] This is a convincing interpretation of the passage and, if correct, rules out any special service of prayer.[4]

The conclusion then seems forced upon us that if the primitive church was a praying community, there was, apart from the eucharist, no organized prayer. Eucharistic celebrations were at times lengthy and included readings, sermons and prayers (cf. Acts 20:7–12). There are mentions of 'vigils' (Acts 12:5; 16:25; 2 Corinthians 6:5; 11:27; Ephesians 6:18 – these last three references give no more than the word 'vigil') but we do not know what was their content and they do not seem to have been regular hours of prayer but rather responses to particular situations. There are also of course mentions of prayer at the third, sixth and ninth hours (Acts 2:15; 3:1; 10:9; 10:30) though Acts 3:1 is a reference to *Temple* prayers and the last two occasions refer to the prayer of individuals (Peter, Cornelius). There are the hymns which modern exegetes seem agreed were once independent pieces: Philippians 2:6–11; Ephesians 5:14; 1 Timothy 3:16 and various texts that are to be found in the Apocalypse, though apart from Ephesians 5:14, which is regarded as a baptismal hymn, we do not know when they were used or if they were used regularly. Finally there are certain Semitic phrases like *Amen*, *Mar anatha* and others which are part of the stock of the prayer-language of Jewish worship.

These words however remind us that the first Christians were Jewish converts, conditioned as everyone is by their past, and brought up in a tradition of piety and prayer that they would not willingly have abandoned. It is now agreed that the Christian liturgy is rooted in Jewish liturgy, especially in that of the synagogue and one writer indeed speaks of the 'genetical link' between the two liturgical traditions.[5] This line of research has been pursued for some years and efforts have been made to establish that the patterns of synagogue worship are to be found in the primitive prayer-services of the church. A recent analysis of the Jewish and New Testament material attempts to show that a prayer-service consisted of psalmody, readings from the Bible with homily, the Lord's prayer, the *Sanctus* and some of the (Jewish) 'Blessings'.[6]

The weakness of this and other similar theories is that it is difficult to establish that these hypothetical prayer-services were separate from eucharistic celebrations. The service recorded in Acts 20 seems to have gone on all through the night and will have been made up of various elements which certainly included the eucharist. Again, it seems to be agreed that a service of the word always accompanied the 'breaking of bread' and, given the sociological composition of the first Christians, it seems unrealistic to suppose that they were in a position to gather regularly for other services. There is of course the well-known letter of Pliny to the Emperor Trajan dated in the first decade of the second century but its interpretation is notoriously difficult. From Pliny's garbled account it *seems* that there were two services, the one before dawn (*ante lucem*) when the people sang 'antiphonally' (*secum invicem*) a hymn to Christ as to a god (*carmen Christi quasi deo*) and bound themselves by an 'oath' (*sacramento*) not to commit thefts, robbery or adultery, and the second later (we do not know the hour) when they met again 'to take food'. This seems to have been an ordinary meal (the Christians *said* it was) and may well have ended the *liturgical* vigil which, as in Acts 20, will have included the eucharist. There is little to our purpose, I think, that can be concluded from this text.[7]

We shall be on firmer ground if we consider the known prayer-practices of the Jews at the time of Christ. There can be little doubt that they were also used by the first Christians and can reasonably be assumed to have had a formative influence on whatever patterns of prayer eventually emerged.[8] It is known that the observant Jew at the time of Christ recited morning and evening the *Shema* ('Hear, O Israel, the Lord our God is one God. You shall love the Lord your God with all your heart . . .'), this practice probably having its origin in Deuteronomy 6:4–7: 'These words shall be upon your hearts and (you) shall talk of them . . . *when you lie down and when you rise*'. But the *Shema* was not properly speaking a prayer–J. Jeremias calls it a creed–and for this we have to look elsewhere. In the middle of the second century BC Daniel is recorded as praying three times a day, the times of the principal acts of worship in the Temple towards which he looked. The two practices were eventually fused. By the end of the first century AD with the morning and evening *Shema* had been combined the *Tephilla*, the prayer *par excellence* (also called the Great Benediction), namely the 'Blessings' (eighteen by the end of the century) while the afternoon prayer at about 3.00 p.m. consisted simply of the *Tephilla*. There were two further elements: private petitions, 'intercessions', were added to the morning and evening prayer;[9] and those of the 'priestly course' who were not on duty in the Temple used to assemble in the synagogue at the times of Temple worship and added scripture readings to the prayers. Already then we can begin to see a certain pattern emerging: praise (in Jewish terms, the 'Blessings'), petition and scripture readings. What about psalms? The evidence does not seem so explicit. At least at the Sabbath assembly Psalms 145–150 were recited and these, as is well known, formed the nucleus of the office of Lauds where however it was only the last three that were used.[10] To these we may add without hesitation the Lord's prayer which brings the specifically Christian element into the pattern.

All this is a good deal more than can be gathered from the New

~

Testament material though we do not know in what order the various items were arranged nor how often or who used the formulas. For Jeremias the Greek verb *proskarterein*, used in Acts 1:14 for what is obviously a prayer-service, means 'faithfully to observe a rite' from which we *could* gather that what the author of Acts was describing was an ordered form of prayer.[11] It may be so, though it seems rather early in the life of the first Christian community to have worked out a fixed form of prayer (unless of course Luke is retrojecting his experience into the past!) and the phrase may mean simply that the disciples were observing the three traditional hours of Jewish prayer.

In the time of Christ there were three hours of prayer, in the morning, in the afternoon and in the evening. The church simply took over these by now traditional *times* of prayer but, as Jeremias observes, 'the new life bestowed through the gospel shatters the fixed liturgical forms, especially with regard to the content of the prayers. What is new here can be summed up in the one word "Abba".'[12]

This is already evident from the *Didache* (8) which enjoins that the Lord's prayer, with its liturgical conclusion 'For yours is the power and the glory for ever and ever', should be said three times a day. We are left wondering whether this was the sum total of the prayer. There is a small phrase in what is regarded as the oldest part of this almost certainly first-century document which seems to indicate that even so early there were meetings for prayer: 'Confess your sins *in the assembly (en ekklēsia)* and do not come to prayer with an evil conscience'.[13] Although at this early date we must not press the *en ekklēsia* phrase, it could be said that these prayer-meetings were ecclesial. Further, there was some sort of confession of sins, there was a form of prayer (*proseuchē*) which will have included the Lord's prayer or perhaps ended with it. There is however no indication at all of the frequency of such meetings; it is difficult to suppose that they took place three times a day.[14] Perhaps the injunction to say the Lord's prayer three times a day was meant as a minimum for any and every Christian who would be faithful to the Lord's command.

The development of public prayer: second to fourth centuries

When we move into post-New Testament times the picture for long is no clearer. We can pick up references to prayer in some numbers. There is the long prayer in the Letter of Clement of Rome (*c.* AD 96) which

~

however seems more like a long intercession made in the eucharist (59–61). In the Dialogue with Trypho of Justin the Martyr we are told that by the cross 'and the water of purification' the people are made 'a house of prayer and adoration', which tells us nothing more.[15] In the Pastor of Hermas[16] there is a fairly complete theology of prayer but nothing about hours of prayer. It would not be difficult to continue this list but to do so would yield very little. That the early Christians prayed, that they had an ability for constructing prayers of some nobility is beyond question but we must resign ourselves to the fact that there is no evidence to show what was the structure of their prayer.

We have to wait until nearly the end of the second century before we can glean any further information. This is to be found in Clement of Alexandria (died *c.* 215) and his slightly younger contemporary Tertullian of North Africa (died *c.* 225). It is from them that we discover that in addition to morning and evening prayer there had come into existence prayer at the third, sixth and ninth hours which were not based on the Jewish hours of prayer but on the official Roman division of the day.[17] The basis of this scheme was the saving deeds of Christ. There is at once a breakaway from the Jewish tradition and an intention to sanctify the hours of the secular day. We shall say something about this matter below but meanwhile two points are worth noting. Clement refers to prayer before meals and before sleep at night and reveals that it consisted of praise, of psalms and the reading of the scriptures.[18] The combination of psalms and readings is interesting and is perhaps the first explicit mention of such a pattern. Elsewhere he speaks of an assembly of some size which comes together to form one flock whose scattered and dissonant voices are subjected to the divine harmony so that finally they make one symphony for 'the choir, obedient to its *chorēgos* and master, the Logos, finds rest only in truth itself when it can say "Abba, Father". Then its voice, conformed to truth, is readily accepted by God as the first joy offered him by his children.' Whether or not this passage refers to a eucharistic assembly it is impossible to say but it is evidence of what Clement saw in the gathering. There is a sense here of an assembly whose unity is to be found in Christ who is 'the choir-leader': all are singing and praising through him and there is such an identity with Christ that together they are able to utter the words 'Abba, Father'. Clement is generally thought to be very Hellenistic and indeed Platonic and it is impressive to see the primitive Aramaic substructure coming through the elaborate and platonized description. Unpredictably Clement seems to be reflecting the early Judaeo-Christian tradition though, it would seem, through St Paul.[19]

Though Clement seems to be generally uninterested in liturgical matters, he is an important witness to the existence of Christian hymns, the texts of some of which he gives, in the prayer of this early period. He repeats the (probably) baptismal hymn of Ephesians 5:14 and records an additional verse: '(Christ) who is the sun of resurrection, begotten before the daystar'–which may well indicate that it has become a hymn for morning prayer.[20] If the famous *Phōs hilaron* ('Hail gladdening light') is of Egyptian provenance, Clement might well have known it as a hymn for evening prayer.[21] We can conclude, then, that Clement knew prayer in the morning and evening as well as prayer at the third, sixth and ninth hours and he is not thinking simply of an interior raising of the mind and heart to God. The prayer he speaks of is vocal prayer which is often done with hands raised.[22] For him it can be said too that 'the whole of life is one long day of festival, it is a sort of continual paschal celebration'.[23] In this, as we shall see, he is completely in accord with Hippolytus of Rome.

As well as recording the practice of prayer at the third, sixth and ninth hours, Tertullian is aware of the 'customary prayers' that are said 'at the approach of day and the coming of night'. These he calls *legitimis orationibus* which are said as a matter of course (*sine ulla admonitione*).[24] In a subsequent passage he reveals something of the content of the prayer (27). At least the more devout (*diligentiores*) add the Alleluia psalms (110–113 LXX-Vulg), the rest of the community responding, presumably by singing the Alleluia. For Tertullian, like Clement, prayer is a spiritual sacrifice (28 and cf. Hebrews 13:15, 16) and Christians who are true adorers pray in the Spirit (cf. John 4:24). But unlike Clement, Tertullian knows the prayer at midnight.[25] As is well enough known, Tertullian has much else about prayer but it is not to our purpose here and we can do no more than mention the magnificent peroration to his Treatise on Prayer where he sees the whole world caught up in the worship of God, even the cattle, the wild beasts and the birds 'who make a cross with their wings', giving praise to God (29).[26]

By far the most copious information about the prayer of the hours is to be found in the Apostolic Tradition of Hippolytus, a document that is usually dated about AD 215 and is thus roughly contemporary with

Clement and Tertullian. We may conclude that in regions as different as Alexandria, North Africa and Rome a common pattern of prayer was emerging. There are several points of interest in the Hippolytus document.[27] The first and in many ways the most important is that there is prayer both at home and 'in church'.[28] Hippolytus urges the laity to pray at home the first thing in the morning but if there is a service 'in church' they are to go there to listen to readings from the Bible, to the instructions given by the clergy and to pray 'for he who prays in church will be able to avoid the evils of the day'. For Hippolytus these gatherings were important and the scripture reading and the teaching no formality. The people are to realize that they are hearing God through him who speaks and 'they will profit from what the Holy Spirit gives them through him who gives the instruction'. We note too that there were both readings and prayers, no doubt psalms.[29] The evidence for a regular evening prayer is not so clear. Hippolytus describes what is evidently an *agape*.[30] The lamp is brought in and there is a prayer of thanks for the gift of light, very obviously on the lines of a Jewish prayer of blessing (*berakah*). A deacon then takes the chalice and says one of the Alleluia psalms and 'if the presbyter so ordains' other psalms of the same kind. The bishop then offers the chalice and says one of the psalms appropriate 'to the chalice'. This may have been Psalm 115 (LXX-Vulg): 'I will take the cup of salvation and I will call on the Lord's name', which in the psalter comes between the two sets of psalms that are called 'alleluiatic'. The people are to respond to the psalms with Alleluia, perhaps the oldest way of responding to the singing of the psalms. Here there is a complete ecclesial service whose roots are obviously to be found in the Jewish ceremony of the lighting of the lamps on the eve of the Sabbath. There do not appear to be any readings and most likely this was a weekly service held on the eve of Sunday. At the same time Hippolytus witnesses to the use of the Alleluia psalms which later on in the West became the psalms for Vespers.[31] But by far the most important feature of Hippolytus's evidence is his teaching on the meaning of the prayer of the hours. For him the framework is the paschal mystery with, in night prayer, an emphasis on Christ's second coming. Prayer at cockcrow, at the third, sixth and ninth hours and in the evening are all so many ways of participating in the redeeming work of Christ. Various writers, Clement, Tertullian and later Cyprian, all give various interpretations of the third, sixth and ninth hours. Hippolytus's is firmly paschal and seems to have been particularly Roman in character. Christ was nailed to the cross at the third hour and it has been pointed out that only Mark, perhaps written at Rome, attests this.[32] At this moment Christ is, for Hippolytus, the sacrifice that fulfils and perfects the sacrifices of the Old Law 'for he is both Shepherd and the bread that comes down from heaven'. The sixth hour marks the beginning of 'the great darkness' and Christians are exhorted to make 'a strong prayer' in union with him who prayed on the cross. Here the identification of the prayer of the Christian with that of Christ is very close. The ninth hour has a double significance: from the pierced side of Christ there flowed both water and blood and with the sleep of death he introduces the next day and makes an image of the resurrection.[33] Evidently Hippolytus has both cross and resurrection in mind and with all the writers of his time he sees them as two phases of the one redeeming action. Nowhere better than here do we see that for him the prayer of the Christian community is a celebration of the paschal mystery.

Echoing the New Testament teaching that prayer, especially at night, is to be made in expectation of the coming of the Lord,[34] Hippolytus gives an eschatological emphasis to prayer at midnight. He sees it as a preparation for, and an anticipation of, the *parousia* and refers to Matthew 25:6: 'Behold a cry is heard in the middle of the night saying: Behold the bridegroom is coming; rise and go to meet him . . . That is why you should keep watch [*vigilate*] for you do not know at what hour he will come.' This sense of the Second Coming which had not faded in the time of Hippolytus gave a peculiar intensity to the early Christian prayer at night, which has not been wholly lacking in the later vigil-prayer of the church.[35]

To complete Hippolytus's interpretation of the hours, let it be said that, as we should expect, morning prayer (at cockcrow) is related to the resurrection of both Christ and the Christian. The language is obscure though we note the phrase that 'at this moment we recognize him [Christ] by faith', which would seem to be a quite modern way of saying that it is only the eye of faith that can 'see' the Risen Christ.

Hippolytus then gives a quite complete theology of Christian prayer and his system might seem to us a very demanding one. Whether or not anyone practised it we do not know though Jungmann[36] has pointed out that prayer at midnight was not so demanding when people went to bed just after dusk and had ten or so hours of sleep before them. Nor

~

should we think of this prayer whether of the night or the morning as a purely private and mental prayer. Non-vocalized prayer was something that people at this time found very difficult, just as reading a book silently was also something unusual.[37] The prayer was also 'ritualized'. People prayed with gestures, raising the hands like the *Orante*, or in penitence kneeling. When husband and wife were both Christians they prayed together and of course aloud and there would seem to have been a much stronger sense of family worship than is common now. Hippolytus himself is witness to it and it may well be a practice derived from Jewish worship of which in any case there are traces in the account given by Hippolytus.

Whether it is right to see in the Hippolytan scheme the 'origins' of the Divine Office as it came to be, is another matter. The distinction between the clergy and the laity at this time was less clearly defined than it was two centuries later and there is no reason to suppose that the intervention of the clergy was necessary to make their prayer the prayer of the church.[38] Nor can one suppose that there was any direct line of continuity between the practices of the early third century and those of the fifth. The Decian, Valerian and Diocletianic persecutions intervened and a new factor, the prayer of the desert monks, came in the fourth century to modify the pattern of liturgical prayer.

Indications of public prayer do indeed occur in other places in the middle of the third century though the information to be gleaned is nothing like so complete as can be found in the Apostolic Tradition. Origen speaks of prayer in church, a place that is holy first because of the presence of the angelic powers and secondly and more importantly 'because of the power of our Lord and Saviour himself'.[39] Further on he gives some information about the prayer that was made in the assembly. It begins with the praise of God 'through Christ who is praised together with him in the Holy Spirit'. It continues with thanksgiving for both general and particular benefits and moves into confession of sins with a view to their remission. There is petition that those who are praying will receive the great and heavenly gifts and intercession for people generally and for relations and friends. The whole prayer ends with 'praise to God through Christ in the Holy Spirit'.[40] There is, it is true, no mention of readings though it is difficult to imagine a service which Origen had anything to do with where there was no reading of scripture and no homily. He did however deliver some of his homilies at such

~

gatherings.[41] It is also difficult to discern whether or not the prayer he is describing is part of a eucharistic celebration. What is clear is Origen's well-known insistence that all prayer should go through Christ, our high priest, and not directly to God. If he seems unduly strict we have to remember that he was speaking specifically of public prayer and was in any case voicing a rule that was observed in all the early churches.[42]

At about the same time as Origen, St Cyprian of Carthage was writing his little treatise on the Lord's prayer (*De Oratione Dominica*). He is aware of both private and public prayer as well as prayer at certain hours: 'Our prayer is public and made in common and when we pray we pray not for a single person but for the whole people because the whole people is one' (VIII). People are to pray in the morning 'to celebrate the resurrection' and they are to pray in the evening as well as during the night (XXXV).

Cyprian develops a symbology in connection with evening prayer and with prayer during the night. Prayer is made at the evening hour for Christ is the true sun and we pray for the advent (*parousia*) of the eternal light. Like Hippolytus he urges prayer during the night and he extends his symbology of light. Re-created spiritually and re-born by the mercy of God we should begin to do here on earth what we shall do in heaven. 'In the kingdom' there will be no night, only day (cf. Revelation 21:23, 24) and so we shall keep vigil as it were in enduring light and we shall unceasingly be praying and giving thanks to God (XXXV–XXXVI).

Cyprian of course knows the three hours of prayer during the day; the first two are connected with the Trinity and the last with the Passion. What is more important is that he sketches out a theology of prayer that is echoed in the next century by Augustine. He is commenting on the Lord's prayer 'which our Master taught us'. First then our prayer will be that of a friend, an intimate, 'if our petition is made in his [Christ's] words . . . Let the Father recognize the words of his Son; let him who dwells in our hearts be also in our voice . . . let us utter the words of our advocate' for Jesus himself said that whatever we ask in his name he will give to us (III).

Later writers will elaborate this 'theology' of prayer. Morning prayer is always associated with the resurrection of Christ and this is why Psalm 62 in the Septuagint and Vulgate translations (verse 2: 'I watch for the Lord *at dawn*') appears early in that office. Evening prayer was associated with Psalm 140(141) as that office recalled the 'evening sacrifice' whether the Last Supper (John Cassian) or Calvary (St Augustine, *Enarr.*

in Ps. 140, 5, and Cassian, *De Inst. Coen.*, III, 3). This understanding of these two key hours can be discerned throughout the centuries at least for the Saturday and Sunday offices.

But a change of far-reaching consequence was taking place. From the beginning of the fourth century the practices of the desert monks were affecting church life. When under men like Pachomius the hermits were gathered into communities (*coenobia*), it became necessary to organize a form of common prayer. First, there was the organization of regular hours of prayer and then the allocation of psalms to them. Finally, there was the institution of the night office, known as Vigils, and here the number of psalms varied in different places from 30 to twelve. This office took place at cockcrow and preceded the now ancient prayer of praise at dawn. The institution of the regular night office and the recitation of the whole of the psalter 'in course' in a given period of time were the two main features of the monastic office. They would have a considerable influence on the development of the Divine Office in the centuries that lay ahead. These monastic practices came to the church in the West and are described by Cassian (died 435). They can be seen as the basis of the arrangements of the *Regula Magistri*, which was perhaps pre-Benedictine, and had their influence on the office of St Benedict himself.[43]

Henceforth there would be two systems of prayer in existence, the first that which scholars have called the 'cathedral' office and the second that known as the monastic office. The first consisted of morning and evening prayer, both with a limited number of psalms, of 'hymns', a reading from holy scripture and prayers. The second added the night office with its recitation of the psalms 'in course', an extended use of psalms in morning and evening prayer and eventually a regular course of the reading of the Bible, the *lectio continua*. The hours of Terce, Sext and None were incorporated into the daily course and Cassian records the institution in Bethlehem of what some think to be Prime, an office that came between morning prayer and Terce.[44] The whole system was devised for a stable community and not for the generality of the people who obviously could not be present for every office every day. But through the centuries the monastic office steadily exerted its influence on the 'cathedral' office until both the daily course of offices and the regular recitation of the whole psalter within a given space of time came to be accepted as the Divine Office or the prayer of the church.[45]

But this development was a gradual one and the more popular offices of morning and evening prayer remained for some time. There is a description in one of St Basil's letters that seems to witness to a 'cathedral' type of morning prayer. Basil of course is the author of one of the great monastic 'rules' in which he laid down certain prescriptions for the office of his communities. The interest of the letter is that it does not seem to have such communities in view.[46] It reveals a mixed community as well as something of their form of prayer. The people (*laos*) who are with us (evidently the clerical–lay body forming the bishop's *familia*), he writes, go to church to keep vigil. First there are prayers of a penitential kind, then psalms, sung both 'antiphonally', it would seem, and responsorially and divided by 'prayers'. There is meditation on the scriptures and so presumably the reading of them, and at dawn the morning office which included Psalm 50, one of the permanent psalms for this hour though it is sometimes difficult to discern at what point it was recited.[47] No doubt the traditional Psalms 148–150 were also sung. Basil is writing to answer the objections of a neighbouring church though it is difficult to see quite what the point of the objections was. It may be that the vigil part of the office was regarded as a monastic practice which the clergy had no intention of adopting and this would not be the last time that that objection would be heard. What is interesting is that it was the *laos* who were present for both the Vigil and the morning prayer which seems to have been of the traditional kind.

The fullest description we possess of the offices is to be found a little later in the travelogue of the loquacious nun from (probably) southern Gaul who was perhaps called Egeria.[48] If the offices she describes were affected by monastic usages and if the nucleus of those attending were the ascetics (male and female), morning and evening prayer were definitely of the 'cathedral' type. There was a vigil service before dawn, attended principally by the ascetics. Morning prayer followed at dawn when considerable crowds were present. The assembly sang the *matutinos hymnos* after which the bishop with the clergy appeared to lead the prayers for different categories of people. The office ended with the dismissal which was prolonged, all coming to kiss the bishop's hand. Evening prayer, of a similar pattern, was very solemn and attended by all.

Though Egeria does not enumerate the psalms sung, we know from contemporary sources that they included Psalms 62 and 148–150. Possibly at the *Orthros*, the *Gloria in excelsis*, still a prayer of the Byzantine morning office, was also sung. In the evening the *psalmi lucernares*, which included Psalm 140, were used though whether the *Phōs hilaron* was sung, as it seems to have been in St Basil's church, is uncertain.[49] The prayers of intercession, led by a deacon and repeatedly responded to by boys with *Kyrie eleison*, were lengthy and there was the same sort of dismissal as in the morning.

One further feature may be noted. On Sundays, after a short vigil office at cockcrow there was the solemn proclamation by the bishop of the gospel of the resurrection.[50] Apart from this there is no mention of readings for any of the offices. Some scholars see this as an indication that in the early office there were no readings at all. They hold that there were two separate kinds of service, one they call latreutic, consisting of psalms and prayers, and another they call kerygmatic which was instructional.[51] Even if this were the situation at Jerusalem, since its liturgy had many peculiarities – extreme mobility being one of them and a multiplicity of services another – we may not suppose that what was done there was done elsewhere and in fact we know that there were readings in the offices of some other churches.

By the end of the fourth century morning and evening prayer, attended by the clergy and at least the devout laity, had become customary. Augustine speaks of his mother Monica going to church twice a day, in the morning and the evening, that she might hear God in his word and he might hear her in her prayers. He also speaks of the devout Christian who 'like an ant' runs to church to pray, to listen to the lesson, to sing the hymn and to ruminate on what he had heard.[52] Clearly then there were readings as well as psalms and this is borne out by what we know of the office at Milan in the time of St Ambrose.[53] There was prayer in the morning and evening and Ambrose frequently exhorted the people to attend, which seems to indicate that often they did not. As was traditional, morning prayer was related to Christ's resurrection – he is called the Sun of Righteousness – and consisted of psalms and canticles as well as of 'modern' hymns when Ambrose had written them. It would seem that there was a reading of the beatitudes, which may reflect an earlier custom, though it is difficult to believe that they were used daily.[54] No doubt, as was now the custom everywhere, morning prayer included Psalm 50 and Psalms 148–150. Evening prayer was sung 'at the lighting of the lamps' – it was the old *lucernarium* known to Hippolytus and retained in the Ambrosian rite to this day. It was also called the 'evening sacrifice' which seems to indicate that Psalm 140 was used, as in the East.[55] As in morning prayer a hymn was sung, e.g. *Deus creator omnium*, composed by Ambrose. There was also an hour of prayer at mid-day before the eucharist when Psalm 118 seems to have been used. If this is so, it witnesses to the ancient custom, preserved by Rome even until today, of using this psalm in sections for the offices of Terce, Sext and None. Ambrose also speaks of a night office when there were readings.[56] These preceded the prayers, it would seem, and witness to the increasing influence of monastic practices.

That there were popular vigils or *solemnes pernoctationes*, attended by large crowds (some of dubious character), can be gathered from Jerome who writes to Laeta and tells her to keep her daughter near her.[57] Of these vigils the greatest was that of Easter and there were others during the year on the great feasts. They were not the monastic Vigils which took place every night and had a different form.

From a different area and right at the end of the fourth century we have other evidence of an office that was attended by the people. Niceta of Remesiana, the most probable author of the *Te Deum*, wrote two small treatises, *De Vigiliis* and *De Psalmodiae bono*, which yield some interesting details.[58] He was bishop of this small town, now in Yugoslavia, on the main road to the East and his congregation was made up of a very miscellaneous collection of people. There do not seem to have been any monks of any sort. He expects his people to attend week-end vigils which consist of 'prayers, hymns and readings'. From his treatise on psalmody it is not clear whether he has Vigils or morning prayer in mind. No doubt by this time and at least for week-end vigils the two services had been combined. What he gives and what I think no one else of this time gives is information about the canticles used in his office. He details the following: Exodus 15:1ff.; Deuteronomy 32:1–44; 1 Samuel 2:1–10; Habakkuk 3; Jonah 2:3–10; Isaiah 26:9ff.; and possibly one from Jeremiah. These, as we know, have been found in the Roman office for centuries and their number has recently been increased. Finally, he refers to the Canticle of the Three Young Men in the furnace (already known to Cyprian and others as a canticle for morning prayer). In addition, he mentions a considerable number of psalms though it is difficult to discern when these or the canticles were used. In any case, he seems to record a transitional stage.

From yet another area, Spain and southern Gaul towards the end of the fifth century, there is evidence that morning and evening prayer were still regarded as the prayer of the church. The whole of this considerable evidence is summed up by Jungmann as follows: '. . . from Spain's southern tip to the banks of the Rhone, not only were Morning Hour and Vespers regular church services but they had a form of ritual which was regarded as legitimate'.[59] The synods exhorted the clergy to attend but the services were meant for the people and were accordingly comparatively short. The psalm-content was small though morning prayer always included Psalms 148–150. There was also a reading from holy scripture which came after the psalms and for Caesarius of Arles at least there was a homily. From the Synod of Vaison (529) we learn that the prayer included the *Kyries*, for the use of which it invoked Roman custom. So this element existed at Rome too. The office ended with a collect and the Lord's prayer but a blessing was given only when a bishop was present. To sum up, we may say that these offices consisted of psalms, reading (sermon), hymns in some places, intercessions and the concluding prayers. Apart from a tendency to increase the psalm-content, these offices are of the genuine 'cathedral' type and show little trace of monastic influence.

The situation in Rome was, it seems, rather different. As early as the first half of the fifth century the Popes (Xystus III and Leo I) had invited monastic groups to take over the office in the great basilicas though the clergy were required to take part in morning and evening prayer. There is no mention of the people being present though we could argue that from what is known of Milan and Ravenna at the same time, they were. According to Jungmann, as well as intercessions, witnessed by the presence of the *Kyries*, there was also a reading at morning prayer, and it is his view also that by the sixth century this had been incorporated into a system of readings belonging to the vigil: 'The Morning Prayer had acquired a preamble'. This is one explanation of how the night office acquired the element of Bible reading.[60]

By the end of the fifth century then the main lines of the prayer of the church are clear. Essentially it consisted of morning and evening prayer made up in the manner we have described above. These are what the Constitution on the Liturgy (89, a) calls the two focal points of the Daily Office and they almost wholly stand outside monastic influence. They are the prayer of the gathered church both clerical and lay. But alongside it there developed the office of 'Vigils' which was celebrated every night and sometimes had a very large quota of psalms – 36 in the

Regula Magistri!—with a regular course of Bible reading. To this were added the offices of Prime, Terce, Sext, None and Compline so that practically the whole day was covered. Thus was achieved obedience to the gospel injunction to pray always. Even so, for long enough there remained the offices of morning and evening prayer celebrated by the bishop's *familia*, clerics of various degree, as well as by the as yet unorganized ascetics, virgins, widows and other devout laity who lived in or near the church buildings. Here we have in both content and celebration an office which, *pace* the late Dom Gregory Dix, was not the creation of monks, and which modern scholars now see as the nucleus of the prayer of the church, or, as it is now called, the Liturgy of the Hours.[61]

The Divine Office in the early Middle Ages

The sixth century is the watershed in the development of the Divine Office. Until then churches everywhere celebrated the 'cathedral' office for the cathedral with the clergy gathered round the bishop was the real parish of those times. But at this time they had no sense of obligation to recite all the offices that were customary in the great basilicas of Rome, where, as we may have seen, monks had already taken over that duty. But from the sixth century onwards there was steady pressure on clerics to celebrate all the hours. In fact what we witness in the next two centuries is the monasticization of the prayer of the church. But we must dispel two illusions. In the sixth century and for a long time to come there was no notion that there should be but one office which should be celebrated all over the Western church. The great centres in Italy, Gaul and Spain all retained their own traditions, their own books and their own ordering of the office. Development there was and it was all in the direction of a monastic type of office but it was sporadic and uneven. The second fact was that it was some time before any 'secular' community felt that it ought to use all the hours that had become part of the monastic office. The clerics of Rome for instance resisted attempts to get them to celebrate Vigils[62] and especially in Gaul (Auxerre, Tours), when the various hours were adopted, they were shared out among the clergy of the various churches in the same city. Finally, no one at this time thought of an individual obligation to 'say' the office. It was clearly understood that the office was the prayer of the ecclesial community which as such gave praise to God.

~

But when we speak of the monasticization of the office in this period we must be clear what we mean. It is now agreed that an office of the monastic type existed in the Roman basilicas before St Benedict's time and it is this basilican office that is the origin of what became the Divine Office of the Western church. In the course of its development it was affected by the Benedictine office but it always had an independent existence. In view of its importance it will be useful to detail its content. The whole psalter was recited every week and, with a few exceptions (to provide psalms for Lauds, for example), it was arranged in the following order: Psalms 1–108 were allocated to Vigils and Psalms 109–147 to Vespers. The daily vigil office consisted of twelve psalms and of four lessons in winter (three in the summer). On Sundays there were eighteen (or even twenty-four) psalms distributed over three nocturns, and nine lessons with nine responsories. For festal days there were only nine psalms (three to each nocturn) and nine lessons with eight responsories, the ninth being replaced by the *Te Deum*. This is a thoroughly monastic office. Lauds had four psalms, one canticle (Old Testament), the 'praising' psalms, 148–150, and the *Benedictus*. For Vespers there were five psalms specially chosen to fit the hour, and the *Magnificat*. Psalm 118, divided into sections, provided the psalmody for Terce, Sext and None. Each office ended with *preces* and the Lord's prayer since in the basilicas the collect was reserved for the Pope or his deputy. There were no opening versicles and responses, no hymns, and no chapter or short reading. The office of the last three days of Holy Week until the recent reform gave an adequate idea of what the ancient Roman (festal) office was like.[63]

The office of the Rule of St Benedict

Since the Benedictine office exerted an important influence on the development of the office it is necessary to give some account of its content.

It is now generally accepted that Benedict adapted and added to the office already in possession in the Roman basilicas.[64] He grew up in Rome and was familiar with the Roman *ordo psallendi*. In spite of a few additions (the opening versicle and responses and the hymns), Benedict's office was in some ways shorter than the Roman. There were never more than twelve psalms at Vigils, only four at Vespers and at Compline three.

In the summer, when dawn comes early, the scripture readings were reduced (the missing portions being read in the refectory) and in the second nocturn there was no more than one short reading. On Sundays and festivals however there were in addition three canticles and four lessons from the New Testament with responsories, this last part looking rather like a vestige of the old cathedral week-end vigil. The whole was concluded with the *Te Deum* and the chanting by the abbot of a gospel passage.[65]

Lauds however, especially on Sundays, was rather long. Apart from Psalm 66 (to be said every day to allow the brethren to assemble), there were three psalms (one being the classical 50), the *Benedicite* and Psalms 148–150. On weekdays there were two psalms, an Old Testament canticle (after the Roman custom) and Psalms 148–150. We note too that there was a reading (short, for it was to be said by heart), the responsory, the versicle, the *Benedictus*, the *Kyrie eleison* and the conclusion which consisted of the Lord's prayer and possibly the collect though the Rule does not say so.[66] In all this the reading, perhaps the responsory and the hymn seem to be additions to the Roman office which apart from ferial days seems to have lost the *Kyries* and the Lord's prayer which together formed what Benedict called the *supplicatio litaniae*.

Though Benedict kept the distribution of the psalter over the week, he had to modify the Roman *cursus*. He needed psalms for Prime (a monastic office) and to this he allocated Psalms 1–19 (with the exception of three used elsewhere). Psalm 118 was used for Terce, Sext and None on Sundays and Mondays and for the rest of the week he took Psalms 119–127, used in the Roman system for Vespers. Benedict too seems to have been the first to make a systematic use of psalms for certain hours on account of their appropriateness. Thus he allocated Psalms 117 (a resurrection psalm), 62 (long traditional for this hour), 5, 35, etc. to Lauds.[67]

Such in broad outline was the office that Benedict provided for his monks. For a community that lived by the rhythm of an agricultural society it was a reasonable and manageable form of prayer, much more reasonable than that of the *Regula Magistri* or the later one of Columbanus, both of which Benedict's office gradually ousted.

There were now two models of the Divine Office in existence, the Roman–basilican and that of St Benedict's Rule. But it does not follow that either was in *use* everywhere. Not to mention the East, the Roman office was in use in certain churches in Rome but other great centres in Italy, Gaul and Spain had their own traditions. The Benedictine office was confined to the Benedictine family and that family developed slowly. Monte Cassino itself was destroyed in 580–581 and Benedict's work had to be begun all over again. Here St Gregory the Great played an important role for it was from refugee monks from Monte Cassino that he learnt the Rule and it must have been the office of the Rule that St Augustine brought to England. Another centre from which the Benedictine office was propagated was the monastery of Fleury-sur-Loire in the seventh century.[68]

Where however the Benedictine office exerted its influence was on *celebration*. Benedict gave the example of a community which made itself responsible for the recitation of all the hours from Vigils to Compline in one day. This, if not a new idea, was a practice that stable communities of monks could undertake and gradually their example affected practice in other and different places. Thus in Gaul, notably in Auxerre, an ancient centre where there were several churches, the bishop arranged that the clerics of different churches should recite in turn different parts of the office. The episcopal city was still regarded as the nuclear community of the diocese and it was this whole community that undertook the daily course of prayer. When and wherever the Benedictine rule was established, its influence on single communities to undertake the whole course of daily prayer was powerful.

In this respect England, thanks to St Gregory and the mission of St Augustine, played a significant role. As is well known, he and his monks brought the Roman tradition of liturgy to England[69] which was endorsed a century and a half later by the Synod of Clovesho (747) where it was decreed that the *cantilena romana* should be the practice of the Anglo-Saxon church.[70] It was this tradition that Boniface took with him from England to Germany and eventually he powerfully supported the efforts of Pepin to restore regular liturgical practice in his dominions. It was at the same time that Chrodegang of Metz, a relative of Pepin's, after a visit to Rome, brought into existence his 'canons' who lived in community and undertook the celebration of the Divine Office but who unlike monks engaged in certain diocesan work. Thus the way was paved for the far-reaching liturgical reform of Charlemagne.

The reform initiated by Pepin, Boniface and Chrodegang shows that the history of the Divine Office is very much a history of its celebration.

~

For want of the necessary books a solitary priest could not recite the office and both in the eighth century and again in the eleventh communities of priests were formed to maintain a regular life of which the celebration of the Divine Office was an essential part.

Before Pepin and Boniface began their reform there was a lack of liturgical books of any kind. The slow decline of the Merovingian kingdom had left Gaul in disarray and invasions from the East and the West had destroyed monasteries and churches and all that they contained. The *scriptoria* too where the books could be copied had suffered with the rest so that there was no centre left to provide texts of the Bible and the liturgical books. Such as remained were corrupt. This was one factor that prompted recourse to Rome for liturgical books. Another was the continuing prestige of Rome and the close relations that Boniface maintained with it. It was these factors that led to the extinction of the Old Gallican rite and the gradual introduction of the Roman liturgy.

The reform of Pepin seems to have been only partially successful and it needed the vision and energy of a Charlemagne to bring about a lasting change. He had created a vast empire which stretched from Italy to central Germany and although it was only loosely held together, he thought of it as a unity. Furthermore, he came gradually to think of himself as the successor of the ancient Roman emperors and the equal of the emperor who reigned in Constantinople. He was determined to produce liturgical uniformity in his dominions and he too saw Rome as the only possible source of that uniformity. He sent to Rome for a further supply of liturgical books which when they arrived included the famous Gregorian Sacramentary (the *Hadrianum*), and set up a *scriptorium* where authentic copies could be made of biblical and liturgical texts. In all this work the English monk Alcuin played a leading part.

But that was not enough for Charlemagne. He was a ruler and what he wanted must be achieved. For more than twenty years by legislation and by pressure on bishops and synods he sought to impose liturgical uniformity. As early as 789 he was insisting that all candidates for the ministry should study the Roman chant for both the Mass and the office and later, in 805, he explicitly included a knowledge of the Roman *Ordo*, that is, the Roman manner of celebrating the liturgy.[71] The Roman books were adapted, copied and distributed and there must have been an immense improvement in the celebration of the liturgy. But dictation from a monarch is one thing, practice another and we know that there was resistance in certain places like the ancient liturgical centres of Milan and Lyons. What the ordinary clergy of the time made of it all is another matter and the fact that the legislation had to be repeated for years shows that the reform made headway slowly and with difficulty.

What then was this office that Charlemagne sought to impose? Although everything is not certain it can with some probability be reconstructed from the writings of Amalarius of Metz (died *c.* 850) who was familiar with both the Roman and the Gallican traditions.[72]

Sunday Vigils retained the Roman pattern of eighteen psalms and twelve lessons, daily Vigils consisted of twelve psalms and three lessons. The hour was preceded by the versicle and response and the *Venite*. To Lauds had been added a short reading and a collect now replaced the Lord's prayer. Prime had been imported from the monastic office and its *preces* had become extensive: the *Kyries*, the Lord's prayer, the creed, the *Miserere* (Psalm 50) and a fixed collect. Vespers remained the same with the addition of *preces*, and Compline consisted of four psalms without antiphon but with a versicle and the *Nunc dimittis*. Clearly the Benedictine office had been exerting its influence. The daily *cursus* of hours was now complete, the monastic hours of Prime and Compline forming part of it. There was also some use of antiphons but as yet, it would seem, no hymns. Rome would not adopt these until the twelfth century. But it was also a clerical office for the distinction between the cathedral office and the monastic is no longer apparent. Its importance is that basically it was this office that became the office of the Roman rite until the reform of 1911.

The organization of the liturgical books

How far the Carolingian reform was successful is something on which we can only speculate. As far as the office was concerned, it has been reckoned that a small library of not less than ten books was necessary for the celebration of the office. Among them were the Bible, the homiliary, the book of 'sermons', the collectar, the antiphoner, the *ordo* and of course the psalter. If then the office was to become a regular practice of the clergy some organization and simplification of the liturgical books was necessary. This, that might seem to be but a material factor, is important for it eventually affected the shape of the office.

The Bible and the psalter are the two fundamental books of the office and these had to be adapted for liturgical use. At first the reading of the Bible at Vigils was continuous with the exception of the greater feasts when 'proper' passages were read. But it was necessary to indicate the length of the readings and this was first done by the marking of the Bibles in such a way that the reader would know when to begin and end. St Benedict is the first witness to this procedure and it is interesting to learn that one of the first extant Bibles to be so marked is the famous *Codex Amiatinus* which was written in Northumbria about 700.[73] The next stage was (probably) the formation of *capitularia*, giving the beginnings and endings of the passages to be read. The third stage was of course the composition of lectionaries containing the passages to be read day by day and on the great feasts.[74]

Although monks and clerics were expected to know the psalter by heart, the office demanded a different arrangement of it from that of the Bible. So came into being the *psalterium liturgicum*. Another factor making its existence necessary was the addition of antiphons. Although at first these were grouped together in one place and not attached to individual psalms, it would obviously be convenient to do so.

As we have seen above,[75] in the time of Caesarius of Arles, there was a sermon at morning prayer and the notion that commentaries on the scriptures 'by well-known and orthodox Catholic writers' should be read at Vigils was established by the sixth century.[76] Books of homilies from the Fathers thus became necessary and there were several collections current in the early Middle Ages. On saints' feasts it was customary to read the 'passion' or the 'legend'[77] of the martyr or saint being commemorated. For this yet another book was necessary.

The first book however that can be said to represent a convenient arrangement of certain texts was the book of collects or collectary. The origins of this kind of book can indeed be seen in the collects of the Gelasian and Gregorian Sacramentaries where they are gathered together obviously for the convenience of the user.[78] But the first examples of the book properly so called appeared in the eighth and ninth centuries. What are described as complete collectaries are two well-known English books, the Leofric Collectar, which goes back to an earlier, ninth-century, examplar, and the collectary of St Wulfstan of Worcester.[79] The latter was a good deal more than a collectary; it contains whole offices as well as the psalter, litanies and a hymnary though the collection of collects is considerable. There are collects for daily use, collects for morning and evening prayer, prayers for the little hours and *preces*. It looks like the combination of the celebrant's book with sundry private prayers. The collectary was in fact the book of the celebrant whose function it was to conclude each office with a collect. Their very number and variety made a book necessary.

All told, this organization of the books did not go very far and for a more convenient celebration of the office a further stage of development was necessary.

The formation of the breviary

Although there was a growing tendency to insist on the private recitation of an hour by an individual monk or cleric who for some reason had to be absent from choir, the office continued to be regarded as the celebration of a community. But if the office was to be recited conveniently, especially for small communities, some further simplification was necessary. Not only had the books to be gathered into some convenient format but a guide through the complexities of the office was also necessary. These two factors led to the formation of the 'breviary'. Until recently it was thought that the breviary was an abbreviation of the old choir office reduced to the compass of one or two handy volumes for a clergy that was becoming more mobile. Such a view is no longer tenable. First, by far the greater number of early 'breviaries' are monastic and were in fact choir books, regularly noted for singing. Secondly, they were books of from two to three hundred folios which could hardly be said to be portable.[80]

The impetus for the formation of 'breviaries' came from changed circumstances in the life of the church. After the decadence of the tenth century and with the coming of the Gregorian reform in the eleventh, there appeared smaller communities of clerics, later known as canons regular, who sought by the common life to improve the status of the clergy. If large monasteries with their precentors and other officers could find their way through the office, this was a task that was beyond the smaller community. They needed a guide which would enable them to assemble the necessary texts for different feasts and seasons and also to provide a clear 'order of service'. As we have seen above, the collectary contained certain texts for the celebrant and others that it is not easy to account for: e.g. whole offices that seem to have been models to

~

indicate the succession of texts for other occasions. This was the book to which was eventually attached what was called an *ordo* 'indicating for each day and each liturgical hour the texts that were to be sung with their *incipits'*. It first appears in a number of *monastic* manuscripts which shows that even the monasteries needed help in this matter and the title of the document is significant: '*Breviarium* sive *ordo* officiorum per totam anni decursionem' ('A short conspectus or order for the offices of the whole year'). This, says Salmon, is no doubt the origin of the word 'breviary' that eventually came to be used for the book containing the whole office.[81] It is to be noted that only the beginnings (*incipits*) of the texts to be used were given. For the formation of the breviary all that was necessary was to insert the full texts.

This procedure however had its disadvantages. There were the three lectionaries: the scriptural, the patristic and the hagiographical. A considerable quantity of material in themselves and the individual lessons were far longer than those of the breviaries that came into use in the thirteenth and subsequent centuries. It was here that abbreviation had to take place, to the great detriment of the office. Throughout the centuries the lectionaries have remained its weakest element. Likewise, in the older choir office there was a great variety of antiphons provided for optional use and a similar variety of collects to be used for different hours. The breviary eventually brought about the elimination of great numbers of them. It was in this way that the need for convenience brought about a change in the content of the office.

Towards uniformity

The formation of the breviary was a gradual process and as yet there was nothing like uniformity. Religious families all had their own traditions and the great liturgical centres retained theirs. Apart from the monasteries – and they had different customs – no one thought that the same office should be used by everyone everywhere. Even in Rome there was a degree of liturgical pluralism. There was the office of St Peter's which retained the old Roman psalter, and there was the office of the Lateran which almost certainly did not differ greatly but which had a certain prestige as the office of the Pope's residence. In the eleventh century with the reform and centralization of church administration a third centre emerged. This was the *capella papalis* where the Pope with his chaplains celebrated the office on all days when the former was not celebrating the liturgy in one of the stational churches. In the eleventh century the office of the papal chapel was the old Roman office[82] but as the chaplains became curial officials they will have had less and less time (and perhaps inclination) to celebrate the office with song and ceremony. There was a subtle change of emphasis. Although the papal chapel was very splendid, known as the *Sancta sanctorum* on account of the many relics collected there, the celebration of the office became quasi-private. The public office went on in the church of the Lateran while the 'papal' office was recited with reduced solemnity in the papal chapel. The final stage came when the office of the *capella papalis* superseded that of the Lateran Basilica. What the differences were at this time it is a little difficult to discern. It seems to have been austere and Roman. Three-lesson feasts were excluded in Lent and there was a sparing use of antiphons. Hymns were adopted in Rome only in the twelfth century. We may suppose too that responsories were reduced in number as these required a considerable degree of musical skill which the papal chaplains could not be expected to have.

With the coming of Innocent III (died 1216), who was himself interested in the liturgy, a further stage in the formation of the breviary was reached. First the *capella papalis* came to be known as *curia romana* and finally as *ecclesia romana* with the result that anything emanating from the papal chapel/curia came to be known as 'Roman' *tout court*. This is in fact why the thirteenth-century breviary was known as the office of the *ecclesia romana*.

But what was this office of the papal chapel that became the basis of the thirteenth-century office that was propagated throughout Europe by the Franciscans? It has been described as an office which is 'the result of a mixture of Roman, Germano-Gallican and monastic customs' but it was substantially the old Roman monastic office. There is the same distribution of the psalter over the week, there were antiphons and responsories and a modest collection of hymns. The lessons were much longer than those of the thirteenth-century book and the place given to the reading of scripture was generous: e.g. the whole of the Letter to the Romans was read in one week, the first after Christmas, its traditional place. The patristic lectionary was richer than that found in the earlier Roman office. The *Kyries* and the Lord's prayer were included in Lauds and Vespers though the concluding prayer had to be the collect of the day.[83]

The breviary known as the 'office of the *curia*' was the result of a codification that took place in the pontificate of Innocent III. For the convenience of the curial chaplains all the elements of the office, of which the *Ordo* of Innocent III seems to have been the nucleus, were gathered together though it is not clear whether the result was one book or two.[84] It was this office that in a complicated process became that of the Franciscans and which they propagated throughout Europe.[85] It was however not left untouched. It was adapted to the needs and new spirituality of the thirteenth century. To produce a book that could be said to be portable, abbreviation became necessary. The scriptural and patristic lectionaries were shortened. The importance of the Sunday liturgy was forgotten and offices of new feasts, which were shorter than the Sunday office, often superseded it. In fact, there was a steady invasion by saints' feasts of the Proper of Time and when they occurred on ferial days, they eliminated the obligation to say the supplementary offices.[86] This process would continue through the centuries, right up to the time of the reform of the rubrics in 1960. The office became the curious combination of obligation and devotional exercise. If you were not devout, you said it out of a sense of obligation; if you were, you 'enjoyed' the new offices that were so much more appealing than the old and austere texts of the classical liturgy.

The contents of the book, which hardly varied for the next seven centuries, are familiar to those who used the Roman Breviary until the appearance of the *Liturgy of the Hours* in 1971. The scattered elements that had existed in various books, the calendar, the psalter (with the canticles), the Proper of Time, with all the texts belonging to it, the sanctoral, both 'proper' and 'common', and the supplementary offices of the Blessed Virgin Mary and of the Dead, all were now combined in one book. Unlike the Pius V Breviary the rubrics came in the last place. The structure of the old Roman office did indeed remain but it was obscured by a profusion of new offices and overlaid in practice by the celebration of feasts that too often replaced the ancient offices of the Proper of Time.[87] Increasingly it was regarded as the personal obligation of the cleric and the celebration in common of the office tended to take second place to private recitation. In England, it is true, there was a certain insistence on the public recitation of the office at least on Sundays. Numerous episcopal visitations of the last part of the Middle Ages reveal that 'Mattins, Mass and Evensong' were regarded as a primary obligation of the parish priest and many were the parishioners who complained at one time or another that the clergy did not do their duty in this respect. Nor did this 'new' office escape criticism. Salimbene of Parma, a Franciscan, complained of the length of Prime and found the eighteen psalms of Mattins too long 'especially in the summer when the fleas annoy you, the nights are short and the heat intense'.[88] On the other hand, Ralph of Tongres, a conservative and a secular priest, objected to the shortening of the office for which he blamed the papal court. For him it was a new-fangled affair, no more acceptable because it was being 'imposed' by the Franciscans.[89]

Salimbene's complaint about Prime was justified. The *officium capituli*, a purely monastic element used in monasteries as the occasion for the allocation of the day's work, had by now become part of the hour for all the clergy. The long Athanasian Creed had to be said on most of the Sundays of the year and *preces* had become a lengthy and miscellaneous collection of psalm-verses and petitions of one kind or another. It could take longer than Lauds. But there were other grounds for complaint. The calendar and its rules were imperfect, feasts acquired 'octaves' to give them greater 'solemnity', and that meant at times the commemoration of a feast for eight days. Local calendars of saints grew all the time, their offices frequently replacing that of the feria or even that of the Sunday. Non-organic elements like the gradual psalms which in Cluniac houses had been said before Vigils since the tenth century as well as the penitential psalms (6, 31, 37, 50, 101, 142) on certain days, had come to be regarded as integral parts of the daily quota of prayer for the secular clergy too. Nor was that all. The supplementary offices of the Blessed Virgin Mary and of the Dead had to be recited *in addition* to the office of the day on certain days of the week.[90]

When we remember that this whole mass of verbiage had to be written by hand, that the calligraphy of the Middle Ages became less and less legible in the fourteenth and fifteenth centuries, when we recall that often only references were given to the texts to be used and the texts themselves were full of the conventional abbreviations, it is no wonder that clerics felt that the office was rather a burden than a prayer. Cranmer's was not a lone voice when he said in the preface to the Book of Common Prayer that often 'there was more business to find out what should be read, than to read it when found out'. With the coming of the Renaissance the Latinity of the breviary came under fire and the

~

unhistorical absurdities of the 'legends' were the subject of criticism not only in the sixteenth century but in all the centuries that followed until the present day. As late as the *First* Vatican Council the lessons of the office came in for angry criticism.[91]

Not only was the Roman office in a state of confusion, there was a multiplicity of 'uses' or rites which may not have differed very greatly from one another but sufficiently to make any talk of uniformity a dream. There were in England the 'uses' of Sarum, Hereford, York and others. Everywhere there were the offices of the great religious families, the Benedictines, the Carthusians, the Dominicans and the rest and the great liturgical centres like Milan had their own offices. But a new, material, factor came into play, the invention of printing. This not only made possible an infinitely better presentation of the texts of the office but it also made possible that uniformity which was to be the mark of post-Tridentine liturgy.[92] Given the criticism of the office that was widespread at the time and the ability to produce books quickly, a reform of the office in the sixteenth century was inevitable.

Attempts at reform – the Quiñones breviary

We can ignore the futile attempts of some Roman humanists to 'classicize' the hymns of the breviary and their efforts to get rid as far as possible of the Christian Latin of the liturgical books. *Salvator* was not good enough for the Saviour; he had to be *Servator*.[93] The book that caught the attention of men at the time was the breviary of Quiñones, a Franciscan and a cardinal. If his book represents a quite radical reform it is not without importance to know that it was commissioned by one Pope, Clement VII, and authorized for use by another, Paul III.

Where Quiñones's breviary marked a radical change with the past was that it was intended for private recitation by the individual cleric and the fact that it was taken up by so many for so long – over thirty years – shows how weak the understanding of the prayer of the church had become. Because it was intended for private use, all the choral elements such as antiphons and responsories were suppressed.[94] The psalter was to be recited in a week but without regard for the appropriateness of certain psalms to particular hours. Each office consisted of three psalms, no more, no less. For the night office to these he added three readings, one from the Old Testament, one from the New and a patristic or hagiographical one. A good deal of the Old Testament was read during the year and the whole of the New though his allocation of the books of the Bible to different seasons was largely traditional: thus Isaiah and the other prophets were read in Advent. The night office and Lauds were combined, as had indeed been permissible since the thirteenth century. Hymns were retained (a choral element surely!) though they were placed at the beginning of every hour. The calendar of saints was much reduced and their feasts were not allowed to break the rigid system of the psalter. The supplementary offices of the Blessed Virgin and the Dead were suppressed. Substantially Quiñones had reduced the office to the recitation of the psalter and the reading of holy scripture.[95]

The two charges that can be brought against the Quiñones breviary are that it was too austere and too rigid in its arrangements of the material. The possibility of different understandings of the psalms which made them adaptable for use on the greater feasts was denied by the rule that the psalter must be used every week exactly as Quiñones had arranged it. The 'colour' thus given to different feasts, seasons and hours was eliminated. The elimination of almost all the choral elements made of it a book of private prayer. The suppression of these elements gave scandal in certain quarters and although the book had a remarkable success and was even used for choral recitation, the reform that followed the Council of Trent was in conscious reaction to it. On the appearance of the Pius V breviary its use was forbidden and it looked as if this attempt at reform had proved abortive. Jungmann's article on the subject is entitled 'Why was Cardinal Quiñones's reformed breviary a failure?' Perhaps it was not such a failure as he thought. It had an immediate though modest influence on the formation of the Book of Common Prayer[96] and a more far-reaching influence on *The Liturgy of the Hours*.

The reformed breviary of Pius V

The Fathers of the Council of Trent demanded a reform of the liturgical books, including the breviary, but they were aware that a council cannot carry out so complicated a matter as liturgical reform must be. It was remitted to the Pope. We know little enough about the commissions set up by Pius IV and Pius V[97] and all we can do is to judge their intentions on the results of their work. It is best described as a restoration. The office they produced was the old Roman office shorn of some, not all, of the medieval accretions. The night office, now officially called *matutinum*,[98] for Sundays still had eighteen psalms and twelve lessons and the daily (ferial) office twelve psalms and three lessons. Hymns, antiphons and responsories were of course retained. Sunday Lauds consisted of eight psalms, including the Old Testament canticle, or six if you count Psalms 148–150 as one (they were in fact recited straight through). Vespers remained the same with five psalms. The lectionaries remained those of the later Middle Ages and the hagiographical readings went largely uncorrected.[99] The long and shapeless *preces* were retained for Lauds, Vespers and Prime and there were shorter sets for all the other hours. As before in the Roman tradition, Compline had four psalms. The supplementary offices were swept away and replaced by one or two 'suffrages' (i.e. commemoration of all the saints and in Eastertide of the cross), as in fact in the Quiñones breviary. On the credit side was the drastic reduction of the sanctoral for it was evidently the intention of the revisers that the ferial office with its weekly course of psalmody should in fact be used.

All this was held in an apparently unbreakable system of rubrics which seemed to make variation impossible. In fact this system soon proved to be so imperfect that by the seventeenth century the situation was much as it was in the fifteenth. Saints' feasts could quite legitimately replace the ferial office and often enough the Sunday office, and since these offices were a good deal shorter, there was every temptation to have resort to this device. In addition, what Pius V had taken away, his successors spent several centuries putting back so that the calendar by the end of the nineteenth century was largely filled up for the whole year. The Sundays after Pentecost often disappeared altogether and even Lent was not sacrosanct. Here a series of 'votive' offices (e.g. that commemorating the 'Holy Winding Sheet') could supersede the liturgy of the day.

The office the revisers produced was not without its nobility. It had something of the Roman sobriety, it retained ancient texts like responsories which date from the seventh to the ninth centuries, one of the most creative periods of the Roman liturgy, and of course it was essentially a *choral* office. This kept before the mind of its users the fact that when they recited it they were engaged in the prayer of the church. When we recall what happened in the next three centuries, with its subjective devotions and sentimental pieties which all too frequently were allowed to overlay or even obliterate the liturgy of the church, we

~

can be grateful that the revisers did what they did. Unhappily, their office proved to be pastorally impossible. If it had been intended for clerics or religious living in community, there was something to be said for it though eighteen psalms in one office is more than most can stand if we are thinking of the office in terms of *prayer*. The whole quantity was all-but crushing and when one remembers that the rubrics of the old Roman missal strongly urged that every priest should have said Mattins, Lauds *and* Prime *before* saying Mass, they were manifestly asking for something that could not be prayer even if it was physically possible to 'get through' the appalling amount of verbiage. In the centuries succeeding the Council of Trent when among other things the pastoral clergy, including the missionaries, were busier than ever before, the office came to be regarded more and more as simply a burden. The devout did their best to say it, others freely resorted to the use of the offices of saints' feasts and some got dispensations. For few was it a creative element in the spiritual life. A summary judgement on the work of the revisers must be, I think, that they 'did not take sufficient account of pastoral needs and human possibilities'.[100]

From Pius V to Pius X

In view of this situation it is not surprising that in subsequent centuries efforts at further revision were made. There was the revision of the hymns made at the behest of the Barberini Pope, Urban VIII, who himself had a weakness for writing hymns in classical metres. The rough rhythms and unclassical language of the medieval hymns, some of them great poetry like the *Vexilla regis*, offended his sensibilities and so he ordered four Jesuits to put them into a classical strait-jacket. Incongruous as some of the results were, the church was at any rate saved from the irreverent stupidities of the humanists of Leo X's time who would have had us pray to the Holy Trinity as *Triforme numen Olympi* or address the Mother of God as *Nympha candidissima*.[101]

The most notable attempt at reform was initiated by Benedict XIV (died 1758) but it came to nothing. There were the successive and varied reforms of the Neo-Gallicans of the seventeenth and eighteenth centuries which, however irregular from Rome's point of view, anticipated a number of changes that can be paralleled only in the *Liturgy of the Hours* of 1971.

~

The only revision of any importance in this period is that of Pius X. He (or his advisers) decided to take the old festal pattern of the Roman office for Mattins: that is, nine psalms, nine lessons (three from scripture, three patristic and the last three called 'the homily' on the gospel of the day, also from the Fathers and other ecclesiastical writers). Ferial Mattins had nine psalms and three lessons (all from scripture except in Lent). Lauds was reduced to five psalms, including the Old Testament canticle. The ancient custom of always reciting Psalms 148–150 at this hour was changed. They were replaced with a single *Laudate* psalm. Vespers remained the same and the Compline psalms were reduced to three. The whole of the psalter was considerably altered in its arrangement though the psalms that were traditional for certain hours remained in place. The intention was that the whole of the psalter should normally be used in the week. This was effected by an improvement in the rubrics. Here the greatest gain was that, with rare exceptions, the Sunday office could always be said. In fact the Pope brought about a reform of the whole temporal cycle. But, alas, much of his work was negated by his successors who increased the number of feasts and even imposed some of them for use on Sundays: e.g. the Feast of Christ the King. The rank of the 'octaves' of other feasts was raised so that at times the priest was condemned to saying the same texts (with a few variations) for a whole week. This in turn led to an accumulation of 'commemorations' so that at times, e.g. towards the end of June in certain years, there might be three or four of them. Even for the offices of modern saints (and there were many of them between 1925 and 1950) the 'legends' continued to be written in the old style and were often at once long and singularly uninformative. These matters and a number of others, like the length of Prime on ferial days, became increasingly the targets for criticism. Likewise, the language of the office, Latin, came to be regarded by a great number of the clergy as a barrier to prayer. Some of these criticisms were met by the decree on 'The Simplification of the Rubrics' of 1955 and further relief was afforded by the Code of Rubrics of 1960. But the whole system was manifestly breaking down and a radical reform had become necessary. This was decreed by the Second Vatican Council.

Notes

~

[1] See now Annibale Bugnini, **The Reform of the Liturgy** (Eng. trans., Liturgical Press, Collegeville, MN, 1990), pp. 491–576, for a detailed account. For the history of the Divine Office see: **The Study of Liturgy** (rev. ed., London, New York, 1992). Essays by Paul F. Bradshaw, W. Jardine Grisbrooke, J. D. Crichton covering the history of the office from the beginning to the issue of the **Divine Office** (London, Sydney, Dublin, 1974), pp. 339–440. Also other accounts of the 'Office in the Anglican Communion' by G. J. Cuming and the 'Office in Lutheran, Reformed and Free Churches' by David Tripp. George Guiver, CR, **Company of Voices: Daily Prayer and the People of God** (London, 1988).

[2] If the composition of Acts is about the year AD 80 and if it is not granted that this prayer of this passage is 'primitive', though its very Jewishness would seem to show that it is, it is clear that a use of psalms for Christian prayer was **already** in existence when Luke wrote.

[3] Cf. Mark 14:26 for the psalms and for intercessions cf. 1 Tim 2:1, 2.

[4] See J. Jeremias in **The Eucharistic Words of Jesus** (Eng. trans., London, 1966), pp. 118–122. The writer in JBC **in loc.** (p. 176) rejects Jeremias's interpretation and sees the passage as no more than a general picture of the primitive community. Presumably he feels unable to pronounce on the meaning of 'the prayers' and elsewhere shows a regrettable indifference to the prayer-practices of the early church.

[5] See Alexander Schmemann, **Introduction to Liturgical Theology** (Faith Press, London/The American Orthodox Press, Portland, ME, 1966), p. 43. On the next page he lists the scholars who hold this view: Oesterley, Jeremias, Dix, Gavin, Baumstark and Dugmore, though it must be remarked that as far as the prayer of the church is concerned there are considerable differences between them.

[6] See Geoffrey Cuming, 'La base néo-testamentaire de la prière commune', LMD, 116 (1973), p. 28. Further on (p. 38) he gives another scheme which he has derived from the Pauline writings: greeting, thanksgiving, Bible reading(s), instruction and exhortation, psalms (ancient and modern), doxology, kiss of peace and dismissal.

[7] Canon Cuming, **art. cit.**, p. 26, seeks to support his view that the decalogue formed part of the early services on the basis of the 'oath' not to commit various sins. But **sacramento** is more likely to refer to baptism when, as we know later, the candidates did undertake to avoid sin and lead the Christian life. The service may have included baptism as it did in the time of Justin the Martyr forty years or less later.

[8] In the following paragraph I am largely dependent on J. Jeremias, **The Prayers of Jesus** (London, 1967), and especially on his chapter 'Daily Prayer in the Primitive Church', pp. 66ff.

[9] There is indeed a strong element of petition in the Blessings from 4 onwards, evidently the official 'asking-prayers' of Judaism. Cf. C. W. Dugmore, **The Influence of the Synagogue upon the Divine Office** (2nd ed., Faith Press, 1964), pp. 115–24.

[10] See L. Bouyer, **Eucharistie** (Desclée, Tournai, 1966), pp. 63–4, and A. Baumstark, **Comparative Liturgy**, Eng. trans. and ed. F. L. Cross (Mowbray, 1958), p. 38. Bouyer points out that the Hallel psalms 113–118 (Hebrew numbering) were used

~

after the evening meal and that here 'we have the origins of Christian "Vespers" '.
This is more doubtful and does not take account of the fact that it was the 110–113 group of psalms that from the sixth century at least formed the nucleus of (Sunday) Vespers. Also, in the East the evening office seems to have been built up round Psalm 140. See Baumstark, *op. cit.*, p. 112.

11 See *The Prayers of Jesus*, p. 79; but see also *The Eucharistic Words of Jesus*, p. 118, where the word is translated rather differently as meaning 'to attend worship regularly'.

12 *The Prayers of Jesus*, p. 81. And see Paul F. Bradshaw, *Daily Prayer in the Early Church* (Alcuin/SPCK, 1981), pp. 4–9.

13 *Didache*, 4. Maxwell Staniforth translates 'to your prayers'. Neither the pronoun nor the plural is justified (see *Early Christian Writings*, Penguin Books, 1968, p. 229). J. B. Lightfoot (*The Apostolic Fathers*, ed. minor, 1893, p. 231) has of course quite correctly 'to prayer'.

14 In the same passage however there is an injunction to 'frequent the saints *daily*' (*ibid.*, p. 229).

15 *Dial.* c. 86. Cf. J. A. Jungmann, *Christliches Beten in Wandel und Bestand* (Munich, 1969), p. 12.

16 Cf. F. L. Cross, *The Early Christian Fathers* (London, 1960), pp. 23–4; and A. Hamman, *La Prière*, 2 (Desclée, 1963), pp. 66–73.

17 Cf. P. Salmon, EP, p. 794.

18 Cf. Jungmann, *op. cit.*, p. 12. He refers to *Stromata*, vii, 49. Cf. also Hamman, *La Prière*, 2, p. 291.

19 For the text see *Protrepticus*, IX, 84, cited by Hamman, *La Prière*, 2, p. 285.

20 *Protrept.*, IX, 84, in Hamman, *op. cit.*, p. 285.

21 Cf. J. A. Jungmann, *The Place of Christ in Liturgical Prayer* (Geoffrey Chapman, 1965), p. 181, n. 3, who records a fragmentary text in an Oxyrhynchus papyrus which is 'allied' to the *Phōs hilaron*.

22 Hamman, *op. cit.*, p. 290, and Jungmann, *Christliches Beten* referring to *Stromata*, VII, 40.

23 Hamman, *op. cit.*, p. 290.

24 See *De Oratione*, 25, ed. and trans. Ernest Evans (SPCK, 1953), pp. 34–5. Mr Evans translates 'statutory prayers' which seems to say too much.

25 *Ad Uxorem*, II, 4.

26 *Ed. cit.*, pp. 37–41.

27 *La Tradition apostolique*, ed. B. Botte (LQF, Münster, 1963), section 25 (for the *agape*) and section 41 for the hours. Eng. trans. and ed. by Gregory Dix (SPCK, 1937), XXVI, 18 and XXXV, XXXVI. Questions have been raised about the authenticity of section 41 in the Apostolic Tradition. Some features like prayer at cockcrow seem to belong to the fourth century. However others are primitive and some scholars see Jewish origins for them. See Bradshaw, *Daily Prayer in the Early Church*, pp. 54, 55. For the text of the Apostolic Tradition see G. J. Cuming, *The Apostolic Tradition: A Text for Students* (1976), 41, p. 29.

28 *Ap. Trad.*, Botte, 41, p. 89; Dix, xxxv, p. 61. If the Greek was *en ekklēsia* it could mean 'in [the] assembly', as Botte translates it though *a place* is obviously meant.

29 Whether there was a daily service for the people is not certain. Hippolytus urges deacons and presbyters to gather *daily* with their bishop when they are to teach and pray though who is to teach whom is not clear.

[30] Botte, 25, p. 65; Dix, xxv, p. 50.

[31] It is noteworthy that Hippolytus **expects** hard-working people to go to the assembly before work. Perhaps it was all part of his perfectionism.

[32] See Balthasar Fischer, 'La prière ecclésiale et familiale dans le Christianisme ancien', LMD, 116 (1973), p. 43, who describes Hippolytus's interpretation as 'a commemoration of the paschal mystery' and refers to an article by J. H. Walker in **Studia Patristica**, 5 (Berlin, 1962), pp. 206–12, for the observation about Mark.

[33] For reasons that are obscure the language is tortuous, but the meaning is clear.

[34] Cf. Mark 13:33; Luke 21:36; 1 Thess 5:17, etc.

[35] Hippolytus has another notion: the whole of nature, the stars, the trees, the waters and even the angelic hosts, stop their activity at midnight to pay homage to God. Christians should do likewise. He calls this a tradition though whence it comes it is difficult to say but it seems to be related in spirit to the long passage (29) that comes at the end of Tertullian's treatise on prayer.

[36] **The Early Liturgy** (Notre Dame Press, 1959), p. 100.

[37] Even Augustine was surprised to find Ambrose reading silently when he called on him. Cf. F. Homes Dudden, **The Life and Times of St Ambrose** (Oxford, 1935), 1, p. 112.

[38] As Pierre Salmon contends in several places in his treatment of the subject in EP.

[39] **De Oratione**, xxx, 5, and cf. **Origen on Prayer**, ed. and trans. Eric George Jay (London, 1954), p. 213.

[40] **Op. cit.**, xxxiii, 1; Jay, pp. 216–17.

[41] See Bradshaw, **Daily Prayer in the Early Church**, p. 70, referring to Origen, **Hom. in Gen.**, 10, 3.

[42] Jungmann has pointed out that he was writing to Ambrosius, a recent convert from Gnosticism, which rejected the Old Testament Jahweh and put Christ in his place. See **Christliches Beten**, pp. 18–19, and his **The Place of Christ in Liturgical Prayer**, pp. 158–9. Hymns and (private) prayers were addressed to Christ.

[43] For Cassian see **La Prière des Heures**, ed. Mgr Cassien and Bernard Botte (Paris, 1963), pp. 117ff., for the **Regula Magistri** see M. D. Knowles, 'The **Regula Magistri** and the Rule of St Benedict' in **Great Historical Enterprises** (London, Edinburgh, etc., 1963), pp. 135ff.

[44] Dom J. Froger's view that Cassian's **novella solemnitas** was Lauds has not generally been followed. For a sufficient refutation see J. M. Hanssens, **Nature et genèse de l'office des matines** (Rome, 1952). See W. Jardine Grisbrooke, 'The Divine Office, the Formative Period' in **The Study of Liturgy** (1992 ed.), p. 416, n. 17. Robert Taft, LHEW, pp. 206–7, favours Froger. The **novella solemnitas** was morning prayer, i.e. Lauds. Bradshaw, **Daily Prayer in the Early Church**, makes a strong case for this view (pp. 106–9).

[45] See Salmon, EP, pp. 804–10, and B. Luykx, LMD, 51 (1957), pp. 55–81.

[46] **Ep.** 207; PG 32, c. 764.

[47] Baumstark holds that this is the first attestation of Psalm 50 for morning prayer: **Comparative Liturgy**, p. 40, n. 1.

[48] See John Wilkinson (trans.), **Egeria's Travels** (London, 1971), p. 236; for the offices, pp. 123ff.

[49] For the **Orthros** see **Apostolic Constitutions** (ed. F. X. Funk) I, vii, 47, as also for the hymn **Te decet**; for Psalm 140, I, viii, 35. The compiler, usually regarded as a Syrian, also witnesses to the long dismissal at morning and evening prayer.

For the **Phōs hilaron** see Basil, **De Spiritu Sancto**, xxix, 73. For Psalm 62, see
Ap. Const. I, ii, 59.

[50] See **Egeria's Travels**, p. 125.

[51] See B. Fischer, LMD, 116 (1973), pp. 42–51, and especially the thesis of R.
Zerfass, **Die Schriftlesung im Kathedraloffizium Jerusalem** (LQF, Münster,
1968). See also the reservations of the editors on the subject in the same number
of LMD, pp. 12–13.

[52] **Confessions**, Lib. V, ix, 17; PL 32, c. 714, and **Enarr. in Psalm 66**, 3 as given
in J. A. Jungmann, **Pastoral Liturgy** (Eng. trans., London, 1962), pp. 151–2.

[53] For a convenient summary with references see Homes Dudden, **St Ambrose**, 2,
pp. 442–6.

[54] **Exposit. in Ps. 118**, 18, 32. Cf. Homes Dudden, **op. cit.**, p. 443.

[55] Cf. **De Virginibus**, iii, 18. Homes Dudden (p. 444) refers to Jerome: Ep. 107, 9:
accensa lucernula reddere sacrificium vespertinum.

[56] **Ep.** 20, 11, 13; PL 16, c. 1039.

[57] **Ep.** 107, **Ad Laetam** (Loeb Classics, London, New York, 1933), p. 359.

[58] See A. E. Burn, **Niceta of Remesiana: His Life and Works** (Cambridge, 1905).
A critical edition, full of information.

[59] See Jungmann, **Pastoral Liturgy**, p. 131 and cf. pp. 122–57.

[60] See **ibid.**, pp. 147, 152, 153. Little is known of the office of the non-basilican
churches, i.e. the presbyteral churches. We are safe in assuming that it consisted
of morning and evening prayer, for the clergy of Rome resisted attempts in the sixth
century to make them attend Vigils. No doubt the people attended morning or evening
prayer in the presbyteral churches. Cf. P. Salmon, LMD, 27 (1951), p. 118.

[61] See G. Dix, **The Shape of the Liturgy** (London, 1945), pp. 319ff. For the
modern scholars see Jungmann, **op. cit.**; Pierre Salmon, 'Aux origines du
bréviaire romain', LMD, 27 (1951), pp. 114–36, and OD; B. Luykx, 'L'influence
des moines sur l'office paroissial', LMD, 51 (1957), pp. 31–51, an article of
crucial importance though the author tends to press the evidence too far and the
word **paroissial** is anachronistic.

[62] Salmon, EP, p. 818.

[63] See P. Salmon, EP, pp. 819–20; C. Callewaert, **De Breviarii Romani Liturgia**
(Bruges, 1939), pp. 51–63.

[64] Cf. Salmon, EP, pp. 819–20; Callewaert, **op. cit.**, pp. 52–5; M. Righetti, **Storia
Liturgica** (2nd ed., 1955), pp. 492, 499–502, 504–5.

[65] Does this derive from the Jerusalem custom of singing a gospel **de resurrectione**
on Sunday mornings?

[66] See **The Rule of St Benedict**, ed. and trans. J. McCann (London, 1972), ch. 13,
p. 57.

[67] Cf. S. Bäumer, trans. R. Biron, **Histoire du Bréviaire** (Paris, 1905), 1, p. 248.

[68] See L. Bréhier and R. Aigrain, **Grégoire le Grand, les états barbares et la
conquête arabe, Hist. de l'Eglise**, ed. Fliche and Martin, 5 (Paris, 1947),
pp. 506–20.

[69] If there is some doubt whether he brought the Gregorian Sacramentary with him
(which may not have been compiled by this time), in the next century St Benet
Biscop brought back quantities of Roman books and what is more important
secured the services of John, the Chief Precentor of St Peter's, a basilican church.
Whether the office was 'pure' Benedictine is, I imagine, impossible to establish.
See H. Ashworth, 'Did St Augustine bring the "Gregorianum" to England?',

Ephemerides Liturgicae, 72 (1958), and other papers by the same author.

[70] From the text of the decree it is clear that the whole of the liturgy was meant by *cantilena romana* and indeed if you used the Roman chant you had to use the books in which it was found.

[71] Cf. MGH *Scriptores,* 1, pp. 106, 131, as given in DACL, s.v. 'Charlemagne', c. 722. Also Rosamund McKitterick, *The Frankish Church and the Carolingian Reform* (Royal Historical Society, London, 1977).

[72] Cf. *Opera Liturgica Omnia,* ed. I. M. Hanssens (Rome, 1948), 2, pp. 403–65; 3, pp. 13–17, as given in Salmon, ODMA, pp. 33ff. His reservations should be noted.

[73] At least it is marked for the Lamentations of Jeremiah used from an early time for vigils of the last three days of Holy Week.

[74] Cf. Salmon, ODMA, pp. 26–7. The last are Gallican books. Salmon however thinks that Roman ones existed also though, as he remarks, Rome was more interested in the *order* in which the books were read.

[75] P. 49.

[76] Rule of St Benedict, ch. 9.

[77] From *legenda,* 'something to be read'.

[78] Gelasian: nos. v, lxi, lxxxi; Lib. II lxxxiii, lxxxv (ed. Mohlberg); Gregorian: nos. 202, 204 (ed. Lietzmann).

[79] *The Leofric Collectar,* ed. E. S. Dewick and W. H. Frere, HBS, 45, and *The Portiforium of St Wulstan,* HBS, 56. And see M. D. Knowles, *The Monastic Order in England* (2nd ed., Cambridge, 1963), p. 553 n. 5. Cf. also Dame Laurentia McLachlan, 'St Wulstan's Prayer Book', JTS 30 (1929), pp. 174–7.

[80] See S. J. P.van Dijk and J. Hazeldene Walker, *The Origins of the Modern Roman Liturgy* (London, 1960), pp. 32–4; Salmon, ODMA, p. 68.

[81] See ODMA, pp. 53–60.

[82] Cf. M. Andrieu, *Les Ordines Romani du Haut Moyen Age* (Louvain, 1931), 1, p. 519 n. 1.

[83] See ODMA, p. 151; pp. 152–70. This office can be reconstructed from an early Franciscan breviary belonging to the cathedral church of Assisi. For it and the development of the Franciscan breviary see Van Dijk–Walker, *Origins,* part 3.

[84] See Salmon, ODMA, p. 154.

[85] See *ibid.,* pp. 152–7, and Van Dijk–Walker, *op. cit.,* part 3.

[86] For these see p. 6.

[87] See Salmon, EP, pp. 839–41.

[88] See Van Dijk–Walker, *Origins,* p. 1.

[89] *Ibid.,* p. 3.

[90] All these texts remained in breviaries until recently. They were offered for 'optional' use!

[91] Cuthbert Butler, *The Vatican Council 1869–1870* (2nd ed., London, 1962), pp. 196–7. It is interesting to learn that an English bishop, Clifford of Clinton, urged that the psalter should in fact be recited in the week.

[92] The same was true of the Church of England. The Book of Common Prayer could be imposed quickly because it could be printed. Even local printers had the facility to do so, like Oswen of Worcester who had the Prayer Book very quickly in circulation. See S. Morison, *English Prayer Books* (3rd ed., 1949), p. 61.

[93] One has noticed this ridiculous use in even some recent Roman documents.

[94] Some were put back in the second edition.

~

[95] For a description of the Quiñones breviary, see Jungmann, **Pastoral Liturgy**, pp. 200–14.

[96] G. J. Cuming, **A History of the Anglican Liturgy** (1969), pp. 52, 69, 72–3.

[97] For what is known see T. Klauser, **A Short History of the Western Liturgy** (Eng. trans., OUP, 1969), pp. 124–9.

[98] The adjective has apparently become a noun; see the first rubric in the psalter: **Ante Matutinum** . . .

[99] A little later Baronius was allowed to make a few timid corrections but substantially lessons remained the same until their suppression in the reform of 1971. They were a scandal to the critical and edifying to the pious.

[100] See the present writer's 'An Historical Sketch of the Roman Liturgy' in **True Worship** (ed. L. Sheppard, 1963), p. 76.

[101] See Bäumer–Biron, **Histoire du Bréviaire**, 2, pp. 117–23; Salmon, EP, pp. 849–50.

Additional note to Chapter 3

~

Although as we have seen the New Testament seems to witness to the use of psalms in Christian worship, the matter is not as clear as one had supposed. Professor Fischer, writing in 1951 (LMD, no. 27, p. 88, nn. 5, 6, 7), sums up scholarly opinion as it was at that time:

1. The theory that the apostolic church took over the psalter *en bloc* from the synagogue is no longer tenable.

2. Up to about the year 200 the hymns sung in the liturgy were composed by Christians (the *psalmi idiotici*, i.e. private compositions e.g. the *Phōs hilaron*).

3. The psalms were used as lessons and read.

We can readily admit that the early church did not take over the whole psalter *en bloc* for *prayer*, though they took it over with the rest of the Old Testament as 'holy scripture'. It must be a long time since anyone contended that the primitive church *sang* the whole of the psalter. It assumes an order of prayer which, as we have seen, did not exist.

Nor is there any difficulty in admitting the existence and use of 'hymns' in the second or even the first century. Clement himself is witness to their use. But both he and Tertullian (*Apol.* 39, 18, as given in *art. cit.* p. 89, n. 11) were hardly innovators and they witness to the use of psalms as prayer and, in the case of Tertullian, as sung prayer. Hippolytus too, an arch-conservative, witnesses, as we have seen, to the same use of psalms. It seems likely then that psalms were used in this way as early as the second half of the second century.

~

The chief text that Fischer alleges to show that the psalms were used as readings, a text that he calls 'le témoignage très probant', is the *Didascalia* V, 19, 1 in the edition of F. X. Funk, pp. 288ff. (the actual phrase is on p. 291). Here we read '*legentes* Prophetas et Evangelium et *Psalmos*'. That looks 'probant' indeed. But it is a Latin translation of the Greek as it is to be found in the *Apostolic Constitutions*. Unhappily, the original Greek no longer exists and that in the AC is unreliable. Dom Hugh Connolly (*Didascalia Apostolorum*, Oxford, 1929, p. v) says that the 'compiler . . . dealt so freely with his source, making perpetual additions, omissions and alterations, that we can seldom feel sure that he has left a sentence exactly as he found it'. In his own translation (p. 189), which is from the fourth-century Syriac (which Connolly holds is accurate), the phrase reads, 'You shall come together and watch and keep vigil (it was the Easter Vigil) all night with prayers and intercessions, and with the *reading* of the Prophets, and with the Gospel and with Psalms'. Obviously this does not say the same as the Latin–Greek versions of Funk. It does not say 'with the *reading* of psalms'. You can read it this way: 'You shall . . . keep vigil with prayers . . . and with the Gospel and with psalms', which is not at all the same thing. Perhaps some Syriac expert will have another look at the matter (though Dom Hugh Connolly was an extremely exact scholar) but as things stand the text cannot be regarded as 'probant'.

Supporting evidence, Professor Fischer alleges, is to be found in the *Peregrinatio Aetheriae* (37, 6, ed. Pétré, p. 236), of the late fourth century, in which we find that on Good Friday psalms (*de passione*) were *read*. But this evidence is rather late and we know from the same source that psalms were also sung. Reading evidently did not necessarily exclude singing. The article of J. A. Jungmann (*Zeitschrift für katholische Theologie* 72 (1950), pp. 223–6), to which he refers, adds no new evidence.

What perhaps can be deduced from all this is that we should not be surprised at Clement's mention of hymns and that he, with Tertullian and Hippolytus, does indeed, as Fischer holds, mark a turning point. The hymns had become 'radicalement compromises par les abus gnostiques' and they fell into disuse, under official church pressure.

Writing in 1992 and to clarify my views I would add that 'hymns' like *Phōs hilaron* and the *Gloria in excelsis*, the first sung at evening prayer and the second (which of course is originally a Greek text) sung (as

~

it still is) in the Byzantine morning office, were indeed used in the second and following centuries (e.g. the *Te Deum* and the *Te decet laus*), that these so-called *psalmi idiotici* (the compositions of private persons) became doctrinally suspect and tended to disappear. Secondly, it seems to me that some psalms were chanted early on (cf. Colossians 3:16: 'sing *psalms* and hymns and spiritual songs'). Even if psalms were 'read' they were declaimed in a kind of chant (cantilated) and sometimes very agreeably (cf. St Augustine, *Confessions*, X, xxxiii, 50, trans. H. Chadwick, p. 208). The main point however is that until the fourth century there was no *cursus psalmorum*, no fixed arrangement of psalms, no thought that churches or clerics should have to sing the 150 psalms of the psalter in a fixed interval of time. That came later with the monastic communities as did also the reading of the whole Bible (at Vigils) from beginning to end in, say, the year. The singing of the psalms 'in course' came with the emergence of the monastic office in the fourth century.

As for readings, always in the early centuries from the Bible, it must be said that there were readings in Egypt and Cappadocia and in the West in Gaul but there was no *course* of readings. At most in either morning or evening prayer of the cathedral office there was one and one only and scholars seem to be generally of the opinion that this reading was inserted under early monastic influence (e.g. Caesarius, bishop of Arles, had been a monk of Lérins). The course of readings as in the Rule of St Benedict was intended to provide material for meditation. This too is the main purpose of the Office of Readings which now forms an 'hour' of the *Liturgia Horarum*.

FOUR

~

'The Liturgy of the Hours'

~~~~~~

IN THE LIGHT OF the foregoing we can now consider the revised office and see where it is traditional and where it has innovated. But first we may ask why it is called 'The Liturgy of the Hours'.[1] First, it is pretty clear that the revisers had no desire to perpetuate the use of the word 'breviary' with all its misleading and unhappy associations. Perhaps too they thought that, although the whole of the liturgy in the Middle Ages was called *divinum officium*, 'divine office' was too legalistic a term. *Officia* for Cicero, as for St Ambrose after him, meant 'duties' and the office is much more than that. The revisers make clear first, that the Divine Office is above all prayer and is the means by which the church may fulfil the gospel injunction to 'pray always'; and secondly, that it is a prayer that is intended to consecrate the hours and the work of the day: 'Compared with other liturgical actions, the particular characteristic which ancient tradition has attached to the liturgy of the hours is that it should consecrate the course of day and night' (GI 10). This is clear from what has been said in a previous chapter and the revisers in their commentary on Lauds and Vespers repeat that the office is a celebration of the mystery of Christ in his passion, death and resurrection (GI 38, 39) and declare that the office engages the priestly intercession of Christ: 'This voice is not only that of the church, it is also Christ's. It is in the name of Christ that she prays, that is, "through Jesus Christ our Lord", and so the church continues to offer that prayer and entreaty which Christ offered during his life and which therefore has a unique effectiveness' (GI 17). What the Introduction wishes to stress is that the office is not just a pious filling up of time or even a means of personal edification. It is a celebration of the paschal mystery and we may draw the conclusion that the relationship between the eucharist and the office is a real and not simply a mental one. The office is the means by which throughout the day Christians may appropriate to themselves, through a prayer that engages the intercession of Christ, the redeeming power and love that are made available in the daily celebration of the

~

75

eucharist.[2] As the Introduction has suggested, this gives to the prayer of the Divine Office a unique effectiveness and psychologically should give its users a great confidence.

It is however in its commentary on Lauds and Vespers that the Introduction gives the traditional teaching that the office is the celebration of the paschal mystery. Lauds 'recalls the resurrection of the Lord Jesus, the true light, enlightening every man (John 1:9)' and the Introduction quotes the words of St Cyprian: 'We should pray in the morning to celebrate the resurrection of the Lord ...'.[3] Vespers, 'the evening sacrifice', continues the thanksgiving of the Mass and 'through the prayer (which) we offer like incense in the sight of the Lord', we recall the sacrifice 'which was given in the evening by our Lord and Saviour when he instituted the most holy mysteries of the church with his apostles' (GI 38). These are the considerations that in the beginning led to the choice of the psalms for these hours, psalms which though now distributed over a longer period are still used at these times. But perhaps the paschal character of Vespers is seen most clearly in the Sunday office which runs from Saturday evening to Sunday evening, thus keeping the ancient Jewish pattern, transposed by one day. Here the canticle from Philippians 2, the 'resurrection' psalms of Lauds (92, 117, etc.) and the psalms of Vespers (109, the great priestly psalm, and the Hallel psalms that follow), all emphasize that the church is praying through Christ who by his passion, death and resurrection brought salvation to the world.[4] This office of the Christian Sunday (for evidently Saturday is regarded as part of it) makes explicit what was contained in the old office but it does so in no uncertain manner. It must be said to be one of the most successful parts of the new office.

The Introduction also wishes to emphasize that if the office is the prayer of Christ in his church, it is also and must be prayer on the part of those who use it. This indeed is the condition of its being spiritually profitable. The office is not and never was the recitation of a certain quota of holy words. But the Introduction goes on to point out that it is a particular kind of prayer and this is an aspect of it that is often overlooked: 'The sanctification of man and the worship of God is achieved in the Liturgy of the Hours by the setting up of a *dialogue* between God and man, so that "God speaks to his people ... and the people reply to God by song and by prayer".'[5] Worship, and particularly prayer, is a two-way traffic and the approach of God to us is far more important than our approach to him, an approach that is indeed impossible without the divine initiative. Yet our movement towards God is the very condition of our being able to take into ourselves the divine word. In practice, a realization of this truth transforms the celebration of the office and the recommendations for times of silence throughout the new liturgy point in this direction.[6] We need to *listen*. Even the psalms convey a message for all that they are prayers addressed to God, and for that message to be heard and for the prayer to come from the heart we need calm and quiet. In the tradition that Cassian records, every psalm ended with a silence and a deep prostration. Likewise we know from experience that a silence after readings whether at the eucharist or the office allows us to assimilate the word we have listened to. In the intercessions of Lauds and Vespers silent prayer is allowed for after the official petitions of the day. It is in this general atmosphere of recollection and silence that we may expect to hear the voice of God – or to put it in another way, we may expect to receive insights for our life and situation.

The structure of the office

When we come to consider the structure of the office as a whole we find a surprising mixture of the old and the new. There is the insistence on the pivotal importance of Lauds and Vespers, which takes us back to the old pre-monastic 'cathedral' office. Then, none of the hours has more than three psalms (including the canticles) and the Office of Readings, replacing the former (and misnamed) 'mattins', is exactly the pattern of the Quiñones breviary with its three psalms and three readings and never any more. If Quiñones is aware of these sublunary matters he must be smiling wryly. Lauds and Vespers have become identical in structure, a process that was started by Pius X. Thirdly, as in the Quiñones book, hymns are placed at the beginning of every hour, including Compline. The sanctoral, already reduced by the Calendar of 1969, again brings the new office into line with that of Quiñones, though the rigidity of his system is avoided. All these changes represent innovations that cannot be traced back further than the sixteenth century. This is not to say, however, that they are either good or bad. Traditional elements are represented by the retention of antiphons and responsories, hymns at every hour (a non-Roman tradition) and the addition of the Lord's prayer at Lauds and Vespers is the restoration of a very ancient custom that was never wanting in the ancient office. The recitation of the psalter (except for three psalms and parts of others) 'in course' and the continuous course of scriptural and patristic readings show that this office is basically monastic, i.e. of the old Roman basilican style. The daily course of prayer, that is the number of hours to be said, represents a compromise between the monastic and the cathedral traditions. The Office of Readings evidently derives from the old monastic Vigils and is presumably intended for the clergy and those religious congregations who undertake the celebration of the Divine Office, but are without an office of their own. On the other hand, Prime, a monastic office, has understandably been suppressed and Compline, also a monastic office, has, with some reason, been retained. Of the day hours, Terce, Sext and None, only one need be said (at the appropriate time) and thus one element of a form of prayer that was institutionalized by the monasteries though, as we have seen, it goes far beyond them in time, is partially kept.

Although this office is a mixture of the old and the new, it has a character of its own. No previous office has been quite like it. As to length, it could be said to be adapted to the needs of the pastoral clergy for, at a guess, the whole of it could be recited in something less than three-quarters of an hour—if anyone was so stupid as to want to do so. Whether it is adapted to the needs of the laity is another matter. One cannot but notice the multiplicity of elements of very different literary forms that are to be found in the office: antiphons in great numbers, responsories, versicles and responses, hymns as well as of course the whole of the psalter, and the three lectionaries. All this is rather a lot to take in. True, all these elements can be found in the tradition and if any *apologia* for the revisers is needed it is to be found in their terms of reference. The Constitution on the Liturgy (89, 90) decreed that the office should be 'revised' and not created anew. As usual, the revisers have been faithful to their commission though this should not prevent a commentator from viewing their work objectively or from making criticisms of it if they seem called for. It is now more than twenty years since the Constitution on the Liturgy was promulgated and the situation of the church in general and of the clergy in particular is very different from what it was then and it would be surprising if in that period, which has been one of the most turbulent for the church in modern times, we had learnt nothing new.

Since the pattern of the office will be well known by now, there is no need to give descriptions of each of the hours. It will be more profit-able to consider the rationale of the hours along the lines of the Introduc-tion (41–80).

The psalter

Although more will have to be said about the psalms later on, since they are so important an element of the office it is necessary to say a little about their arrangements here. The distribution of the psalter over four weeks undoubtedly makes the office more manageable as prayer for it is all but impossible to pray many psalms on end. It is difficult to keep one's attention and their literary genres are so various that one cannot respond to them individually as presumably one should. This re-arrangement, which has lightened the burden of the office, also meets the desires of the pastoral clergy who found the long series of psalms in 'mattins' difficult to handle. Moreover any over-rigid pattern has been avoided. The psalms for the Office of Readings are 'in course' over the four weeks but those for Lauds and Vespers have been chosen as more appropriate to the meaning of those hours. Certain psalms have also been reserved for Compline. The danger of monotony is largely avoided though the regular occurrence of certain psalms is not always helpful. Thus when in Psalm 36 the psalmist is wrestling with the problem of evil within the terms of Old Testament revelation and comes to no very satisfactory conclusion, one does not approach it with any enthusiasm every second week. The sentiment that the wicked 'wither like grass and fade like the green of the fields' hardly seems a Christian one. Their disappearance from the face of the earth does not solve anything and as Christians we are required to convert them or to try to do so. But this is all part of a bigger problem to which we shall return.

From a practical point of view, three psalms for every hour and never any more is probably right and if you distribute the psalter over the month, you are going to run short, even with the addition of canticles. But as far as the Office of Readings is concerned this pattern sometimes gives the impression of strait-jacketing. This is particularly so in the office of the last three days of Holy Week. The 'mattins' and Lauds of these days consisted of some of the richest texts and chants of the whole year and the pattern of the former was the old 'festal' office of the Roman church. These texts, and with them their chants, have almost wholly disappeared and the lack is not made good by the 'vigils' that are suggested for these days. These vigil offices are supplementary to the Office of Readings and here if anywhere the old pattern with its texts could have been retained for the convenience of those who are in a position to use them.[7] Another oddity of this three-psalm arrangement for every hour is that sometimes the office said during the day is almost as long as Lauds or Vespers.

As for the allocation of psalms, on the assumption that you wish to use the whole psalter,[8] it must be said to be reasonably satisfactory. The traditional morning and evening psalms all find their place in Lauds and Vespers and evidently some thought has been given to the allocation of the psalms for the day hours. Psalm 118[9] has been distributed over a number of days so that it is not necessary to recite a great deal of it on a single occasion. But two of the greatest psalms, 21 and 44 (though the latter does occur in the Office of Readings and Vespers for Monday, Week 2), are allocated to a day hour on a Friday and Saturday respectively. They merit the best recollection one can bring to them and they would be better coming either in the Office of Readings or even in Vespers. But this may be a subjective judgement.

In the liturgical use of the psalms the Christian or fulfilled sense of holy scripture is of crucial importance and from the beginning the psalms have been used as Christian prayers.[10] But as anyone knows who used the old office it was, apart from certain great psalms like 21 or 109, impossible to carry round in your head the messianic sense or the Christian interpretation of 150 psalms. To facilitate understanding of the psalter the revisers have done two things. They have indicated the original subject of the psalm, e.g. for Psalm 103 'Praise of the God of merciful love' (which seems obvious enough in that case) and, secondly, they have added what centuries ago were called *tituli*[11] which were a device to enable worshippers to pray 'in Christ'. Some of these are from the New Testament and some from the Fathers or early Christian writers. The former are nearly always well chosen, some of the latter say little enough. However, they are worth attending to and almost certainly in the mind of the revisers they help towards a prayerful use of the psalms. They provide a moment of recollection before reciting the psalm. To sum up, if the revisers have kept the monastic pattern of psalmody, they have done what they can to secure that the psalms will be prayed rather than merely recited.

Antiphons

There is yet a third element of the psalmody that requires consideration. Every psalm throughout the psalter has its antiphon which is to be said before it but need not be repeated after it. The church of the East and the West has since the fourth century felt the need to 'actualize' the psalms so as to adapt them to different seasons, feasts and occasions. Antiphons have been used in various ways and the history of their use is not yet fully elucidated[12] though the short antiphons coming before and after the psalms derive from the Roman tradition.[13] The longer ones that still occur in Lauds and Vespers at the *Benedictus* and *Magnificat* are of Gallican and Spanish provenance, some few of them are from the Greek. For the great seasons and feasts the antiphon both gives a Christian sense to the psalm and reflects the chief significance of the celebration. In this they perform a valuable function.[14] Others, for the ferial office, usually underline a particular thought of the psalm and may have a purpose though their constant recurrence enfeebles their effect. Now that we have a title giving the subject of the psalm and another indicating its Christian sense, it is less easy to justify this considerable multiplication of texts. However, they may be used very freely. Most ambitiously they may be repeated after the strophes of a psalm and throughout its singing. For this musical settings of some complexity are needed. On the other hand, it does not appear that the whole assembly must sing or recite them. They could be sung or read by a cantor with a short pause for reflection before going on with the psalm and, as we have observed, it is not necessary to sing/recite them after the psalm. It is to be regretted however that the device has been pressed into service so relentlessly. For the daily offices where the subject of the psalms soon becomes known, they seem to be hardly necessary. In practice, their inclusion gives the office a greater appearance of complexity and makes the book bigger than it need be.

The canticles

A feature of the new office is the great number of canticles, 44 if the index is correct, provided for both Lauds and Vespers. For the former they are from the Old Testament and for the latter from the New. As we have seen in a previous chapter, Old Testament canticles, notably the *Benedicite*, were used in the morning office from at least the fourth century. The use of them was extended, by St Benedict especially, and they are not to be regarded as merely supplementary to the course of psalms. They have always been regarded as poems of spiritual value and like the psalms have been interpreted in a Christian sense. A good example is the Canticle of Jeremiah (31:10–14) whose meaning is indicated by the two titles: 'The joy of a liberated people'; 'Jesus had to die to reunite the children of God who had been scattered' (John 11:51–52). From the New Testament (an innovation) seven canticles have been chosen, with two extra ones, 1 Peter 2:21–24 for Sundays in Lent and 1 Timothy 3:16 for Epiphany (a happy touch this) and the Transfiguration. For Saturdays Philippians 2:6–11 is selected and it is wholly suitable for the office.[15] For *every* Sunday Revelation 19:1, 2, 5–7 is a bit high-pitched and over-decorated with numerous Alleluias. Ephesians 1:3–10, set for Mondays, is over-used (with a feast of Our Lady and an apostle it can appear three times in a week) and again the translation needs looking at.

The lectionaries

Of the Office of Readings the lectionaries are clearly important constituents and they must be considered at greater length further on. Here we consider them as elements of this office and take in with them the short readings of the other hours.

The reading of the scriptures 'in course' has always presented problems. To repeat a truism, the Bible is a large and very miscellaneous collection of books and at some point the decision has to be made whether you are going to include the whole of it or only part. If the latter, which parts? And then we are in danger of subjective judgements. One thing seems clear: the revisers have decided that some parts are not suitable for use in the office – which is essentially prayer – and these have been omitted. We are spared genealogical lists and catalogues of objects that run remorselessly through, for instance, the book of Exodus. Judges has been ruthlessly pruned though one wonders whether even what is left is appropriate for the office. Its barbarity strikes hard. But if you use a Bible for your scripture readings, you discover some rather odd things. The book of Ben Sirach for example is not read at all in full. Extracts from it take us over two weeks and the reasons for the selections made are sometimes far to seek. That apart, there is a case here for 'extracting', for there is something relentless about the continual moralizings (of various quality) that run through 51 chapters. In some cases, the readings resemble a mosaic of texts from one or even two chapters. It is an odd procedure and one does not know whether it is done on critical principles or simply to make the reading more comprehensible. Perhaps the custom of reading the Bible continuously is no longer regarded as important as it once was but there are those who like to use it in that way and it is the only way you can come really to know the Bible.

However, the matter of this lectionary is a very complex one. As we see from the Introduction (146), the original intention was to provide a two-year cycle but this had to be abandoned on account of the extra bulk this would give to the book when it came to be printed.[16] The result, we are told, is that 'we have more Old Testament and less New Testament reading than originally planned'.[17] What exactly has happened to the Old Testament lectionary is difficult to discover. A prolonged examination of the texts in all three volumes would be necessary to discern the principle of selection. As it is, we have fairly evidently a truncated lectionary. Then, the two-year lectionary for week-days in the missal had to be taken into account and here the revisers have been successful in preventing over-lapping. Altogether, the problem of the biblical lectionary cannot be said to have been solved and the root cause of the failure must be said to be the practical impossibility of printing anything like an adequate lectionary in an office book even if it is four volumes.[18] And it may be asked, why try to? Every church presumably has a Bible and all that was needed was references to the appropriate passages. For clerics who have to move about a good deal, there are handy pocket-editions of the whole Bible which are easily portable.

In spite of these imperfections, the lectionary is a great improvement on the old one where the readings were sometimes reduced to mere snippets. Each reading in the new book makes sense and the length is about right. The New Testament lectionary proves in use to be very satisfactory. The divisions of the text conform for the most part to the modern critical editions which however have not been followed slavishly.[19]

Of the short readings the Introduction (45) says that they are to be regarded as true proclamations of God's word and are intended to focus attention on short sayings whose significance might be missed in the

~

continuous reading of the Bible. This they do. Those chosen for Vespers, always from the New Testament, are sometimes quite substantial and almost always apt. For Sundays, Fridays and the greater seasons of the year, the character of these times has dictated the choice (GI 156–158).

For the second reading, from the Fathers and other ecclesiastical writers, the revisers have drawn on a very wide variety of sources from the East and the West (the proportion of Greek writers is particularly notable), from ancient and more modern writers, though apart from Paul VI (homily for Feast of Holy Family), no recent writer has been included.[20] Some may regret this and there may well be a case for the inclusion of contemporary writers. They can often 'speak to our condition' as a writer of the fourth century does not. There were no doubt good reasons for the decision though one cannot but regret the exclusion of so famous and spiritually profitable a writer as Newman.[21]

One at least of the reasons why the revisers have drawn largely on the Fathers is that they wish the patristic reading to be, as far as possible, a commentary on the scripture reading. This is apparent both for the greater feasts and seasons and also for certain weeks during the year. But with the baggage of modern critical scholarship that one carries in one's mind, these commentaries are not always as acceptable as one would like them to be. There seems indeed to be an opportunity here for a new kind of spiritual writer, namely one who is completely competent in modern scriptural exegesis and who yet can draw out the meaning of the passages in question for the spiritual life.[22]

One of the most criticized parts of the former breviary was the 'legends' of the lives of saints that appeared in the second nocturn. They were not only inaccurate but sometimes sheer fabrications like the one about St Cecily of whom next to nothing is known. Again, the legends were written in a conventional literary form. Certain virtues were made pegs on which to hang a meagre amount of information about the saints' lives. Requests for their revision have been heard throughout the centuries and now the revisers have solved the problem by cutting the Gordian knot. A brief biographical note, duly reserved where facts are meagre, precedes the lesson which is either an extract from the saint's writings (if any) or an account of his life by a contemporary or near contemporary, or finally an appropriate passage from a contemporary writer. The results nearly always make acceptable reading. The *fervorino* of St Methodius of Sicily ('With full awareness this virgin empurpled her lips and cheeks and tongue by dabbing them with the light and colour of the blood of the true heavenly Lamb . . .') stands out as an unwelcome exception.

Responsories

As is now well known, the readings are followed by responsories which were one of the richest but, musically speaking, the most difficult texts of the old office. The principle underlying their use is admirable: we listen to God's word and then we ruminate on it and pray about it. The best responsories of the old system did precisely that. The chant dwelt on key phrases from the readings and turned them this way and that. But when the office is recited, they say little enough. As we know, in private recitation they may be omitted and other texts with similar content may replace them.

Hymns

When we come to consider the pattern of the individual offices we are immediately confronted with the question of the place of the hymn. From the time of St Benedict the hymns of Lauds, Vespers and Compline were placed within the body of the office. In the new office they come at the beginning of every hour. The reasons for this, according to the Introduction, are that the hymn sums up 'the particular characteristic of each hour or feast' and helps to 'draw the people into the celebration' (GI 42, 173). That is, the hymn is a popular element and it may be agreed that it is so when an office is celebrated with a community. The opening versicle and response is hardly sufficient to engage the people's attention. On the other hand, the revisers might have gone one step further and put the hymn *before* the versicle and response so that it could be sung in procession. However, there is a case for keeping the hymn where it was, at least in Lauds and Vespers. There at best it served as a meditative commentary on the short reading that preceded it and came as an interlude after the long stretch of psalmody. This function is now performed by the short responsory which in the form given has its difficulties. How is it to be set to singable music? However, it may be replaced by another hymn or verse(s) of one, so the principle is saved.

The collection of Latin hymns is extensive and drawn from many sources not hitherto used in the Roman breviary. All the great hymns of the past appear but there is much undistinguished stuff among them. All are in their pre-classical, pre-seventeenth-century form and while this is satisfactory when they are sung to their proper chants, too frequently their rhythm is uneven. However, other collections of national hymns may be used (GI 178) and the editors of the English book have not hesitated to do so.

The patterns of the hours

Public prayer, as we have indicated above, must have a certain definable pattern if it is to be an adequate vehicle of worship for a community. It will be useful then to examine some of the individual offices. Lauds and Vespers have the same pattern and may be taken together. It is to be supposed that the revisers thought that three psalms for these offices would be sufficient and psychologically manageable though once the decision had been made to distribute the psalter over four weeks, some reduction was inevitable. The text that follows, the short reading, is of a quite different literary genre and if read slowly and followed by silence, it introduces a meditative element into the office and in this the new office marks a decisive change from the old tradition when an hour was 'gone through' without pause and sometimes almost breathlessly. The responsory prolongs the prayer. Perhaps the full value of this part of the pattern will be seen when there is a longer reading, followed by a homily which will be aimed at leading the community to prayer.[23]

Lauds and Vespers rise to a natural climax with the singing of the evangelical canticles and here, especially on the greater feasts, the antiphons that go with them and that are often of great antiquity and beauty, perform their function very well, though it must be said that in translation they sometimes appear rather pedestrian. Often they sum up the whole meaning of a feast, as for instance the antiphon to the *Benedictus* on the feast of Epiphany.[24]

In public recitation the singing of these canticles may be marked by some ceremonial and the censing of the altar at the *Magnificat* is obviously appropriate.

Up to this moment the movement of the prayer has been Godward even if in the course of it the community have recalled God's saving deeds, that is, his love towards us. But now the prayer moves in the direction of the community, of mankind who needs God's help. Hence the intercessions, the Lord's prayer and the collect. The intercessions have obviously been thought out with great care and in the course of the year they suggest petitions for almost every conceivable human need. They indeed represent a petitionary element in the office which was long desired and which was astonishingly absent from the old office.[25] If the form seems over-elaborate, first (and usually) the statement of a need, then a petition and finally a response, they may in fact be used very flexibly. The response may be omitted and from time to time it will be better to do so as it is not always on all fours with the petition following the statement. Finally, time is allowed for private prayer after the official petitions and this should be used. It would also seem indicated that pauses should be made between the petitions. In this framework the Lord's prayer appears as the summing up of the whole hour and its restoration to these offices, after a long absence, can only be greeted with gratification. The collect particularizes the prayer of the feast or the hour and the addition (i.e. restoration) of so many collects to the individual hours is also something to be welcomed.

There is no significant change in the hour(s) to be said during the day. The number of texts, notably the short readings, has been increased and the selection of psalms, which of course is dictated by the re-arrangement of the psalter, is somewhat different though many that were in the Pius X breviary for these hours will be found here also.[26] Compline however has suffered a considerable change and is the chief victim of an unimaginative systematization of the liturgy which had been prevalent since the post-Tridentine reform. If you make a change in one part of the liturgy, you must make the same change everywhere else. If you think it 'a good idea' to put the hymn first in other offices, it must be put first in that of Compline. Compline has always had a special character, quiet, contemplative, summing up the day and looking on to the sleep of the night. The old office suggested this by its very pattern: a reading (even if formalized in the Roman office), from which naturally proceeded an examination of conscience, a general confession and absolution. The psalms moved forward quietly and the hymn continued in the same mood. The little chapter (which could with advantage have been varied) and the responsory turned one's thought to the coming night and the *Nunc dimittis* followed by the collect with the anthem of the Blessed Virgin Mary brought the hour to a fitting close. The place of the hymn in the new office wrecks the pattern. The examination of conscience (or in public recitation[27] the penitential act) has no obvious connection with the hymn that immediately follows it. Since the beginning of the hour has been changed and the 'blessing' (for the reader) suppressed, it was thought necessary to salvage the sentence asking for 'a quiet night and a perfect end' and this appears at the end of the office. Altogether an untidy affair. It will be said that the new Compline has the same effect. Perhaps it has, but not without jolts and bumps.

Like every liturgy the new office will reveal its virtues and defects through use over a considerable space of time. Experience may well show that if it is to become the prayer of the *people* a good deal of simplification will be necessary. This is particularly true of seasons like Lent and Advent where the pattern adopted by the revisers makes the arrangement of the book a complicated matter. The editors of the English edition have done their best to produce a reasonable arrangement but it can still be puzzling. One reason for this would seem to be the policy of the revisers in providing a very considerable number of proper texts for these seasons and the division of the seasons into two parts: the first four weeks of Lent and the special days of Advent from 17 to 24 December. The former is the more troublesome and some re-thinking of this period would seem to be necessary. Much could be done for both seasons by reducing the variety of antiphons and responsories. On the other hand, there is the fact that the office may be used with great flexibility and in the course of time there will no doubt be those who will be able to find solutions to the problems presented by the existing complexity. Already there are some who see the new office as a basis on which to build a prayer of the church for the people.[28] There is however another feature of the new office that deserves great attention. It is simply that it allows for and indeed encourages a calm, recollected manner of celebration. The titles of the psalms demand at least a moment of reflection, silences may be kept after the readings and there would seem to be no reason why similar silences should not be made at the end of the psalms before the *Gloria Patri*, especially when as in Psalm 21 its content is rich. Likewise full opportunity should be taken to provide moments of silence in the course of the intercessions and if these are said kneeling (as I think they should be) the possibility of recollected prayer is real. This is one of the ways in which the unfortunate gap between public and private prayer, 'meditation' or whatever it has been called, can be closed. In the past it was not always realized that you cannot pray out of a vacuum. You need something to pray about and the office with its psalms, readings and intercessions provides jumping off points for personal prayer. Perhaps too it has not been sufficiently realized that the prayer of petition is essentially an approach to God, a recognition of his power and love and when that approach is made in humility of heart, the one praying is open to the movement and inspiration of the Holy Spirit. In more recent years when there has been more than a tendency to set charismatic prayer against liturgical prayer, it is important to realize that with the silences of the Divine Office there is a place in it for charismatic prayer. It would be a pity if the charismatic movement became associated with certain phenomena whether they be the speaking with tongues or healing. If it is anything at all, it is a movement that wishes to give free play to the movement of the Spirit in the human heart and this may be, and probably usually is, totally imperceptible to the senses or the outside world. A waiting on the Spirit within the context of liturgical prayer will strengthen both the charismatic element in the life of the church and the prayer that is called and is the prayer of the church.

Notes

~

¹ The official Latin edition has two titles: **Divinum Officium (ex sacrosancto concilio . . .)**, at the top of the page and in the middle **Liturgia Horarum, iuxta Ritum Romanum**. But **Liturgia Horarum** appears on the spine and it is clear from the Introduction that the revisers intend it to be called by that name. The English translators opted for **The Divine Office** and have put 'The Liturgy of the Hours etc.' as a sub-title (see **The Divine Office**, Collins, Dwyer and Talbot, 1, 1974, the edition used here). The reason was that 'Liturgy of the Hours' sounds odd in English and is over-technical. On the other hand 'The Divine Office' has long been used in English-speaking countries.

² Even if a Christian is unable to be present at the eucharist every day, it is being celebrated continually.

³ Gl 38 and Cyprian, **De Orat. Dom.**, 35.

⁴ Of Terce, Sext and None the Introduction simply says that they commemorate the events of our Lord's passion and the first preaching of the gospel (75).

⁵ Gl 14 and cf. CL 33.

⁶ See Gl 201–203.

⁷ I have noted only one of the famous responsories of **Tenebrae** and there are two meagre extracts from the Lamentations of Jeremiah which have been sung on these days for about fifteen hundred years. Nor should it be said that these texts, because they can only be sung in Latin if you are to retain the chants, are 'no good to the people'. They are so moving that anyone with a bi-lingual text (if he needs one) can

profit from them. It may be that there are few churches able to sing them. But if they are abolished, there will be none.

[8] Short of three, 57, 82, 108, the 'cursing' psalms which have been omitted 'because of certain psychological difficulties' (GI 131 – which must be regarded as a deliberate understatement) and verses from a number of others.

[9] Which it is so difficult to **like**.

[10] Cf. for example Acts 4:23–31; and also Ephes 5:19; Col 3:16.

[11] Not the 'titles' found in the Hebrew psalter. See P. Salmon, **Les 'tituli psalmorum' des manuscrits latins** (Paris, 1958).

[12] See P. Salmon, EP, pp. 822–3, and J. Gelineau, **Voices and Instruments in Christian Worship** (Eng. trans. C. Howell, Collegeville, MN, 1964), pp. 107–8.

[13] See Salmon, EP, p. 823.

[14] For the **seasons** however the system does not always work. Thus for I Vespers of 1 Advent the antiphon 'Behold the Lord will come and all his holy ones with him . . .' is in no way related to the psalm (141) which is about deep suffering and affliction. Likewise, 'Rejoice and be glad, new Zion . . .' attached to a section of Psalm 118 is totally out of key with it. Examples could be multiplied.

[15] The translation is not always happy: 'Jesus did not count equality with God a thing to be **grasped**'. 'Grasped at' would be more correct but that was evidently too much for the RSV translators though the phrase would seem to mean 'cling to' – so JB.

[16] For details see Dom Placid Murray, 'In Season and out of Season', **The Furrow** (February 1975), pp. 100–1.

[17] **Ibid**.

[18] The typical edition of the **Liturgia Horarum** is in four volumes. A fifth was planned and is expected, containing among other things the psalter collects. See below, Chapter 9.

[19] These editions do in fact differ from one another but the revisers do not seem to have followed the Vulgate.

[20] In the draft lectionary there was one extract from Thomas Merton, but recently dead, and one (in French!) from Newman, both **ad libitum**.

[21] Because he is not canonized?

[22] A beginning was made by German scholars some years ago and some of their commentaries have been made available in English. Cf. for example **Das Evangelium nach Matthäus** by W. Trilling in the series Geistliche Schriftlesung (Patmos Verlag, 1962); Eng. trans. **Gospel according to Matthew**, 2 vols (Burns and Oates, 1969). The series has been continued by Sheed and Ward.

[23] GI 46 suggests that this reading may be taken either from the Office of Readings or from the Mass (and indeed from other places). But what happens when the priest-celebrant has to use these texts before or after the office? What, I think, was needed was a supplementary lectionary, no more than references to the Bible, to be used for these longer readings.

[24] A good deal could be said about the revised liturgy of the Epiphany which has heavily emphasized the Western aspect of it as a feast of mission. In the Eastern church, from which it came, the emphasis is on the marriage between Christ and his church. In the revised office this antiphon is distinctly isolated. The emphasis could be corrected by the substitution of Isaiah 62:1–5 (a bridal text) for Isaiah 52:7–10 (a missionary text).

[25] With the exception of certain parts of the **preces** and these were stereotyped to an intolerable degree.

[26] Proper antiphons for these hours seem to be an unnecessary luxury.

[27] Is not public recitation of Compline something of an anomaly? For St Benedict it seems to have been a domestic act: it was said wherever the brethren were gathered for the reading of Cassian's Conferences or the Lives of the Fathers (Rule, ch. 42).

[28] The French for instance who have not (yet) committed themselves to producing a large and expensive office book. Père Roguet recorded that in Notre Dame, Paris, large congregations gathered on Sundays for Lauds (!) and Vespers according to the new office. But he did not describe exactly what was done (see his essay, p. 78, n. 1 in **The Liturgy of the Hours**, trans. Peter Coughlan and Peter Purdue, Geoffrey Chapman, 1971). For England see S. Dean, **Celebration Hymnal: New Songs of Celebration** (Great Wakering, Essex, 1989); P. Inwood, **Evening Prayer** (London, 1986). For the USA, J. A. Melloh and W. G. Storey, **Praise God in Song** (GIA Publications, Chicago, 1979).

For a full account of the revision of the **Liturgy of the Hours** with the many difficulties and complications involved see A. Bugnini, **The Reform of the Liturgy** (Eng. trans., The Liturgical Press, Collegeville, MN, 1990), part 4, pp. 491–558.

FIVE

~

The Prayer of the Psalms

~~~~~~

I T IS CLEAR THAT in the new office the psalter has a dominant place. It is the spine of every hour. In addition to canticles from the Old and New Testaments, we are required to say eleven psalms or parts of psalms a day which means 77 during the week and, as we know, the whole psalter (short of three which have been omitted) during the month. If this is a notable alleviation of the burden of reciting 150 during a week, it still amounts to a good deal and unless we have an adequate understanding of them, it is not going to be easy to use them as prayer.

It would seem that there are many modern Christians who have difficulties in this matter, difficulties that have come from various quarters. Several generations of scholarship have revealed the psalms in all the starkness of their primitive meaning. Even the not very profound knowledge of the psalms that an average theological student acquires in the course of his studies is sufficient to show that the psalms are *Hebrew* poems, the expression of a culture to which he does not belong. The God of the psalms is so often the God of battles who is fighting for a small and insignificant tribe. Up to a point we can rationalize this and then we are brought up sharp with an utterance that strikes one as barbarous: 'O give thanks to the Lord for he is good, for his great love has no end . . . The first-born of the Egyptians he smote, *for* his great love is without end . . . he flung Pharaoh and his force in the sea, *for* his great love is without end . . .' (Psalm 135). A strange way of showing love, and all we can think of is the poor babies of the Egyptians and hope that the accounts of their death are no more true than the events of the Aeneid. Then in the psalms we find God manipulating nature for his own purposes; storm and flood, the crashing of trees, smoking mountains and earthquakes are all caused by God to put fear into errant Israelites or their unspeakably wicked enemies. For the psalmist sometimes sees God as his ally, set against the people of Canaan or the invading hordes from the North: 'We have heard with our own ears . . . of the things you did long ago . . . To plant them you uprooted the nations: to let them spread

~

92

you laid peoples low . . .' (Psalm 43) and we are reminded unhelpfully of the carnage of the Book of Joshua. The same psalm goes on relentlessly: 'Yet now you have rejected us, disgraced us . . . though we had not forgotten you . . .'. Here the note of *self*-righteousness that we hear from time to time in the psalms appears. A little too frequently the psalmist affirms that he–or the people–have done all that was required of them, and yet and yet . . . This seems to be in direct contradiction to the gospel saying: 'We have done all that we should and (yet) we are profitless servants' (Luke 17:10). It would not be difficult to prolong the list which would perhaps look like an indictment.

Underlying these objections there is a deeper problem. As soon as you begin talking of prayer, you raise questions about God. On the one hand, our notion or image of God conditions our prayer and on the other our prayer will say much about how we regard God. The psalms can often voice the deepest and most anguished emotions known to man (Psalms 21 and 68) but God dominates the scene and there is apparently little reference to 'neighbour'. To put the matter in another way, the psalms emphasize the transcendence of God giving the impression that he is all and man is nothing. It is the problem of transcendence and immanence that runs throughout religious history. Today many seem to have lost the sense of God's transcendence. God has been declared dead some time ago and by that is meant (at worst) that God is no more than part of the human process. At best, it means that modern Christians are more keenly aware of God in others, their fellow human beings, than in the traditional out-going of man to God in worship, praise and adoration. The resolution of the tension and the solution of the problem are to be found in the incarnation where God, the Lord of all things, becomes Immanuel, the God who is with us. It is perhaps for this reason that as soon as the church began using the psalms for prayer (and before that, for *kerygma* and teaching), by what seems a kind of instinct it christianized them. Of this we say something below but first we must attempt some answers to the other points.

It may be conceded that when we are confronted with the psalms and are constrained to use them we have to make a transference from one culture to another.[1] But it may be remarked that if we are to use any part of the Old Testament profitably and for that matter much of the New, we have to make this transference. Moreover, it needs to be said that the modern understanding of the psalms, the possibility of putting

~

at least some of them in their *Sitz-im-Leben*, helps us to use them. If there are psalms, and there seem to be many of them, that are to be dated to the time of the exile, and if we remember something of the circumstances that accompanied it, if indeed we project back into that far-off age something of the experience of the millions who have suffered exile in our own times, we can appreciate the anguished accents of the psalmist who becomes the voice of his whole community. In turn, such psalms can become *our* voice, our prayer for those same people. Spatial and temporal parochialism which restricts our horizon to our own affairs is not only not true to the New Testament but it is not true to the deepest insights of the Old. It may indeed often be difficult to discern whether and if the psalmist is expressing simply his own experiences or those of the community. Yet even in psalms so deeply personal as 21 and 68 there is a sense that the sufferer is the representative of the people and that he is suffering in them and they in him. This in fact reminds us of a dimension of the psalms that at times seems to have been overlooked. Nineteenth-century exegetes, who were usually brought up on a very individualistic kind of Christianity, did not, it would seem, always realize that they were dealing with the prayer book of a community. Whatever may have been the origins of certain personal psalms – and it is a perfectly proper exercise to try and discover those origins – by the time they were incorporated into the psalter they had become the expression and prayer of the people.[2] One reason why the psalter could become the prayer of the church was because it was first the prayer of the old Israel of God.

A more difficult problem is that of the relationship of God to the world and to historical events. As the merest tyro in exegesis knows, the Old Testament by-passes secondary causes. If anything happens, it is God who does it. Where natural phenomena are concerned perhaps the difficulty is not so great. In the Old Testament God was involved in the human process which was not simply something that went on without him. If God was too close to natural and historical events in the Old Testament, nowadays he is thought of even by Christians as being absent from the course of history. The difficulty of course is that in the Old Testament view, God seems to be responsible for *evil* and this the Christian cannot accept. The only solution to the problem would seem to be that we must realize we are reading about God through the mentalities of successive generations of people of the Old Testament. We need to remember that when the prophets said 'Thus says the Lord' they had not a hot line to God, that the sometimes blood-curdling utterances that are part of that word are the expression of the human speaker or writer and that he is saying as best he can what the message entrusted to him is. Thus when the writer of Psalm 135 seems to be exulting in the death of innocent Egyptian babes we need to remember that he was calling on an ancient and primitive tradition that is recorded in the Book of Exodus. His emphasis is not on the destruction of infants but on the power of God who brought the people of Israel out of the slavery of Egypt. It is in *this* that his love is revealed.

Perhaps in any case the Old Testament writers were not so naïve as we imagine. They could see the obverse and the reverse of the same event. *What* caused the death of the Egyptian children I think we must say we do not know. All the 'plagues' are put in a conventional framework and some are no more than the natural phenomena of Egyptian climatic conditions. The deaths happened and they were the other side of the epic story which tells of the deliverance of the people whom God loved. The same could be said of the destruction of the Egyptian army. We have to make the same considerations in our own day. Were the issues about the Second World War so clear-cut in 1939? There were many who thought they were not. They were aware that even if the war was necessary it would cause a loss of life and a destruction of industry and property that would be incalculable and in the event they were right. But the Western nations thought they must resist a tyranny that would have brought to an end a whole way of life which, if far from perfect, guaranteed certain fundamental human liberties. This end was achieved. This was the positive good but the evil remained and is not yet effaced.

Then there is the question of God as the 'God of battles' or even of the God of vengeance, the tribal God of this little Iron Age people who are slowly and painfully emerging into something that can be called civilization. It may seem a poor consolation to be told that the God of the Old Testament is infinitely superior to the gods of contemporary religions but it does put us on to the track of a better understanding. In the Old Testament we have a progressive revelation of God, his image is being gradually purified and in the deepest understanding of the Old Testament writers he is not a tribal God. And so many of the psalms proclaim he is Lord of heaven and earth, the whole of creation is his and the destiny of the whole human race is in his hand. His 'jealousy' (and there is not a great deal about this in the psalter) is not an unworthy

~

human emotion of which any decent monarch would be ashamed. It is the expression of the great love he bears to the people he has chosen. Nor are they chosen simply for their own sake. As so many of the psalms show, as so much of the prophetic writing shows, the Israelites are at once the representatives of the human race and the means chosen by God to carry his message of salvation to the whole of mankind. As we see from psalms like 95, 97 and 102, and from Isaiah 61 and 66, to mention no other passages, the final message of the Old Testament is universalist: all shall see the salvation of God. One day the posterity of Abraham will no longer be a tiny people dwelling precariously on a strip of land constantly overrun by the heathen. They will be a great nation, a universal people who will flow into a new Temple which will no longer be the shrine of a small tribe but the house of God's people. In this perspective God is the God of the whole human race whom he loves and who is the object of their love.[3] He is the God who one day will come among them, set his tent among them and indeed be one of them. It is this broad vision we need to keep in mind as we use the psalms rather than concentrating on the apparently arbitrary behaviour of God which is no more than an imperfect expression of his transcendence.

Perhaps 'transcendence' is the root of the trouble. As everyone knows there has been a vast and as yet an unended debate about this matter. In recent decades the horizontal relationship between man and man in religion and even in worship has been emphasized at the expense of the vertical relationship with God. At its simplest, the case is stated by the modern Christian in this way: he can find God in others or in the service of others and prayer has at times and by some been pronounced a useless activity. Not all in that view is to be repudiated but if the divine transcendence is rejected whether in theory or in practice, then it is difficult to see that worship and prayer in any real sense can survive. Perhaps this trend is now reaching its close, though rather from exhaustion than from a resolution of the problem.

Yet the question of the divine transcendence remains one of crucial importance. It is impossible to accept that the God of the Bible, the God of Jews and Christians alike, should be part of the world process to be conceived as in a constant state of self-perfection. That way lies either pantheism or atheism.

The reasons why some have wished to get rid of the divine transcendence are no doubt various but one of them is probably that it has seemed to deny the validity of this world order or to undervalue its importance. It is just at this point that we can see the value of the psalmists' emphasis on the involvement of God in the natural processes and in those of human history. Nowhere is the transcendence of God thrown into such high relief and yet nowhere is the sense of God being with the world and concerned in its events so strong as in the psalms. No doubt the 'science' is primitive, no doubt philosophical analysis is totally absent, no doubt we, with our post-Copernicus model of the world in our minds, need to 'translate' a good deal of what is there, but the central insight is sound. As Etienne Gilson showed long ago, it is this insight, combined with the Aristotelian philosophy, that enabled the medieval philosophers to work out their rich synthesis in which God is approached through those things that are (*ea quae sunt*), things that form an essential part of the whole reality. Aquinas does indeed in one place speak of all created beings 'emanating' from the Creator in language that seems Platonic (*in exitu creaturarum a primo principio* . . .) but he also sees them returning to their Origin perfected, their potentiality realized, *more* themselves than when they began their journey.[4] Dependent on God for their origin, directed towards him as their last end, they none the less achieve 'autonomy'. They *are* and they are valuable in themselves. But because they derive their being from God, they can reflect his beauty, truth and love (of which they are expressions) and through man's contemplation of them can lead him to God. The distinction between Creator and creature is always clear but so also is their essential relatedness.

This seems a far cry from the psalter but what are the psalms saying, what is Psalm 8 saying ('How great is your name, O Lord our God, through all the earth. Your majesty is praised above the heavens'), if not that? The examples could be multiplied. If modern Western industrialized man cannot respond to the exultation that underlies such expressions it must be because he is spiritually impoverished. For even if you are a Christian, if in practice you *exclude* God from all that really matters, you are not going to be able to praise him, to worship him or perhaps even to believe in him in any real way. Whatever may have been the defects of the people of the Old Testament they did not do that. God was real to them, God was present.

Part of the trouble about transcendence is that people have thought it meant that God was 'far away', 'up there' or 'out there'. Transcendence does not imply spatial images and when the psalmist cried 'I lift up my eyes to the mountains from where shall come my help' it is we who would be naïve in supposing that he thought God dwelt on the mountain. Sometimes one feels that the alleged inability of some to use the psalms comes from a failure to appreciate poetry! Transcendence implies 'otherness' and the radical distinction that must be made between God and things if we are not to fall into pantheism. But it may be admitted that the tension between transcendence and immanence was never wholly resolved in the Old Testament. There was a sense of God's presence, there were intimations of the Immanuel, but there could be no resolution of the tension until God had become man. It was their understanding of this radical change that enabled the first Christians to use the psalms with confidence and without *arrière-pensée* first for teaching and then for worship. This development was no doubt assisted by the translation of Yahweh in the psalms by the word *Kyrios* which the New Testament applied to Christ without hesitation. This brings us to what has been called the christological interpretation of the psalms.

It has been remarked that the office (as it was) was too theocentric, its users were required to glorify God 'as if the incarnation had never happened' and even if the form of the church's prayer derives from the synagogue a Christian will want 'to make it more christological'.[5] This was true of the old office, but, as we have indicated in a former chapter, this is no longer true of the new. The criticism is however made largely with the psalms and the Old Testament readings in view and these still form the major part of the Divine Office. Of the scripture lectionary we shall say something below but something further must be said about the psalms here. How can the psalms be christianized? How can we find Christ in them? How can we become aware that we are praying with Christ, about Christ and to him? These are not new questions though the need to answer them has become more acute in recent years and there has in fact been a vast amount of writing on the subject[6] which unhappily cannot even be summarized here.

Professor Fischer is quite emphatic about what he calls the 'christologization' of the psalms. Without it, it is impossible for the Christian to use them as prayer and he finds justification for his views in the interpretation of the psalms that is assumed in the gospels and the rest of the New Testament.[7] He sees this interpretation being formed in the early church ('the church of the martyrs') in two principal ways. First, there is the christological interpretation that moves 'from above' as when the

Yahweh of the Hebrew is taken as *Kyrios*, the Lord Jesus of the New Testament. The second way is the interpretation 'from below' as when the psalm is seen as giving the words of Christ—as if the *persona* of the psalm were Christ. Or the matter can be put more simply: 'for the church of the martyrs each psalm in some fashion speaks *of* Christ or *to* Christ or finally Christ is seen speaking in it'.[8] But the voice of Christ was not separated from the voice of the church, so the psalm is often seen as the voice of the church, *vox ecclesiae*, which is united with that of Christ. This aspect of the matter was summed up by St Augustine in one phrase: the psalm is the voice of the whole Christ, head and body,[9] a theme that, as we know, he pursued through his vast book, the *Enarrationes in Psalmos*.[10] The whole matter is expressed in the commentary of St Augustine on Psalm 85 which we have quoted in the first chapter of this book: '. . . the Saviour of the Body, (Christ) prays *for* us and *in* us and we make our prayer *to* him. He prays for us *as priest*, he prays in us *as head* and we pray to him *as our God* . . .'.

This understanding of the psalms, which was markedly that of the ancient Roman liturgy,[11] of course involves a major 'translation' and perhaps not everyone will be willing to make it. It may be said however that given the right disposition of mind, continual use of the psalms brings a growing realization that the psalms are, in the deepest sense, Christian prayer. The *practical* difficulty is to discern when a psalm speaks *to* Christ as *Kyrios*, when it speaks *of* him, when it gives voice to the sentiments of Christ or when it is the voice of the church, the body of Christ. One important clue, given by the antiphons,[12] is the use the church has made of the psalms on the great feasts of the temporal cycle. Without going into technical questions of which psalms are truly messianic, it is clear that psalms like 2 and 3 (about the resurrection), Psalm 22 where the Good Shepherd theme links it immediately with John 10, Psalm 21 which no Christian thinks of as anything other than the voice of Christ (cf. Matthew 27:46; Mark 15:34), have a Christian sense. Nor is there any doubt about a psalm like 109 or even Psalm 110 which gives the covenant theme. The list could be greatly extended but there is no space for such a list here.[13] In other words, the easiest and probably the most effective way of learning the Christian interpretation of the psalms is to observe the use the church has made of them in the office of the great seasons of the year. What would be of the greatest assistance to a Christian understanding of the psalms would be a new kind of commentary, based on modern scholarship, which would take into account the whole of the Christian tradition of interpretation. Just as the typological interpretation of the scriptures has undergone close scrutiny in recent years, so we need a similar sifting for the psalms. They would stand to lose nothing and would be made more accessible to the ordinary user.

The new office has done something to bring this Christian sense of the psalms before the user by printing the second title (which may indeed in private recitation be used as an antiphon; GI 115) before the text of the psalm. These titles are drawn often enough from the New Testament (e.g. Psalm 2 'They rose up against your servant Jesus, whom you had anointed' Acts 4:27) or from the Fathers and other ecclesiastical writers. Thus the title of Psalm 1 interprets the 'tree that is planted beside flowing waters' as of the cross, the source of life, a phrase that evokes John 19:34. It is attributed to a writer of the second century. The 'sun' of Psalm 18A is interpreted by the 'The Rising Sun (who) has come to visit us to guide our feet in the way of peace' of Luke 1:78, 79. This too is a very ancient interpretation going back to Justin the Martyr (*Apologia* I, 54) and represents a very bold reference for its time to *Helios*, the Sun god.[14] In a different register, namely the *vox Christi*, we find as the title to Psalm 6 'Now my spirit is troubled . . .' of John 12:27. The psalm goes on 'Lord, do not reprove me in your anger, punish me not in your rage . . . Have mercy on me Lord . . . my soul is racked with pain . . .'. Such a title suggests the interior sentiments of Christ in his passion and the use the church makes of psalms like 21, 37, 68 and some others in the Holy Week liturgy yields the same interpretation. It is indeed one of the stranger features of the early Roman liturgy that it could accept without hesitation or apology a depth of human-ness in the suffering Christ that some even today might think excessive. This interpretation is so prevalent in the liturgy of the time that it is not too much to say that it was an authentic expression of the mind of the church. If that is so, it means that we have an insight into the interior sentiments of Christ in his passion of which the gospels say very little.

All this is helpful and in using the new office we should take due notice of these titles. It is to be regretted however that a few are not really illuminating. Thus the title of Psalm 146 says no more than the text of the psalm itself: 'You, O God, we worship; you, O Lord, we adore', and the psalm goes on: 'Praise the Lord for he is good, sing to

our God for he is loving' which I imagine in the view of Professor Fischer
would be regarded as a christianization 'from above': that is, 'Lord' =
Kyrios. In one place the title contrasts very oddly with the psalm: 'To you
have I lifted up my eyes . . . Like the eyes of a servant on the hand of
a mistress . . .'. For this the title, taken from Matthew 20:30 (and
awkwardly translated), is 'The two blind men cried out: "Lord, have pity
on us, Son of David"'. Yes, well, of course the general sense is clear but
still the point of the gospel incident is that the men could not see. The
titles drawn from patristic works sometimes say little enough. See for
example that for Psalm 60: 'The prayer of a just man who looks to the
things which are eternal' (St Hilary). Or let us take Psalm 98, one of the
most powerful psalms of the psalter which recalls so much of the history
of salvation. To this is attached a saying from St Athanasius, again rather
lamely translated: 'You are higher than the Cherubim; you changed the
bad state of the earth,[15] when you came in a nature like ours'. These
lapses however are comparatively rare and a study of the titles reveals
that on the whole they have been successful in pointing to the Christian
sense of the psalms and, it is interesting to note, they have done this most
effectively by using phrases from the New Testament. There can be no
sounder basis than this and the revisers have rather cleverly by-passed the
scholarly debate about which psalms are 'christological' and which are
not;[16] whatever criticism may be made of details, the restoration of the
titles to the psalms has done much to christianize them in practice, i.e.
for those who are going to use the new book.

However, it may be said that if all this 'theology' and the device
of 'titles' are necessary, that only goes to show that it is difficult if not
impossible for the ordinary mortal to use the psalms as prayer. To this
it can be answered that all prayer needs effort of one kind or another.
Even the post-Tridentine tradition of mental prayer with its composition
of place, its two or three 'points for consideration' and its resolutions or
'spiritual nosegays', demanded a good deal of work as did and do simpler
forms of prayer. Few are they who can fall on their knees and immediately get in touch with God. Most of us need a text either from holy
scripture or some other kind of book to provide the necessary point of
departure. It does not seem a great deal to ask that people who use the
psalms should take some little trouble over them so that they can become
prayer. To this we can add that there are a number of psalms that
present no difficulty at all. For centuries Christians have used Psalm 50

to express repentance, Psalm 129 to express their need of God and redemption; and Psalm 130 'O Lord, my heart is not proud . . .' is the simplest and most moving plea for the virtue of humility which needs no reference even to the New Testament. There are others, like Psalm 22 of which the several metrical versions show that it has in fact become a Christian prayer. In the Anglican tradition, in which the psalter of the Book of Common Prayer has played so great a part, there is similar evidence to show that certain psalms have long been regarded as Christian prayers. Some of the greatest Anglican hymns, such as 'All people that on earth do dwell' (Psalm 99), are simply paraphrases of the psalms.

If we add psalms of this kind to the very large corpus that has received an easily discernible Christian sense in the liturgy, we shall find that we have covered a great deal of the psalter. There remain others that are more difficult to use prayerfully. For instance, the series of long psalms from 104 to 106 and Psalm 77 recalling the chief events of Old Testament salvation history, which from a literary viewpoint can only be regarded as epics and not very promising material for prayer. In the new office they have been spread out and in any case are used only during Advent, Christmas, Lent and Eastertide. They are more suitable for *reading* than for praying and if they were appointed for use as lessons, that would be a return to the earliest use of the psalter.[17] There are others, such as Psalm 36 and Psalm 51, dealing with the problem of evil which is 'solved' in a way that is unacceptable to a Christian, and there are passages of other psalms, some of which have been omitted, speaking of the destruction of the wicked or the 'enemy', which can only be described as sub-Christian. What is to be done about them it is difficult to say. It is hardly satisfactory, as has been suggested, to put such passages 'into parentheses' and presumably pretend they are not there.[18] The only solution to the problem that I can see is that the church should recognize frankly that there are still psalms and parts of psalms in the office that the Christian cannot use or can only use by means of a complicated exegesis. In spite of considerable modifications in the liturgical psalter of the 1971 office, it may be that the church still sees some inherent value in reciting in principle the whole of the psalter. It would seem to be a case that is still to be proved. Part of the problem of the psalter is that there is probably still too much of it in the office, and if the quantity of psalms were reduced, not simply in a single office (that is another question), but over the given period of a month, it might very well be possible to use what is left with greater spiritual profit. If the church made this decision, it would simply be returning to the earliest tradition of the prayer of the church.

Of the arrangement of the psalter in the office we note that for Lauds and Vespers all the psalms that are traditional for those hours have been retained. The ancient group 148–150 has been further divided, a process that began with the Pius X psalter, but in spite of the severe criticisms of Anton Baumstark on the matter,[19] such division is a psychological necessity. To recite these psalms every day is more than most can bear. Otherwise the office follows pretty well the course of the psalter as it is in the Bible with the necessary allocation of psalms for particular hours. Sometimes this leads to uncomfortable results. For the prayer during the day of Thursday of the third week we find juxtaposed Psalm 78, a lamentation over the destruction of Jerusalem, and Psalm 79 which is similar in mood even if its main message is 'Come, Lord Jesus'. With the section of Psalm 118 they make a rather long office. As far as length goes, the same could be said of the same office for Monday of the second week; Psalm 118:41–48, Psalm 39, divided into two sections. There is a great deal to be said for the Benedictine arrangements here, namely the use throughout most of the week of the gradual psalms. They are short and experience has shown that they can be prayed again and again and always have a message to deliver.

One or two other matters in connection with the use of the psalter deserve mention. The most obvious way in which the psalms have been christianized is by the addition of the short doxology (the 'Glory be to the Father . . .') to each psalm.[20] This addition was made apparently in the fifth century and can be regarded as a permanent element to remind worshippers that they are using the psalms as Christian prayers. Dom Vandenbroucke sees in it no more than an 'extrinsic christianization', a term that would seem to indicate that he does not think much of it. It is true I think that it has become so much 'stuffing' and we do not seem to have missed its absence in the responsorial psalm of the Mass. It is to be regretted that the older form 'Glory be to the Father, through the Son, and in the Holy Spirit', which was still current in the time of St Basil, gave way to the present form which is a relic (so old!) of the anti-Arian campaign of the fourth century. The older form would certainly remind us that always we are praying through Christ to the Father and in the Holy Spirit.[21]

~

The psalm-collects

Another means to make the use of the psalms more prayerful was the psalm-collect which was recited after a pause for silence at the end of every psalm. There is a considerable number of these collects in existence[22] and we are told[23] that they will be included in the supplementary volume to the *Liturgy of the Hours* which at the time of writing has not been published. It must be confessed that occasionally they are disappointing because arbitrary. A phrase is snatched from the psalm and prayer is built up round it perhaps regardless of context. But generally speaking they witness to the profound Christian understanding of the psalms that was current in the fifth and subsequent centuries. A few examples will give some notion of these collects.

1. From Psalm 40 ('Happy the man who considers the poor and the weak') the writer expands what is almost its last verse: 'Establish me in your sight'.

'Strengthen me in your sight, Lord, and deliver us not into the hands of the enemy for you once raised us up in Christ the Lord. Send your help to us on our bed of pain; heal our souls for we have sinned against you. Guard us, give us life and make us blessed on the earth' (p. 192).

2. On a not very promising psalm 'O God you have rejected us and broken us' (59) with its curious expression about 'casting a sandal over Idumea', we have this:

'Go forth, Lord, at the head of our armies. May we be strong in the power of the Word who, when he clothed himself in our human nature, took possession of the earth [lit. *extendit calceamentum suum in Idumea*]. Through him help us in affliction and forgive the sins of your people' (p. 142).

3. From the great eschatological psalm, 28, where God is seen enthroned in his temple ('In his temple they all cry "Glory"') the writer has seized upon that notion:

'Strengthen your people, Lord, and make us the temple of your Holy Spirit so that with pure hearts we may prepare for you an acceptable sacrifice (*holocaustum*)' (p. 78).

4. One last sample must suffice. There is much to exploit in the Messianic Psalm 109 and a Spanish writer does so. The phrase *ante luciferum genitus* has caught his attention but it is only a point of departure:

~
104

'Lord, Father almighty, from your own being as from the womb before the daystar you brought forth the Son; grant that he who with you made the light of the whole world from nothing, may enlighten us with his shining glory. May he who was born into the world from the Virgin's womb, though without leaving your side, make us sharers in his passion as he promised us to be his co-heirs in glory' (p. 242).

A little prolix perhaps, as was the Spanish habit, and somewhat complicated, but the prayer links the worshipper with the whole redeeming work of Christ which *began* in the incarnation.

The procedure is clear. The writers of these prayers do not summarize either the theme of the psalm or its Christian meaning. They seize upon a phrase here and there and build up their prayer on it but they bring a Christian mind to the psalms and find in them the Christian message. One is inclined to say that perhaps too often they find what they want. It would be interesting to compare at length these ancient collect-prayers with some which have been written in more recent times. Space forbids but it will be useful to give one example of a modern collect for the same psalm (109) which does in fact sum up and christianize it:

All powerful and ever-living God,
you have enthroned your Son, Jesus, at your right hand.
He was begotten of your being before the dawn
and *was raised up from the dead by the power of the Spirit.*
You have placed his enemies as a footstool under his feet.
Spread his reign by the growth of his church
and by the sacrifice of our eternal High Priest
give us to drink from the torrent of his graces
and make us co-heirs of his glory for ever.[24]

The italicized phrases indicate a thorough-going christianization of the psalm and it is clear that the collect summarizes its themes. It may seem over-elaborate and indeed over-done, but the recitation of a prayer like this at the end of a psalm makes it come alive for the Christian.

Titles, antiphons, the Christian interpretation of the psalms, the *Gloria Patri* and the collects – all this adds up to a great deal and if these 'aids to prayer' have their place, they also show that the praying of the psalms is not an easy matter. If modern people, if the young monks and clerics of whom Archbishop Weakland has written, are unwilling to take this trouble, then I fear they will not be able to use the psalms as

Christian prayer. Whether we like it or not, we *have* to make a transference from one culture to another but in this the psalter is not unique. The whole Bible is involved and with it the question of its *sensus plenior*, the fulfilled sense of the Old Testament.[25] Without this we are condemned to reading the Old Testament as the record of an obscure pre-Christian tribe. At that level, which is not without its importance for scholarly purposes, it can hardly become *lectio divina*.

The canticles

Two new features of the office are the very considerable increase in the number of Old Testament canticles and the inclusion of canticles from the New Testament that apart from the *Benedictus*, the *Magnificat* and the *Nunc dimittis* have never appeared in it before. No doubt the allocation of the psalter to a period of four weeks had something to do with the first and a growing realization among exegetes that there are identifiable canticles in the New Testament accounts for the second. Of these additions the General Introduction has nothing to say except to record their appearance in the office (136, 137).[26]

The difficulties over the Old Testament canticles are neither greater nor less than those that affect the use of the psalms. Titles to help in their use have been added to them as to the psalms. For the most part these canticles are well chosen and include many of the great passages from Isaiah. Daniel 3 also makes a very good prayer. I am not at all sure of the value of Isaiah 38, the canticle of Hezekiah, which was in the old breviary, in spite of the new title added to it: 'I was dead, and behold I am alive and I hold the keys of death' (Revelation 1:17, 18). The lack of a sense of an after-life in all the Old Testament literature until the last books is disconcerting and the christianization of a text like this is unconvincing. Hezekiah did not in fact die and what he feared was complete extinction. The long Canticle of Moses, though much abbreviated (Deuteronomy 32:1–12), remains unappealing. The Canticle of Habakkuk (also abbreviated 3:2–4, 13a, 16–19), in spite of its corrupt Hebrew text which provides great difficulties in translation, is a good paschal hymn (compare its use in the former Good Friday service) but it takes some understanding. The Canticle of Hannah (1 Samuel 2:1–10) makes a good prayer and an explicit reference is made to the *Magnificat* by the title. There seems to have been a re-discovery by liturgicals of

Ezekiel 36:24–28 (as well as of Jeremiah 31:10–14) in recent years; it appears an astonishing number of times everywhere in the new liturgy. A canticle one would like to have seen excluded is Ben Sirach (*alias* Ecclesiasticus) 36:1–7, 13–16, which oddly enough appeared as an epistle in the old missal for the Propagation of the Faith:

> Save us, O God of all things,
> *strike all the nations with terror*;
> *raise your hand against foreign nations* (!)
> that they may see the greatness of your might.
> Our sufferings proved your holiness to them;
> *let their downfall prove your glory to us* . . .

A strange way of converting people one might think. It is plainly sub-Christian and has no place in the Christian liturgy.

The use of New Testament canticles (apart from the traditional three) is an innovation and one to be welcomed. Here we are aware that we have to do with specifically Christian prayers and from this point of view they provide no difficulty. Ephesians 1:3–10 and Colossians 1:12–20 are very dense texts (one reason for using them in the office) but they need help from commentaries if the full richness of their content is to be appreciated. The canticles from Revelation are somewhat fabricated, verses from different places, even different chapters, being combined. The result would seem to show that the procedure was justified. All these canticles are well allocated and of course their use is restricted to Vespers. Ephesians 1:3–10 however is somewhat over-used. It appears in Monday Vespers and is used for feasts of the Blessed Virgin Mary, for apostles and for other saints when their anniversaries are kept as *festa*. This means that you might have to say it on Monday and again for a feast of Our Lady on Tuesday and for a *festum* of a saint on Friday – altogether too much of a good thing. The reason why it has been selected for these occasions is to be found, it would seem, in the phrases 'He chose us in him . . . that we should be holy . . . He destined us in love to be his sons through Jesus Christ. . . .' The whole text in fact underlines the total dependence of the saints on Christ.

There is another question connected with these canticles, especially some of the New Testament ones. It is the matter of translation. In the Greek Ephesians 1:3–10 (all one sentence) goes with a fine swing which is also palpable in the Vulgate. This is made possible largely through the

~

107

use of participles both in the Greek and in the Latin. Understandably modern translations bow to the necessity of breaking up the clauses if only to make the passage intelligible. In the process they have destroyed the rhythm. In the Ephesians passage (the translation is that of RSV) we have a very inelegant repetition: 'according to his purpose which he set forth in Christ. / His purpose he set forth in Christ as a plan. . . .' A different and freer form of translation would seem to be required. These texts are now being used as *prayers*, they are not the subject of learned exegesis, and while keeping as close as possible to the original text translators should be encouraged to produce more rhythmical texts that can be both said and sung with pleasure.

Finally, a word must be said about the canticle from Revelation 19:1–2, 5–7. It is a splendid piece of course and one is glad to see it included in the office. It is the song of the bridal church to Christ and to his Father. But not counting those of the antiphon, it is 'decorated' with no less than sixteen Alleluias of which eight may be omitted in private recitation! I fear the revisers have over-done it. Perhaps if you sing the text in *Latin* and if you have choir/cantor and assembly this could be made effective though even then the thought of doing this every Sunday of the year (except in Lent) makes one blench. In private recitation or in recitation with a small group the continual iteration of Alleluia is bizarre. I think we should be justified in using our own discretion in the matter.[27]

Notes

[1] See Rembert G. Weakland, 'L'homme d'aujourd'hui et l'office divin', LMD, 95 (1968), pp. 66ff., conveying the criticisms of young monks and clerics.

[2] It is sometimes possible to detect the redaction processes. See, for example, the last two verses of Ps. 50 which seem to be a post-exilic addition and something of a contradiction of verses 18–19.

[3] Cf. Deut 6:4.

[4] See G. Vann, *On Being Human* (London, 1933), p. 46, n. 1. The whole passage he translates as follows: 'In the coming forth of creatures from their first principle there is a sort of circling back, inasmuch as all things return as to their end to that from which in the beginning as from a principle they sprang (**prodierunt**)' (**Sentences**, Dist. xiv, q. 2, a. 2).

[5] Weakland, **art. cit.**, pp. 67–8.

[6] The chief authority is Balthasar Fischer. See 'Le Christ dans les psaumes', LMD, 27 (1951), pp. 86–109. It is a summary of his doctoral thesis of 1946. Cf. also a

further study by François Vandenbroucke in QLP, 4 (1952), pp. 149–166; 5 (1952), pp. 201–213. One can also refer to J. Daniélou, **The Bible and the Liturgy** (London, 1960), especially ch. 11, 'Psalm XXII', and L. Bouyer, **Bible et Evangile** (Paris, 1951), ch. 12.

[7] See **art. cit.**, pp. 105–8.

[8] **Art. cit.**, p. 92.

[9] **Art. cit.**, p. 93: **Psalmus vox totius Christi, capitis et corporis.**

[10] PL 36.

[11] See Vandenbroucke, QLP, 5, pp. 207–11.

[12] GI 113.

[13] See Vandenbroucke, **art.** and **loc. cit.**, who gives long lists which however refer to the old missal and breviary.

[14] The same identification is made, if I remember rightly, on an early catacomb painting.

[15] Ecological problems so early?

[16] I am dubious in any case about this term which seems to have been devised by Professor Fischer. 'Christology' is usually taken to mean the theology of Christ, principally in the incarnation. The alternative 'the Christian sense or interpretation of the psalms' is clumsy but, as it seems to me, more accurate.

[17] See Fischer, LMD, 27, p. 88. But see above, p. 73.

[18] See **ibid.**, pp. 102–3. He records that St Thérèse of Lisieux did this with a phrase from Ps. 118: 'Inclinavi cor meum ad justificationes tuas **proper retributionem** ("I bow my heart to your commands for reward" – the reward I shall get!)'. **She** said 'O Jesus mine, you know that it is not for reward that I serve you but uniquely because I love you and to save souls'.

[19] **Comparative Liturgy** (London, 1958), p. 34.

[20] See John Cassian, **Institutes** II: LHEW, p. 59.

[21] See Vandenbroucke, **art. cit.**, p. 150 and n. 1 for the date of its insertion. Cf. also P. Salmon, EP, p. 822.

[22] P. Verbraken, **Oraisons sur les 150 Psaumes** (Paris, 1967). The author has used three collections, African, Roman and Spanish. Salmon, EP, p. 821, states that six series are known.

[23] GI 112. A booklet was published some years ago containing these collects. Some are helpful, some not.

[24] The **Psautier de la Bible de Jérusalem** (Paris, 1961), p. 256. The collects were written by J. Gelineau and D. Rimaud. The whole edition, which does not seem to be well known, is worth attention. It has longish 'titles', is pointed for singing (in French) and of course has the collects.

[25] JBC, II, pp. 614–19 (R. Brown); cf. NJBC, p. 1157.

[26] In A. Bugnini, **The Reform of the Liturgy** (Eng. trans., Liturgical Press, Collegeville, MN, 1990; pp. 525–6), writing of the addition of the NT canticles, the author states that they were added since the psalms speak of Christ prophetically and the NT canticles speak of the reality of the mystery of Christ.

[27] There is a similar difficulty in Eastertide. Frankly, there are too many Alleluias and it is difficult to see why they should have been added to a text like 'Into your hands I commend my spirit' of Compline. In the Latin office they often worked, though even there they sometimes split an antiphon in half. The revisers seem to have retained these Alleluias without giving much thought to the matter.

SIX

The Lectionaries

~~~~~~~

THE EXISTENCE OF THREE lectionaries in an office raises questions and calls for a more extended comment than could be given in an earlier chapter.[1] What is the purpose of a biblical lectionary and need it be printed in the office book? Why should there be a patristic lectionary and why should there be yet another for saints' feasts? We will try to answer these questions in what follows.

As we have seen in an earlier chapter, when the cathedral office was the prayer of the church there was but one lesson in morning and evening prayer and it is improbable, to say the least, that there was a continuous course. But when stable communities were established and the night office came into existence it was obviously possible to use a fixed course of readings and this is what happened. St Benedict witnesses to the existence of such a course as also to the division of the biblical material into *lectiones*. From him too we know that there was a patristic lectionary. The third, consisting of the 'passions' of the martyrs and the 'legends' of the saints, appears, it would seem, in the Gallican region in the seventh century.[2] The inclusion then of a *lectio continua* of the Bible as of the patristic and hagiographical lectionaries is another instance of monastic influence on the office.

When the lessons could be read out in choir from a single book there was no problem about their length and the community or its abbot, no doubt depending on tradition, could make the necessary selection. Difficulties begin when you try to cram a lectionary into a 'breviary'. The inevitable result is, as we know, abbreviation and the problem of the Bible lectionary has never been wholly solved. The revisers of the new office have made another attempt to do so and we shall have to examine their work in due course. But before we do so, it will, I think, be profitable to look at the purpose and pattern of the old Roman lectionaries which reveal a certain understanding of the scriptures as seen in the early tradition.

The Bible lectionary

At least in the Roman tradition the order in which the books of the Bible were read during the year was a matter of greater concern than the details of the pericopes to be used.[3]

The course of readings to be found in *Ordo* XIV (Andrieu), which may go back to the time of Gregory the Great, is as follows:

> From Quinquagesima Sunday (i.e. approximately fifty days before Easter) until the Saturday before Palm Sunday the Roman church read the first six books of the Bible (Genesis to Joshua);
>
> in Holy Week the readings were evidently 'proper': selected extracts from Isaiah and for the last three days the Lamentations of Jeremiah;
>
> from Easter to Pentecost the readings were from the 'Catholic Epistles', the Acts of the Apostles and the Apocalypse;
>
> from then until 17 October the books of Samuel, Kings and Chronicles were read;
>
> then, until 1 December there were the Wisdom books, Judith, Esther, Tobit and Maccabees;
>
> from Advent to the Epiphany Isaiah, Jeremiah and Daniel were read;
>
> Ezekiel, the 'minor' prophets and Job filled up the rest of the time until 13 February (presumably omitted when there was an early Easter).

One book only was omitted, Esdras, perhaps, says Salmon, because of the existing doubts about the canonicity of Third and Fourth Esdras. The letters of St Paul were allocated either to the eucharist or to the end of Vigils or to the first three lessons but in any case the reading was not continuous.[4]

Another lectionary of the eighth century and in use in the Lateran (*Ordo* XIIIA, Andrieu) slightly modifies the former and provides the basis for the lectionary that existed in the office until the recent revision.[5] The Pentateuch, Joshua, Judges and perhaps Ruth were read from Septuagesima to Passion Sunday when the reading of Jeremiah began. After Easter the readings were taken from 'the Acts of the Apostles, the seven canonical epistles and the Apocalypse' and continued until the end of the octave of Pentecost. From then until the first Sunday of August the books of Samuel, Kings and Chronicles were read. To August were allocated the Wisdom books, and to September Job, Tobit, Judith, Esther and Esdras. 1 and 2 Maccabees were read in October and in November Ezekiel, Daniel and the minor prophets. Isaiah occupied the month of December and after Christmas until Septuagesima the epistles of St Paul were read.

The differences between the two series are not very great and we may assume that there were reasons for this pattern. The purpose of the Bible lectionary was not of course the scientific study of the Bible nor yet simply a complete knowledge of the whole text though at this time and for centuries it was regarded with great reverence. In the words of Pierre Salmon,[6] 'the aim was to teach the faithful the history of salvation, its preparation, its types, its prophecies and its fulfilment in the life and work of Christ and its continuation in the church'. It was no coincidence then that the readings began at Septuagesima, then regarded as the beginning of the liturgical year, with the book of Genesis which gives the story of creation which is to be restored by the redeeming work of Christ. Here and in the books that followed are all the great events that prepared for the coming of Christ, and all the types, like Abraham, the 'redemption' from Egypt, the passage through the Red Sea and the making of the covenant in the desert, that were seen as foreshadowings of the redeeming work of Christ. The Christians of that time 'read' the events of the Old Testament in the light of the New (*novum testamentum in vetere latet; vetus testamentum in novo patet*[7]) and accepted prophecy in all simplicity as prediction. As the monks heard the words *Ecce virgo concipiet . . .* read out in the flickering light of a candle they instinctively translated 'Behold the Virgin (Mary) shall conceive . . .'. We have ineluctably become more sophisticated though it is a question whether we are any nearer the truth.

To continue, the oldest part of the liturgical year, the *Pentecoste*, has a lectionary that is as old as St Augustine and perhaps older, basically the Acts of the Apostles and the Apocalypse. The reason is that, as an ancient collect for the Easter Vigil (quoted in the Constitution on the Liturgy (5)) has it, from the side of Christ as he lay in the sleep of death on the cross came forth the wonderful sacrament of the church. The church in Acts is seen as carrying on the redeeming word and work of Christ and that is why it is read at this time. On the broadest view the Apocalypse is to be seen as a cosmic view of human history, under the ultimate control of God, but fraught with pain, persecution and suffering which the church must endure if she is to be faithful to the Faithful Witness and to be gathered to him as his Bride 'without spot or wrinkle'. To put the matter in another way, the Apocalypse is the history of the church as she makes her painful pilgrimage from the time of the resurrection to the consummation. The 'canonical' or 'Catholic' epistles, with their 'household codes' and strong moral emphasis, may be regarded as indicating the behaviour that is proper to members of the Risen Christ.

The readings from Samuel and Kings continue the history of salvation in which David, the type of the Messiah, plays a central role. After this the pattern becomes less clear until we come to November. The Wisdom literature, with which should be included Job, can be seen as a reflection on the great saving events (as indeed so much of it is), and as a recollection in tranquillity (in the hot summer months of southern Europe!) of the significance of those events. The readings for the rest of September are somewhat miscellaneous though Tobit, Judith and Esther can be understood as typical of the great heroes and heroines who in one way or another carried forward the purpose of God. With Maccabees in October we take up again the history of salvation. The last part of the liturgical year is concerned with the Day of the Lord and the consummation of all things in Christ. Evidently, the readings from Ezekiel, Daniel and the minor prophets are appropriate for this time. Isaiah in this scheme becomes understandably the exclusive prophet of the incarnation. It is less easy to account for the letters of St Paul after Christmas but I would hazard the guess that since in the Roman liturgy of the time, as also in the Sermons of St Leo for Christmas, the redemptive aspect of the incarnation is much emphasized, St Paul, who deals with both the incarnation and the redemption in all their depth and richness, can be seen as continuing the message of the Christmas season.

Whatever we may think of the procedure – and it is to be doubted whether it was ever formally thought out – this, as far as we can discern, was the understanding of the Bible that underlay the whole scheme. The modern and more critical assessment of the 'spiritual' or fulfilled sense of holy scripture has made us more cautious in our use of it but has not, I think, invalidated the older view. In many ways it has strengthened it.[8] With minor alterations, and unhappily drastic abbreviations, this lectionary survived the centuries and was to be found in the breviary of Pius V and indeed in the breviary that has only recently been superseded by the new office.

~

This pattern of the lectionary, then, indicated the main purpose of the readings. There was another which is summed up in the traditional phrase *lectio divina*. The primary intent of the readings was not to give a complete verbal knowledge of the whole Bible though this is in fact what the monks achieved. Even a superficial acquaintance with the literature that came from the monasteries reveals a quite astonishing knowledge of the Latin Bible. Its texts in all its parts became part of the mind of the monks. But this was a sort of by-product. The purpose of the readings was that the monks should be able to nourish their spiritual life on the word of the Bible. Like the devout Christian of St Augustine, they listened to God's word and ruminated on it afterwards. Formal meditation of the kind typical of the post-Tridentine church seems to have been unknown in the monastic centuries and indeed for long afterwards. The monks filled their minds with the word of holy scripture and during the night office by means of the responsories meditated on its meaning, a meditation that was continued during the day. Hence the need for silence and the continued reading of the Bible in the refectory. The fruits of this system—if such it can be called—are to be seen in what scholars have called the monastic theology that preceded scholasticism and of which there are a number of examples in the lectionary of the new office. Whether and how far the pastoral clergy, even when they had the texts, were able to profit from this kind of reading is another matter. The drastic abbreviation of the scripture lessons over the centuries certainly made them less attractive.

When we come to examine the lectionary the revisers have constructed we see that they have kept substantially the pattern of the old lectionary though with very considerable changes. Responding to the requirements of Vatican II (CL 92) that a better provision of Bible readings should be made in the revised office, an attempt has been made to include practically the whole Bible in the biennial course (short of the gospels of course which appear in the Mass-lectionary). This at least was the intention of the revisers but they have in fact produced a one-year cycle which seems to be a modification of the two-year cycle.[9] I cannot pretend that I have got the matter clear. All I can do is to summarize the Introduction 145–153 and then make some observations on the lectionary as it has already appeared.

1. For Advent we have Isaiah with the addition of the book of Ruth and certain passages from Micah. This is traditional enough though the

addition of Ruth seems to be an innovation, wholly appropriate as it is in this place (she was the ancestress of David and so of the Messianic line).

2. The period after Christmas which used to begin with Romans is now occupied with Colossians 'in which the incarnation of the Lord is considered in the context of the whole history of salvation' (148). For the second cycle the Song of Songs, interpreted as the marriage between God and his people, is prescribed but does not (yet) appear in the office book.

3. For the period after Christmas the rest of Isaiah and Baruch (absent) are prescribed.

4. Lent (Thursday after Ash Wednesday) begins with Exodus which is read during the first three weeks; then come Leviticus and Numbers, which are followed by the Letter to the Hebrews until the end of Holy Week. What was *intended* is that Deuteronomy and Hebrews should be read in cycle I and Exodus, Leviticus and Numbers in cycle II. In the book as published Deuteronomy now comes in weeks 2 and 3 of the ordinary time of the year and so will normally precede Lent. It is noteworthy that there are no readings from the Old Testament in Holy Week. Yet the revisers intended that two of the Servant Songs and passages from Lamentations should be read in cycle I and extracts from Jeremiah in cycle II.

5. In Easter Week 1 Peter is read and thereafter the Apocalypse (Weeks 2 to 5). The three Johannine letters cover the rest of the period. (There are exceptions for Sunday 2 and of course for the Ascension.) Originally it was intended that 1 Peter, the Johannine letters and the Apocalypse should be read in cycle I and the Acts in cycle II. Since Acts is to be found substantially in the Mass-lectionary this change is not catastrophic.

6. It would be tedious to detail all the books that are read from the Monday after Trinity until Advent. Suffice it to say that the history of salvation is taken up on the Monday after Trinity with readings from 1 and 2 Samuel which are followed by those from 1 and 2 Kings. But all these readings are interspersed with readings from the Pauline epistles and indeed with extracts from the prophets. Thus while the traditional arrangement can still be discerned it is clear that here the revisers have innovated. It was intended that there should be a two-year cycle (152) when these books would have been better distributed and, I suspect,

there would have been a more adequate representation of them. The epistles are read in full and almost always well divided. This cannot always be said of the Old Testament readings.

Finally, the Introduction states that 'the single year arrangement is abbreviated in such a way that every year passages are selected complementary to the two-year sequence of scripture readings at (weekday) Mass' (152). A detailed examination of this would be lengthy and cannot be done here. In any case, perhaps the details do not matter over-much. Sufficient of the traditional arrangement has been preserved to make it possible to use the lectionary as *lectio divina*. At the same time, I have found it profitable to read the lessons directly from the Bible. Then one discovers the context and the many gaps left by the lectionary can be filled in. If one uses the Jerusalem Bible with its invaluable notes, particularly necessary for the prophetic literature and the Apocalypse, the reading becomes more profitable still. It is I believe an illusion to think that we can, like medieval or even seventeenth-century Christians, read the *nudus textus* with spiritual profit. Modern Christians feel that if their *lectio* is to be really *divina*, they must come as close as possible to the original meaning of the text and then go on from there.

In the light of these last considerations and of the difficulty of including a biblical lectionary in a liturgical book, one is led to question the whole policy of providing such a lectionary. Surely the clergy can be expected to possess a Bible and to read it and nowadays vast numbers of the laity have and read a Bible if not always systematically. If the argument is that 'when you are travelling' (another instance of the *argumentum ex turismo?*) it is inconvenient to carry around a Bible with you, it would have been easy enough to include a sufficient selection of Bible readings in the volume to last two or three weeks. However it can be readily agreed that the new lectionary is infinitely superior to the old. Even as it exists it presents a very great part of the Bible and, as far as I can see, the whole of the New Testament. If the insertion of certain books or parts of books here and there is a little difficult to understand, as a whole the lectionary makes sense and is a useful instrument for the pastoral and spiritual life. (The above argument still has a certain strength but since the revisers have for good reasons omitted duplications in the sacred text and long lists of objects–e.g. Exodus, the description of the Tabernacle–and of people–genealogies that crop up everywhere–the use of an unmarked Bible is hardly possible. Some passages are shortened, verses omitted and so on. All these arrangements have been made by scripture scholars and lighten the burden of reading the whole Bible without any aids at all. Still, it would have been pleasant to have had a breviary that is much smaller than the *Divine Office* is, and the French and the Germans have indeed managed to do this by the use of fascicles for the scriptures and other readings.)

The patristic lectionary

The Introduction (163–165) gives three reasons for the inclusion of a patristic lectionary in the office:

1. It offers a meditation on the scripture readings.
2. It gives an authentic interpretation of the word of God.
3. The readings from this lectionary teach Christians the meaning of the feasts and seasons of the liturgical year.

About the last point there can be no doubt at all and if preacher or people are to do justice to the Mass-texts it is usually necessary to look at the patristic texts as they appear in the office. But it is a little difficult to know what weight to attach to the word 'authentic'. Most of the Fathers knew no Hebrew and the Latin Fathers from Augustine onwards knew little or no Greek. Apart from a few giants like Jerome, when he is not being Origenist, Chrysostom on St Paul, and Leo in his homilies where he remains very close to his texts, we cannot look to the Fathers for a *literal* interpretation. Even in the new lectionary there is a certain amount of allegory like this passage of Gregory of Nyssa: 'In this creation the sun is pure life; *the stars are virtues; the air is candid behaviour;* the *sea is depth* and the riches of wisdom and knowledge . . . *the trees bearing fruit are the observance of the commandments*' (Monday, Week 5, Eastertide). It is elegant, as Gregory always is, it is charming and the whole passage is full of New Testament echoes but it remains allegory which we are not required to take *au pied de la lettre*. What 'authentic' evidently means is that broadly the Fathers transmit the continuing Catholic tradition and in this they are peculiarly effective, as the Introduction says, in their interpretation of the greater seasons and feasts.

There are other values in the patristic lectionary. Didactically the Fathers keep before us the broad spectrum of Christian writing which we ignore to our own impoverishment. It is possible for our Catholicism to be geographically broad but chronologically shallow. And the Fathers at their best, like Augustine on St John, have a depth of penetration that takes us beyond any literalist interpretation. In this, as St Benedict saw, they assist the *lectio divina* of the scriptures. At another and less important level they remind us of the history of the church, in the sense that in various ways they suggest the continuing life of devotion and aspiration towards God which is the real history of the church. In this context it would have been helpful to append to the names of the Fathers and other writers the date of their death. Who can lay his hand on his heart and say when Aphraates flourished?[10] Nearer home is Fulgentius of Ruspe. How many of us know that he lived in the late fifth century and is an echo, often a feeble echo, of Augustine?

We must then see the patristic lectionary principally as an aid to *lectio divina* and it is clear that especially in the 'ordinary time' of the year the patristic lesson is a commentary on the scripture reading. For the great feasts it takes up one or other aspect of the scripture reading or conveys the meaning of the feast as a whole. In this respect Leo the Great, Maximus of Turin (on the paschal mystery and its consequences), St Gregory Nazianzen, and St Augustine when he is concerned more with the feast than with the exegesis of a text, are particularly effective. St Gregory the Great too, a difficult writer to 'extract', scores a bull with his homily on the Good Shepherd (Sunday 4, Eastertide). For the Easter season the revisers apparently gave up hope of finding a suitable commentator for the Apocalypse. Possibly there is no suitable candidate. In the vast literature on the Apocalypse, which has attracted every kind of oddity in the church from the second century until now, it would seem that only Andrew of Caesarea (Greek, fifth or sixth century) or Primasius (Latin, African, sixth century) are likely to provide suitable material.[11]

The same rule has been applied to the other great seasons of the year: the writers expound the mystery or the meaning of the period. Thus in the last part of Advent we find Ambrose, Bede and Bernard commenting on the infancy gospel of Luke. Leo remains the chief commentator on Christmas and Epiphany. For Holy Week we find a variety of authors and for Good Friday Chrysostom on the blood and water that flowed from the side of Christ after the piercing of his side.[12]

During Easter week when 1 Peter is read, the patristic readings expound various aspects of the paschal mystery. For Monday there is Melito of Sardis (*c.* 166), perhaps the earliest and most interesting expositor of the paschal mystery. The readings from the last three days of the week are taken from the Mystagogical Catecheses traditionally attributed to Cyril of Jerusalem. More from the same source for this week would have been welcome, especially as the piece from 'an unknown author' (sometimes thought to have been Hippolytus) of the second century does not in fact say very much.

When we leave the great seasons and feasts commentary becomes difficult. The amount of material is vast, writers from East and West, writing in Syriac, Greek and Latin, not to mention a few writing in modern languages, appear in the lectionary. In time they run from Clement of Rome to Vatican II and if the generous allocation of the sub-apostolic Fathers is much to be welcomed, the way they are broken up and used from time to time as commentary (for which they are not suitable) is not so satisfactory. Hippolytus in his scripture commentaries does not suffer extraction very well but Irenaeus, who has been very carefully selected, does. In fact he is the one early writer, much used in the lectionary, who stands out above most of the others. He has important things to say and he is allowed to say them. The translation seems to be excellent, no doubt benefiting from the Sources Chrétiennes edition.[13] Another notable feature of the lectionary is that the revisers have drawn generously on the Greek Fathers, who were poorly represented in the old. Aphraates, Ephrem and Theodore of Mopsuestia represent the Syriac Fathers. The range of Latin writers has been considerably extended and among other things the revisers have been able to take advantage of the discoveries of scholars in, for example, the matter of the sermons of St Augustine. But what is new is that writers of the monastic centuries like Isaac of Stella, William of St Thierry, as well of course as St Bernard, have been used. St Thomas Aquinas, in all the simplicity of his homiletic or expository style, St Bonaventure, and lastly the *Imitation of Christ*, represent the later Middle Ages. There has, I think, been a subtle change. The *Imitation* and the extracts from post-Tridentine writers like St John of the Cross and St Teresa turn the reading into a *lectio spiritualis* of the more modern kind. Tastes and judgements will differ but these writers and some others do not seem to be quite in harmony with the tradition of the liturgy.

But this suggests another consideration. Good as the Fathers are, at least at their best, and helpful as the more modern spiritual writers may be judged to be, often their preoccupations are not ours. It is true that a modern note is sounded by extracts from the Council documents but the question suggests itself: have contemporary writers who share our concerns no place in the lectionary? The decision was made to exclude living or recently dead writers (e.g. Thomas Merton) and perhaps with a good deal of justice. Still, it is a pity that a writer like Newman, who has been teaching the church for a hundred years and whose sermons, the Plain and Parochial, so often provide superb material for the great seasons and Sundays of the year, was not included.[14] In any case there would seem to be no reason why a community or an assembly should not read a supplementary lesson from a modern author after the one given in the office.

In so vast a collection of literature it would not be surprising if there were weaker pieces and that is in fact the case. Hippolytus to Noetus (I, p. 163) does not really say very much in the extract given. Origen on Abraham is more allegorical than typological though it is a moving piece and Hilary on the beard of Aaron is more than a little fanciful. Maximus the Confessor has this on the redeeming act of Christ: 'he offered his flesh as a bait to provoke the insatiable dragon to devour the flesh which he was greedily pursuing' which suggests the 'paying of a debt to Satan' kind of soteriology. Minor and obscure writers do not come off very well. John of Naples, whoever he was,[15] has an 'élévation' of the Bossuet kind of *Dominus illuminatio mea* and Gregory of Agrigentum starts off well with one or two down to earth observations and then goes on to the 'spiritual meaning' which is really allegorical. Zeno of Verona, who can write succinctly on the paschal mystery, is not seen at his best in taking Job as a type of Christ. Dorotheus, a Greek ascetic writer of the sixth century, is not really very satisfactory on the book of Job. Tastes and needs will differ but I do not find Isaac of Stella who provides a reading on the church as the mystical body (I, 95) or William of St Thierry or Guerric d'Igny, all monastic writers, very satisfactory. The lesson of the first is over-contrived and the other two seem to be working in a tradition that is already becoming exhausted. The oddest juxtaposition I have noted is on Deuteronomy 32, the death of Moses, on which the commentary provided is from the Constitution on the Church in the Modern World on the mystery of death. I doubt whether the *death* of Moses is the point of the story.

The translations in the Divine Office of this vast and varied collection of readings seem to be good. Those of Irenaeus, as I have said, are outstandingly good. Where I have been able to test translations of other texts I have found them accurate though at times the style is a little old-fashioned.[16] Wherever possible modern translations of good quality have been used. For the rest the translators remain anonymous. In one place the translator does not seem to be very familiar with the style of St Leo. In his well-known sermon on the Passion (8) Leo has 'ordo clarior *levitarum*, et dignitas amplior *seniorum* et sacratior est unctio *sacerdotum*'. What Leo meant was 'deacons', 'presbyters' and 'bishops' and that is how I believe the passage should be translated. Finally, examination of a number of texts shows that the English translations are sometimes better than the Latin translations in the *Liturgia Horarum* which the revisers often took simply from what was available in Migne.

Obviously much more could be said of this lectionary, both for and against it. We must see it as a remarkable anthology of Christian literature which should prove to be of great value to those who use it. But again, whether or not it was wise to include it in the office book is another matter. The device of a supplementary volume would have met the case and the extracts could perhaps have been even longer. (The supplementary volume that is expected before long will contain a second cycle of patristic readings which will be very welcome. Whether they will be longer than the existing extracts remains to be seen.)

The hagiographical lectionary

The principles on which this lectionary is constructed have been mentioned elsewhere[17] and there is no need to repeat them. But those same principles mean that a very wide spectrum of religious literature is to be found in this lectionary: writings of the Fathers, extracts from the writings (when they exist) of canonized saints and other passages from other writers which comment suitably on the life of the saint. The decision to use this method for the saints' feasts has relieved the office of a whole mass of fiction, much of which had become the target of clerical mockery: 'to lie like a second nocturn' was a hoary clerical joke. Even the most respectable legends, like those for the offices of St Cecily and St Clement, have gone and who can regret the disappearance of the wholly fictitious lesson on St Alexius? Those on the Trinitarian saints (i.e. saints of the Order of the Holy Trinity for the Redemption of Captives) were in the same category. If a little colour has gone from the office, let us remember that it was meretricious. The Introduction insists on 'historical truth' for the lessons of the saints and in doing so is merely repeating what has been said since the sixteenth century. Whether or not these legends had any religious value may perhaps be a matter of discussion.[18] But if there is regret that some of these texts have gone, the loss is amply compensated for by the new lessons. St Gregory Nazianzen on Basil and his friendship with him is worth more than all the second-hand disquisitions from someone who never knew him. It is obviously right that we should have Athanasius on St Antony, the desert father, and who is not moved by reading Cyprian on the martyrdom of Pope Fabian? In another genre St Ambrose on St Agnes, even if all his facts are not correct, has got the spirit of the saint admirably. The contemporary account of the Japanese martyrs, St Paul Miki and his companions, has an immediacy that no other kind of writing can give. Leaping back fourteen centuries we rejoice to read an extract from the contemporary 'passion' of St Perpetua and St Felicity. This is sufficient to show that almost all these readings are apt and can be read with profit and pleasure.

But not all saints are literary geniuses nor necessarily those who write about them. You may not feel moved by reading St Angela Merici's exhortation to her nuns and the literary style of St Brigit of Sweden may be too emotional for you but a great number of these readings occur on optional *memoriae* so one is under no obligation to read them at all. It may be a shock, but surely a salutary shock, to find St Leo with a sermon on the incarnation allocated to the *memoria* of Our Lady of Mount Carmel when we remember what was there before. A reading from the Rule of St Benedict is preferable to even the Dialogues with all their charming naïvety. On the other hand one regrets the absence of St Ambrose's splendid piece of rhetoric on the martyrdom of St John Baptist. It is replaced with something much tamer. Since we must end somewhere, let us rejoice in the inclusion of Thomas More's letter to his daughter Meg for the feast of St John Fisher and St Thomas More.[19]

The biographical notes before the lesson are brief, usually succinct, and help to situate the saint in the history of the church.

Notes

[1] See pp. 82–5.
[2] P. Salmon, EP, pp. 826–8. Its inclusion in the Roman office is attributed to Pope Adrian I (died 795).

3 **Ibid.**, p. 826. For details of the Roman lectionaries described below see his *L'Office Divin* (Paris, 1959), ch. 4.

4 P. Salmon, OD, p. 137.

5 See **ibid.**, pp. 137–8.

6 **Ibid.**, p. 137.

7 'The New Testament is hidden in the Old Testament and the Old Testament is made plain in the New.'

8 Cf. R. Brown in JBC, II, pp. 611–19; considerably modified NJBC, pp. 1153–62.

9 See A. Bugnini, **The Reform of the Liturgy** (Eng. trans., Liturgical Press, Collegeville, MN, 1990). The matter is explained in the above book, p. 536: 'The presidency of the Consilium decided that the amount of material must be reduced by eliminating elements not indispensable and **putting these in a supplementary** volume that would nonetheless be part of the typical edition. But the problem created by the two-year cycle of biblical readings remained, and it was decided to create an annual cycle by selecting from the two-year cycle the parts best suited to each liturgical season. The annual cycle thus developed was included in the typical edition of the **Liturgia Horarum**.' In fact the second cycle of readings has been in circulation for some years: **Two-Year Cycle of the Scriptural Passages for the Office of Readings**. Only references are given and it is not easy to use but when published in full it will give a satisfactory variety: e.g. 1 Advent, year I: Isaiah 6:1–13; year II: Isaiah 1:1–18 (which is the one now in the Breviary; the first is the call of Isaiah).

10 The answer is apparently **post** 345. He was the first of the Syriac Fathers (see J. Tixeront, **Précis de Patrologie** (1927), pp. 2854–5, and ODCC, s.v., p. 68). Between 1927 and 1974 (the latest edition of ODCC) it would seem that nothing further has been learned of his date.

11 See E. B. Allo, **Saint Jean, L'Apocalypse** (Paris, 1933), pp. ccxlvi, ccxlviii.

12 Good as this is one would have preferred the great sermon of Leo (**De Pass**. 8) which gives the whole mystery of the cross. It used to appear for this day in the Dominican office and is of course to be found elsewhere (Lent 5 Tuesday).

13 Sources Chrétiennes nos. 34, 100, 152, 153. Irenaeus wrote in Greek but much of his work survives only in a Latin translation which is so literal that unless you are able to translate it back into Greek it is often obscure. And few of us can be expected to do that.

14 There were one or two extracts – in French – in the draft lectionary. Local conferences of bishops may compile supplementary lectionaries. Cf. GI 162. Such supplementary lectionaries have already appeared, notably that drawn up by the monks of Orval and the lectionary of the English Benedictines (obtainable from Stanbrook Abbey, Worcestershire). An example of an extensive anthology of mostly modern writers for the Anglican Office is C. R. Campling, **The Fourth Lesson**, 2 vols (London, 1973–74).

15 He is unknown to ODCC.

16 I have wondered whether the translations in the **Ante- and Post-Nicene Fathers**, now over ninety years old, have been used.

17 Above, pp. 84–5.

18 See **Notitiae** 103 (1975), 2/3, pp. 83–7.

19 The former has at least one lesson elsewhere.

SEVEN

~

The Hymnary

~~~~~~

O F ALL THE PARTS of the office this is the one I find it most difficult to write about. In the *Liturgia Horarum* there is a vast collection of hymns most of which seem to come from obscure medieval sources. In the *Divine Office* there is yet another collection which coincides with the former only on the greater feasts. To do justice to all this material one would have to be both a prosodist and a seasoned literary critic. The present writer is neither but as it is admitted that hymns need not always be good poetry, perhaps he may be allowed a few observations.

The Introduction (173) states that hymns have had their place in the office from early times, that their lyrical character makes them specially suited to the praise of God and that they are a popular element in the celebration of the office. There is of course a high degree of truth in those statements on the assumption that choral celebration of the office is a regular feature of the church's life. But immediately we are brought up against two problems: the nature of the hymn, and the quantity of hymns that even a community can be expected to sing in the course of a day.

1. Although the matter is not beyond dispute, hymns seem to demand that by their nature they should be *sung*. In private recitation, which is the lot of most of the users of the office, this is obviously impossible. Can they profitably be *said*? There are those who hold that they can but at once we are brought up against the literary quality of the hymn. Everyone knows that many well-loved hymns are of poor literary quality and if you read them or say them their poverty stands out immediately so that they become a barrier and not an aid to prayer. Everyone knows too that a good melody can redeem a poor hymn and that in the last resort is why they are popular. There does not seem to be any solution along these lines.

2. If a community, especially one that is not particularly skilled in singing, is going to celebrate the office chorally, five hymns a day in addition to the psalms and canticles like the *Benedictus* and the *Magnificat*,

~
124

are going to tax their powers. If the material is not particularly distinguished they will perhaps think that the effort is not worth while.

For there is yet a third difficulty. The number of really great hymns in the Western church from the time of St Ambrose until today is not very great. By great hymns one means those that express an insight into a feast or season in memorable language. These because of their depth of meaning and language can be repeated year after year though hymns like *Pange, lingua, gloriosi* or *Vexilla regis* more easily bear repetition in Latin, no doubt because in their original language they are great verse. We are faced with the problem of the shortage of really good hymns and the conclusion that was forced on me after using the office in Latin for some time was that the collection in *Liturgia Horarum* was not a very distinguished one. The Introduction (178) states that local conferences of bishops may adapt the Latin hymns 'to the nature of their language' and introduce new ones *provided* they are suited to the spirit of the hour, the season or the feast. What the editors of the *Divine Office* have done is to draw on the abundant and varied hymnology of the English tradition which to a great extent derives from the Anglican and Free Churches. To hymns from these sources they have added others, usually the translations of Caswall, Knox and a few others. The nuns of Stanbrook Abbey have made some attractive, original contributions.

The construction of the hymnary was in itself a major undertaking. A vast corpus of material had to be examined and hymns appropriate to the hour, day, season and feast had to be selected. Since a great number of these hymns were not written with the prayer of the Divine Office in view, the difficulty of selection was all the greater. If one is not always enchanted with the results it is probably because the compilers had set themselves an impossible task. The dangers of subjective criticism are considerable in this matter and this must be kept in mind in what follows.

Let us look at the provision made for Advent. We find E. Caswall's translation of *En clara vox* though drastically shortened to three verses (a quite constant practice of the compilers). This is followed by what seems to be a translation of *Conditor alme siderum* (though we are not told it is), a quite attractive piece but again only four verses. Charles Coffin's[1] hymn 'The co-eternal Son' stands out in the translation of R. Campbell as a piece of poetry. 'O Come, O Come, Emmanuel' is given in two parts. That is all and not I think sufficient for a season of four weeks.[2] One would have thought the *Verbum supernum* merited inclusion.

The provision for Christmas is more generous. There is the attractive fifteenth-century hymn/poem 'A noble flow'r of Juda', *A solis ortus cardine*, attributed to Sedulius, in the translation of R. A. Knox, and the *Corde natus ex parentis* of Prudentius, translated by J. Mason Neale. Three more are given for Christmastide and two for the time after the feast of Epiphany.

For Lent there are five hymns of which 'God of thy pity . . .' and 'Jesus, think of me', by that curious fourth-century bishop, Synesius, prove to be the most enduring. Among the four given for Holy Week we find of course *Vexilla regis* and 'O sacred head . . .' in the translation of R. A. Knox which seems better than the others one comes across. Eastertide is divided into two parts and if sufficient is given for the first part, a good deal of it is rather conventional. However if a community can manage it, there is nothing to stop them *singing* (it cannot be said!) 'This joyful Eastertide'[3] since it is to be found in an authorized hymn-book. For the second half there is 'Come down, O love divine' and the translation of a twelfth-century text by Robert Bridges 'Love of the Father, love of the Son' which one is glad to see there.

For feasts of Our Lady there are six hymns which one rejoices to see include Knox's translation of Dante's *Vergine madre, figlia del tuo figlio* (he has undoubtedly been underestimated as a translator of verse) which gives one something to think about, and a Stanbrook hymn 'Mary, crowned with living light' which stands out for its freshness. The great Anglican hymn 'The Church's one foundation' comes appropriately for the Dedication of a church.

These are but samples, but I think some of the best of what is to be found in the appendix. Others for use during the year are given in the psalter and it is here that we run into trouble. Some few are good (e.g. 'Be thou my vision') but most of them make no particular impact and some of them are extraordinarily brief. In these hymns particularly, but also in many of the others, we are confronted with another, a literary difficulty. For the most part the diction of these hymns is antiquated and their verse-forms conventional. The religious language of the nineteenth century is no longer ours and the devotional adjectives in particular have become hopelessly deflated. Nor do we any longer take to rhyming couplets as the Augustans or even the Victorians did. All these unhappy features come together in one verse of what was once a great hymn and which can still be *sung* with pleasure: 'Come Down, O Love Divine'. Its second verse runs:

~
126

Let holy charity
mine outward vesture *be*
And lowliness become mine inner *clothing.*
True lowliness of *heart,*
which takes the humbler *part*
and *o'er its own shortcomings weeps with loathing.*

There is the relentless rhyming and the sort of language (perhaps dictated by the verse form) in the last line, 'weeps' and 'loathing', which we can no longer tolerate. Yet I do not think that the remedy is to modernize the diction of such hymns, as was attempted in *The Catholic Hymnal*, by changing the 'thou's and the 'thee's with their verbal cognates to 'you' and 'yours'. They are of their epoch, heavily conditioned by the time when they were written. If Latin hymns whether sung or said in Latin are more acceptable and so repeatable it is perhaps because they have a certain timelessness, even if they were written over a period of fifteen hundred years. Perhaps modern translations of these hymns should be attempted though the thing that should be aimed at is the thought underlying the verse and not simply the words themselves. But what is needed both for the office and for the rest of our liturgy is *new* hymns, new in idiom, new in metrical forms, hymns that are newly conceived and come from new insights into the whole Christian mystery. One of the odder features of Roman Catholic hymn-writing since Faber set his hand to the work is that we have never produced a great hymn on the church. 'Who is she that stands triumphant' is intolerably aggressive and 'Faith of our fathers' is not a hymn about the church at all. It simply reflects the sentiments of the minority of England and Ireland who were emerging from the oppression of three centuries. But, alas, no more than poems do great hymns get written to order and all we can hope for is that since we have begun to use vernacular hymns in our worship we shall also gradually learn what is required.

Perhaps the poems that are included in the appendix are foreshadowings of what might come. Both Hopkins and Eliot experimented with metre and indeed with diction and although they too are now poets of an age that is ending, their example is still important. The selection of poems, which seems to have been influenced by the one to be found in *A Christian's Prayer Book*,[4] is not without significance. They are the choice of an age that had discovered the seventeenth-century 'metaphysicals' and that had taken to its heart their modern equivalents, Hopkins and Eliot. We note that John Donne, Henry Vaughan (two pieces), George Herbert and Robert Herrick (the last two are not 'metaphysicals' at all) have the lion's share of the older poets and Hopkins, Muir and Eliot of the new.

Their inclusion in a book of the Divine Office is interesting. Their very presence suggests that we should use them rather as meditations than as texts simply to be recited. Poems of some religious depth obviously lend themselves to such treatment which may well give us insights into the Christian mystery. But I fear that those who are not familiar with these poets will not find them acceptable and so will not be inclined to use them. Nor are there enough of them to take one through the great seasons of the year. But that again is to raise the question of *bulk*. It is just not possible to include everything that is desirable. And when all is said and done, need there have been a hymnary included in the book? If one is saying the office at home or in church, hymnals are (presumably) available. If one is away, should one be obliged to recite snippets of undistinguished verse?

In the future however things may be different. On the assumption that the prayer of the church will evolve and will be allowed to evolve,[5] the meditative quality of poems could be incorporated in the office as *responsories*. These are intended to 'turn the reading to prayer and contemplation' (GI 106) and such responsories, both long and shorter, are provided throughout the office. For the most part they consist of short passages of scripture which echo the previous reading. But while the lapidary style of Latin lent itself to responsories, at their best pregnant in meaning and at times of great beauty, that does not seem to be the case with responsories in English. Traditionally these texts were not necessarily passages of scripture or if they were, were handled very freely. The Byzantine liturgy has a whole corpus of texts in various forms which are really poetic compositions, some of which were taken over by the old Roman liturgy: thus the *Mirabile mysterium* of Lauds (1 January), the famous *Crucem tuam adoramus*, still used as a responsory in the Good Friday liturgy, and most famous of all the *Adorna, thalamum tuum*, a responsory in fact which remains in the office (unhappily shortened) of the Presentation of the Lord.[6] Texts such as these sensitively handled would have an acceptable place in the office. But there is no reason why we should stop there. Modern poets will respond to English texts and if they were given encouragement, that is, to be brutally practical, some promise that their work would be used in the liturgy, they could produce responsories that would enrich our office. They could even be in hymn-form provided it was not too rigid and the versicle for repetition by the assembly could be a refrain. Such a procedure would, I believe, bring relief to an office that is often prosy and might do something to re-create the whole tradition of hymn-making and hymn-singing.[7]

Notes
~

[1] Of Jansenist sympathies. His dates are 1676–1749.

[2] Other hymns are given in the psalter but they are not seasonal.

[3] *Praise the Lord*, 2nd ed., no. 205.

[4] Ed. P. Coughlan, R. C. D. Jasper, Teresa Rodrigues (Geoffrey Chapman, 1972).

[5] See the interesting remarks in GI 273: 'The Liturgy of the Hours should not be looked on as a beautiful monument of a past age . . . On the contrary it should come to life again with new meaning and **grow to become once more the sign of a living community** . . . We may confidently hope that **new ways** and **new forms may be found for our own age**, as has always happened in the life of the Church.'

[6] For a list of Greek texts taken into the Roman rite see H. W. Codrington, *The Liturgy of St Peter* (LQF, Münster, 1936), p. 3. It does not appear in the rite of the procession of the day but of course may be sung (cf. *alii cantus apti*).

[7] There are a few non-scriptural responsories in the new office which would lend themselves to the treatment suggested above.

~

EIGHT

The Intercessions

~~~~~~

S INCE THE INTERCESSORY prayers that have been added to the office play so important a part in it something needs to be said about the nature of intercession as well as about the texts that have been provided.

In earlier chapters of this book (1 and 5) we have discussed, all too summarily perhaps, some of the problems connected with prayer. In the vast debate on this subject that has been going on for some years one notes that the prayer of intercession is the one that is most questioned. There are several problematic aspects of the matter. What are we doing, what do we think we are doing, when we pray 'for fine weather'? What did we mean when, as we used to in the Litany of Saints, we asked to be delivered from earthquakes and other natural disasters? What do we think happens when we pray for other people? The petitions for innumerable 'temporal favours' like asking for a fine day for a cricket match or for 'success in exams' did much to trivialize the whole business. Much of this seems to have gone (though one wonders whether the young pray *for* anything at all), and that is gain but the problems remain and the answers are not easy to come by.

One answer, which is also a criticism, is that instead of praying for the relief of famine, say, we should get out and do something about it. If you are suffering from toothache, you do not make a novena. You go to the dentist. If someone is in distress, you go and help him in whatever way you can. Indeed, it is said that prayer on the whole is waste of time and that we should get on with the business of living even if by that is meant *Christian* living. We find God in others, we serve Christ in our neighbour and that when all is said and done is prayer. Critics of this sort say that Christians have spent too much time praying about matters they would have been much better occupied in putting right. There is a certain truth in these charges. At one time there was a mystique of suffering among Catholics which was all-but fatalistic. Suffering was 'good' for you, so you did not take the natural remedies or you hesitated to do so.

~

In a way it was Hobson's choice in earlier centuries. You might be suffering but the doctors would make you suffer more and, as like as not, kill you. Even a king like Louis XIV suffered appalling tortures at the hands of his doctors, tortures he endured with an extraordinary stoicism. Natural disasters, which included famine, were 'acts of God', of an angry God, who sent these things to punish sinful mankind. If there had been a Copernican revolution in astronomy, it took a very long time to filter down to theology and the life of prayer. God, in a way, was all too immediate. He manipulated the universe directly and everything, both good and bad, was attributed, again directly, to him.

In other words, he was, from the viewpoint of prayer, the God-of-the-gaps. When man had come to the end of what he thought possible, he invoked God to fill in the gaps. This kind of theology has been slow to disappear though its demise could be forecast with the social encyclicals of Leo XIII[1] which showed that man was not the (intended) victim of economic forces, that he has the right to shape his own destiny and that inherent in him is the power to change the conditions of human society. But it was not until Vatican II with its Constitution on the Church in the Modern World that Catholics were given a new vision of reality. This world is not an expendable extra which we should be glad to get rid of as soon as possible. It has a validity of its own, it is part of the saving purpose of God with whom man is a collaborator, a co-worker. It is his vocation to bring this world, as far as lies within his powers, to perfection and in working for the betterment of human society, in investigating the deep secrets of nature and in using them for the good of mankind, he is working out the purpose of God. All the efforts of man are to be directed towards the good life, towards the enhancement of the dignity and freedom of his fellow-men. He has a certain autonomy and is not the cat's-paw of a manipulative God. All this at the purely socio-economic level. At its deepest the document sees a certain co-inherence of the saving work of Christ and the 'tragedy' of the world. *Jésus sera en agonie jusqu'à la fin du monde*; or if you prefer St Paul, 'the whole world is groaning until it achieves its purpose and is shot through with hope that that purpose will be achieved' (Romans 8:19, 20). In striving and suffering for that achievement man, whether he knows it or not, is sharing in the redeeming work of Christ that lies at the heart of every human endeavour so long as it is not self-orientated, so long as it is 'for others'. The natural and the supernatural are not two self-contained departments—there is but one world and Christ is present to the whole of it. If we need to get rid of the pre-Copernican universe, we need also to get rid of the two-tier system which would have us think that the natural goes one way and the supernatural goes another, as if in the intention of God, they had different ends.

At first sight this view of things does not seem to help in the matter of prayer. It seems to eliminate the need or even the possibility of praying for a whole range of things that used to be regarded as the legitimate objects of prayer. Is there any sense at all in praying for fine weather? What do we expect God to do? What I think it has done is to kill the notion that God is a means and not an end. The response to the manipulative God seems to have been an effort on the part of man to manipulate God—which is magic. If notions like that have gone, so much the better. Again, with the sense that man is a co-worker with God who has entrusted to him the perfecting of this world, he realizes more clearly that in the face of the insufficiencies and evils of this world it is his task, his vocation, to remedy them. He may very well pray for the strength to perform his task, for purity of intention that he may work for others and not for himself, but that is rather different from praying for an intervention of God into the normal course of affairs. Although not all the problems connected with the prayer of petition have been solved, it is unwise to talk about a 'crisis' in the matter. What has been happening is that Christians have been absorbing new insights on prayer which have come from a renewed reflection on God and also those that have come from the new scientific way of looking at the world. In the process we have become more *adult* in our way of looking at God.

How then are we to think of prayer and in particular, the prayer of petition? We can and must eliminate from the discussion any notion of 'moving God' or trying 'to change his mind', notions that seem unhappily to remain current. We must accept that we are confronted with a world that has its own laws which are inherent in the nature of things and it is not for us to seek to 'bend' them. At the same time we are aware that we and all creation are dependent on God which in terms of language means that we are petitioners. Perhaps the basic notion of prayer is that it is a *cry*; we express our need as the infant does for its mother's milk. But this cry is but the symbol of a desire, it is a cry for *love*, a cry for the *person* who loves.[2] Prayer is in fact the expression of an interpersonal relationship: the cry is the desire for love and the response, or the gift, is the expression of a reciprocated love. That is, in her response the mother too is asking the child, the petitioner, for something, namely that the child will accept her gift. But as long as a request, even for love, is thought of in terms of satisfaction, there will always be an ambiguity, for even a mutual desire for satisfaction has an element of selfishness in it: 'it is always possible to maintain that "The Other is only granting me this so that I may duly give him satisfaction"'. The problem can only be solved by stripping the request of the desire for satisfaction of need and seeing it as 'the upsurge of pure desire which is a longing for nothing else but the pure desire of the Other, or rather identification with that very desire'.[3]

It is obvious that this pure and unconditioned desire or identification of wills is something that exists rarely if at all among human beings, but it is a theory that fits in extraordinarily well with the teaching of the gospel and Christian tradition. The whole of the first part of the Lord's prayer, made explicit in the Matthean version, is a petition that God's will may be done. It is an effort on the part of the one praying to identify his will with God's though he does not, or only rarely, know what that will *for* him is, much less how it will be accomplished. It is also possible to see how the petitions for more particular needs fall into place in the second half of the prayer. At an even deeper level, prayer is to be seen as the response in the Spirit to the Other whom I am addressing. Or, as L. Beirnaert puts it: 'The Other to whom my words are addressed is God himself speaking and petitioning within us with inexpressible moans and cries' (Romans 8:26, 27). This too is surely the meaning of those many statements in St John's gospel that we must pray 'in the name of Christ', utterly united with him, identifying our will with his.

This too is, I believe, the teaching of St Augustine (to which I have referred in Chapter 1) that prayer is an expression of desire for God, for *all* he is and wants of us. It seems also to be the final thought of St Thomas Aquinas as expressed in the *Compendium Theologiae* (II, 2). It will be as well to give the whole passage:

The petition we address to man has not the same grounds of necessity as the one we address to God.

When directed to a man, the petition serves to inform him of the applicant's desire or need, then *to sway the heart* of the one solicited until it yields. For prayer addressed to God, the same does not hold true. He knows our ills and our desires. And *there is no question of modifying the divine will* by means of words so that God may grant what was previously against his will. If petitionary prayer is necessary to man, the reason is that *it exercises an influence on the one who resorts to it.* When he considers his weakness, his *heart ardently desires the goal which alone matters* to the one who prays. He thereby *renders himself capable of attaining it.*[4]

This is a noble teaching on prayer and even if it does not answer all the modern objections to prayer, it states some essential principles. No question for Aquinas of 'moving' or 'changing' the divine will, no question of swaying God's heart. Secondly, he sees prayer as affecting *man*. It may shock some to hear that *man* is the object of prayer, but it is he who has to be changed if he is to be capable of attaining the goal, namely God. Thirdly, in terms that remind one of Augustine, Aquinas sees man as desiring the goal, what Augustine called the beatitude or blessedness that is to be found in God and that is God.[5] And given St Augustine's teaching in his commentary on St John's gospel on 'praying in the name', it would not be going beyond the evidence to say that for him the desire of the petitioner involves identification of his will with God's.

There is another view of prayer which throws into relief an important aspect of it though in the end the solution it offers comes close to the one set out above.[6] Prayer is the response of faith to the message, the call, the address of God, in the last resort the response to *God*, to a Person, who has revealed himself in words, the word of holy scripture. Prayer then is an expression of faith: 'faith itself is prayer, the basic form of prayer'.[7] But since we have faith in a Person, it means rather 'I believe in you' than 'I believe in it', that is teachings or doctrine.[8] But since faith means a total commitment to the Other, prayer will be an expression of that commitment.

Prayer is also spoken of as a 'conversation' or a 'dialogue' but it is important to remember that that dialogue is *initiated* by God and that our part of it consists of *listening*, in silence. We are not to look for 'a verifiable answer' from God. Then out of that silence we respond to God in faith and can only grasp the import of the message by faith. But this response can take various forms and use a variety of expressions: 'If prayer is conceived of as "verbal faith" whose basic form is "I believe in you", then every prayer – regardless of the words or form it chooses –

must continually repeat this phrase in endless variations, or else it is
nothing more than the "empty phrases" of the Gentiles which Jesus
criticised so sharply (Matthew 6:7ff.).' This emphasis on faith in prayer
is very valuable and does more than anything else to raise it from a
sub-Christian level. In language with which we may be more familiar, it
means that all prayer, since it is a response to God in his self-revelation,
is prompted by the Holy Spirit, who alone inspires our believing. Thus
we come back to Romans 8:26, 27.

But if this view is valuable it seems to need further development. Faith
seems to be the cannibal virtue; the New Testament speaks also of hope
and love. We respond 'in faith' but we must also respond *with hope*, i.e.
trust, a particularly important matter when we are dealing with the
prayer of petition, and also *with love*, for it is only then that we begin to
identify our will with that of God. We can and do also respond with joy
and praise and thanksgiving and that is presumably what is meant by
'endless variations'. Perhaps it would be best to say that we respond to
God with all that we have and are, giving ourselves to him who gives
himself to us.

Two other matters must be briefly dealt with. If it is asked why we
need to express our faith/desire in words, the answer is that God has
approached us to reveal himself in words and that language is of the very
stuff of human nature. If faith were never expressed in words it would
become unreal. Words are not mere counters of information, they are
what are called 'performative'. They bring about effects, they modify atti-
tudes and to pray in faith is to increase faith and in prayers of petition to
increase our concern for others.[9] Faith and the prayer that springs from
it would be less than a human activity if it were never expressed in words.
However odd then some of the words used in prayer and worship may
seem, they are all expressions of man who is responding to God in faith.

Then there is the question of life and prayer. If prayer normally
expresses itself in words, must it always do so? It is a question that did
not escape the notice of St Augustine: since prayer is desire, the desire
for God, the Christian can and does continue to 'desire' God, to have his
will directed towards union with God, *all the time*. This, for Augustine,
is what the saying 'pray without ceasing' means. This desire for God,
then, is to be found in all that we have to do, in all our daily tasks.
But since our 'desire can grow cold', we need to withdraw from our
work from time to time to renew our desire, to reflect on the life of

blessedness (*vita beata*) towards which by desire and will and work we are tending.[10] The moderns do not seem to have gone much beyond this: 'By this (continual and inexplicit prayer) we mean that a Christian to a certain extent sees his entire work . . . as an indirect form of prayer without words . . . for . . . if a person accepts his life and work in faith, then everything he does and experiences will be pervaded by faith.'[11] Put like that the statement seems to make things too easy. We need to stand back from our work from time to time, we need to try and see it under the eye of God and, as Augustine suggests, we need to renew our desire (or faith) and this we do by prayer. Without that kind of prayer we may very well live in the illusion that our life and work are 'pervaded by faith' or, if you like, permeated with love and unless we *offer* our life and work to God – for all that the offering will be prompted by 'faith' – it is all too likely to be directed towards self or to the achievement of purely materialistic purposes.

From all this we may deduce the following:

1. Prayer is the response of faith to God who has revealed himself and since God takes the initiative and our response is prompted by the Holy Spirit, prayer by its nature exists in the order of grace. It is the expression of the inter-personal relationship between God and ourselves.

2. But the response of faith can take many forms, praise, thanksgiving but also petition where adherence to God in hope and trust is peculiarly important.

3. But if the inter-personal relationship is to be one worthy of the name it is above all a response of love through which we are able, though no doubt with great and continued effort, to identify our wills with God's.

4. In prayer, including the prayer of petition and whatever we may ask for, we are seeking God's will and not our own.

5. In praying for 'the development of the peoples', for the progress of a truly human world order, we are seeking to co-operate with God, for this world is not an historical accident but is part of the saving purpose of God. There is no question of our manipulating God for purely human ends.

6. When we pray and especially when we make petitions, our prayer has an effect on *ourselves*, disposing us to attain the goal of all things, God. It will open us out to God, no doubt enlighten our minds so that we may see something of what God intends, that is, his will. With St Augustine

~

we may say that such prayer is necessary if our desire to identify our wills with his is to be maintained.

7. When we pray for others we are asking that they may be made more capable of seeking union with God, opening their hearts to him so that they may 'desire the goal which alone matters'. Our prayer cannot bend their wills (as some seem to think) nor is it some strange 'influence' playing upon them (as others have thought) and when 'we commit others to God' we are asking that by his grace they may open themselves to him to do his will.

Against this background we can, I think, see that there is an adequate justification for the prayer of petition. Understood in this way it is not unworthy of God, it does not turn him into a benevolent dictator and it respects, without exaggerating, his transcendence. It removes prayer from the sphere of magic and it remains profoundly Christian. Perhaps not all will be satisfied with this justification but that would not be surprising. God is a mystery, the radical mystery, we know him only 'in part', dimly as in a mirror, and prayer is a mystery for it is the expression of our relationship with God. Of its effects, if we think of those as *results*, we know nothing and that is one reason why 'prayer-in-faith' and 'prayer-as-the-response-of-faith' is so supremely important. If a St John of the Cross, who had a sense of the immediacy and presence of God that is given to few, could say that in the dark night of the soul he could only cling to God in the darkness of faith, we should not be surprised if prayer is a matter of faith for us.

By what seems to be a kind of instinct Christians have felt the need for the prayer of petition throughout the centuries. Perhaps this 'instinct' is evidence of a relationship with God that is not wholly definable. It is none the less deeply rooted in the heart of man and whatever may be the imperfections of the image of God to whom he has prayed, his prayer is witness in itself of the reality of God. But if it can be described as an instinct, it has been deepened and immeasurably enriched by the revelation of the New Testament. The importance of the prayer of petition and the commands to pray are so patent in the pages of the New Testament that there is no need even to summarize them here. A single phrase of the First Letter of St John (1 John 5:14) expresses all that is of the essence of the prayer of petition: 'We are confident that if we ask him for anything, and *it is in accordance with his will*, he will hear us'.

There is also the unbroken witness of the church from the Letter of

Clement to the Corinthians through the innumerable statements of Christian writers, early and late, to the liturgies of every kind which have always included prayers of petition. In our own time they have been restored to our liturgy, first in the Mass with the inclusion of the Prayers of the Faithful, which, *pace* those who write to the newspapers, have been very acceptable to the generality of the people, and now to the Divine Office in the form of Intercessions in morning and evening prayer. The amount of material of this kind is very great and any adequate commentary on it would run to many pages. All we can do here is to single out one or two dominant features and comment upon a certain number of details.

First, there is the matter of the term: Intercessions. In the Latin they are called simply *preces* with the intention presumably of suggesting that they are the continuation of the curious amalgam going by that name in the old office. The editors of the English *Divine Office* felt that 'prayers' was insufficiently explicit. There are other prayers in the office, there is the 'Concluding Prayer' that comes at the end of each hour. It seemed that the *preces* should be distinguished from all others. Then if you look into the prayers you find that they are almost wholly prayers *for* particular purposes and people. It is true that the prayers provided for the morning office are often expressions of praise, thanksgiving and dedication. But there are others that can be rightly called intercessory. Those for the evening office are almost wholly so.

A second feature of these prayers throws light on what is meant by 'intercession'. One notes with satisfaction that again and again in the introduction to the prayers the mediatorial role of Christ is prominent. The sense indicated is that the Christian, not merely as an individual but as a member of the great community of the church, is making intercession in and through Christ for the needs of mankind. All petitions are made 'in his name' and all petitions are enfolded in the unceasing prayer of Christ who is ever-living to make intercession for us. Some of the prayers are addressed to Christ himself (and in this they are different from the Prayer of the Faithful in the Mass) but he is constantly seen in relation to his Father. In a broad and general way I would say that these prayers are in the deepest sense of the New Testament *Christian* prayers where the presence of Christ is always apparent. This, I think, is one reason why they have been so warmly welcomed by those who use them.

An inspection of whole series of these prayers reveals a third feature.

~

Although they cover almost every conceivable human need, they ask for things that are evidently in accordance with the will of God. If we are invited to pray for the betterment of the world, we do so in terms that underline our co-operation with God. If the subject of the prayer is the feeding of the hungry we ask that *men* may do what is required of them, that is, in the language of St Thomas, that they may be made capable of attaining the goal, in this case the love of others which is an integral part of loving God. If we pray for a good harvest we are asking that men will co-operate with the forces of nature to the best of their ability. There are some direct petitions for the 'healing' of the sick but they are in a distinct minority; more often they ask for God's comfort and support of the sick. Again and again the prayers ask that God may be *with* people in this or that situation or need. Equally often the prayers turn our attention and concern to others and are constant reminders of the sense of service we should have for them. A typical example is this: 'May our lives today be filled with your compassion; give us the spirit of forgiveness and a generous heart'. In this they are doing what liturgical prayer is among other things meant to do, namely they help us to realize that we are members of the community of the church and also of the human community that surrounds it. In these intercessions we pray *for* the church but often enough they show us that we are praying *as* the church: 'In the name of the church we pray . . . Be mindful of your church; keep her free from evil and make her perfect in your love' which echoes phrases of John 17. Finally, for the list could be very long, the prayers show a realism about life and its problems and an especial concern for those engaged in heavy and perhaps unrewarding work.

If the prayers are very varied, they are also adapted to the liturgical seasons. They draw out the implications of the mystery of Christ in his incarnation, passion, death, resurrection and ascension and before Pentecost there are almost continual invocations of the Holy Spirit. This again helps us to realize that the celebration of the mystery must have consequences in our living. Here are one or two examples: 'May our lives express what we celebrate at Christmas; and may its mystery enrich your church this year'; 'By your coming you showed us the faithfulness of God; keep us faithful to the promises of our baptism'; 'King of peace, your kingdom is one of justice and peace; grant that we may seek those things that will further harmony among men'. For Holy Week: 'Christ, our Redeemer, let us share in your passion by works of penance; let us attain

~

the glory of your resurrection'; 'Lord and master, for us you became obedient even to death; keep us faithful to God's will in the darkness of our lives'.

One for Eastertide illustrates another feature of these prayers: they are constantly echoing or quoting holy scripture and very frequently are related to the readings of the Mass or office of the day: 'Let us cast out the leaven of corruption and malice; let us celebrate Christ's passover in purity and truth'. Here is another for the week before Pentecost which recalls Romans 8:26, 27: 'Through the Holy Spirit you have made us sons of God; at all times let us pray through the Spirit to you (Christ) and the Father'. In the 'ordinary' time of the year the prayers are perhaps more practical and down to earth: 'Lord, give us your strength in our weakness; when we meet problems give us courage to face them'; and again (from the old Prime collect), 'Direct our thoughts, our words, our actions today so that we may know and do your will'. Nor do the prayers overlook certain aspects of life which too often have not figured in Christian prayer: we are invited to pray for artists and writers and all who in any way reveal the beauty and glory of God: 'Pour out your Spirit on artists, craftsmen and musicians; may their work bring variety, joy and inspiration to our lives'. Even the town-planners are not forgotten: 'We pray for all who plan and build our cities; give them respect for every human value'.

In this vast corpus of prayers it is possible that there are some that could be criticized from one viewpoint or another and that would not be surprising. It is possible that some could have benefited from further thought and revision: God is asked a little too often to do things directly that other prayers see as being done by his creatures. What is a matter for some criticism (though I realize what an appalling task they had) is that the translators have not always been very happy in the way they have turned phrases. For instance, in the example given above for Holy Week 'works of penance' with its unhappy overtones is not the best way of translating the simple *per paenitentiam* of the Latin; 'by penitence' or even 'by repentance' would have been better. Penitence is both a state of mind and will and expressive of an intention to proceed to action. Another example is from Thursday Vespers (Week 3): 'Turn sinners back to you'. This is very odd English. Surely it should be 'back to *yourself*' if you are going to keep that sort of sentence. It is a reflexive verb; it is the Father who is being addressed. There are several other examples of the same kind not only here but in the ICEL translation of the missal. I have to presume that it is but another example of the decline of the English language. The Latin is *Da peccatoribus conversionem, lapsisque virtutem; omnibus paenitentiam et salutem concede.* Very neat! For the first phrase why not 'conversion of heart': 'To sinners grant conversion of heart'? Perhaps the whole sentence could go like this: 'To sinners grant conversion of heart, to the fallen the power to rise from their sins (this phrase is omitted) and to us all true repentance and the salvation that comes from Christ'.

Then there is the question of certain words. In Lauds for Friday of the third week (of the psalter) we find: 'You sent your disciples to preach the gospel . . . *Bless* those men and women. . . .' This word occurs quite frequently and I would contend that it is unblessedly vague, especially when in the Latin there is a good strong verb: *adiuva*. The word comes in other places where the phrase goes 'Bless our families . . . Bless these and those'. What I find very extraordinary throughout these prayers is the use of the word 'brothers'. A good word of course when applied to *men* but with the exception of one or two isolated phrases (as above) women nowhere appear. 'Brethren' I suppose was regarded as archaic though it has deceived far too many people into thinking that it meant both men and women whereas of course it is merely the plural of 'brother'. For some strange reason 'sisters' was regarded as an improper word – and yet there are thousands of religious sisters throughout the world using this office who are not allowed to pray for each other but only for their 'brothers'. Elsewhere too 'sons' (of God) could often be turned 'children' who are both male and female!

When we turn to the form of the petitions, at first sight they seem a little over-complicated: the petition, divided into two parts, the whole followed by a response. The form of course is useful for those who in an assembly have no books – they can merely repeat the response but in private recitation it seems to be overloaded. However, the way we may use the petition is very flexible: 'The priest or minister says both parts of the intention and the congregation adds the invariable response, or pauses for silence; otherwise the priest or minister says only the first part and the congregation the second part of the intention' (GI 193). In private recitation then the response may be omitted. In practice it will often be best to make a silent pause after each petition and turn it into a personal prayer. One of the things that the sometimes despised prayer of petition can do for us is 'to raise our mind and heart to God'. However, if there are responses, they ought to be appropriate to the petition that has preceded them and this is not always so. Thus the response for the Second Sunday after Christmas is 'Let your birth bring peace to men' and yet in the petitions we pray (a) for the church, (b) for the Pope and bishops that they may be faithful stewards and (c) that Christ will help us in our weakness and give us a share in his kingdom, all of which does not seem to have anything to do with 'peace to men'. Another petition reveals where the source of the trouble lies: 'Jesus our Saviour, in the body you were put to death . . . grant that we may die to sin and live in the power of your resurrection. *Lord, restore your kingdom in the world.*' The response which has no evident relevance to the petition is too specific. Where the responses are short and general, like 'Lord in your mercy, hear our prayer' or simply 'Lord hear us', there is no difficulty at all.

However, it must be emphasized that the intercessions are for the most part well thought out and agreeably expressed. The criticisms made here are offered in the hope that in the event of a second edition the intercessions may be reviewed and perhaps revised. Local conferences of bishops have the faculty to approve new prayers though these must follow the rules laid down in the General Introduction (184–186)–a salutary precaution! Nor should the permission to add petitions in ordinary celebrations be overlooked (188). In this way the prayers can be adapted to local needs and conditions. It is also helpful to allow a period of silence when the prayers are finished so that individuals can make their own petitions and pray to God in their hearts.

Finally, it should be noted that the intercessions are part of a whole pattern; intercessions, the Lord's prayer and the collect. All these elements, while at one time or another and in various ways giving praise and thanksgiving to God, turn the prayer of the whole hour towards ourselves so that we may appropriate and apply to our lives the content of all that has gone before. It is a sound formula, making the new office far more personal than the old and keeping a nice balance between the upward thrust of praise of God and the needs of the human community who are approaching him for help.

A note on collects

The very numerous collects of the new office deserve prolonged consideration but that cannot be done here. Their very number and the great variety of their content and style prohibit any adequate treatment. All we can do is to point out that they perform their proper function admirably in summing up the whole hour either in the context of the day, feast or season or in that of a particular time, e.g. mid-day prayer or Compline. One feature that is very welcome is that apart from the greater feasts and some parts of the greater seasons, the prayer of the Mass is used only for the Office of Readings and even there there are some variations. In the daily office Lauds and Vespers, as well as the midday prayer and Compline, have their own collects and we are no longer required to repeat the collect of the day again and again. This has been done very deliberately not only to relieve monotony but to make the point of a particular hour (199).

The problems of translations were as great as those for the collects of the missal and it is for the users of the office to judge their value. Very generally they seem to have been welcomed.[12]

Notes
~

[1] In the secular sphere Hegel and Marx seem to have been the precursors of a 'theology' of social progress which largely turned on the meaning of history – a subject that has preoccupied Christian theologians for some time.

[2] See L. Beirnaert, 'Prayer and Petition for Others' in *From Cry to Word* (Lumen Vitae Press, Brussels, 1968), pp. 29ff.

[3] *Ibid.*, pp. 30, 31, which I have been summarizing.

[4] As quoted *ibid.*, p. 36. Emphases mine, inserted to show the difference between human requests and prayer to God.

[5] St Thomas quotes part of the Letter to Proba in II–II, 83, 6. In the previous article (55, ad 2) he speaks of prayers as a conforming of our will with God's.

[6] For what follows see *The Common Catechism* (Search Press, London/Seabury Press, New York, 1975), pp. 352–61.

[7] P. 357.

[8] *Ibid.*

[9] On the subject of language, see *ibid.*, pp. 354–6.

[10] PL 33, 501.

[11] *The Common Catechism*, p. 361. Note the characteristic prevalence of 'faith'. We can accept our work in love and indeed in hope too. As Augustine (*loc. cit.*) says, 'In faith, hope and love we pray always by unceasing desire'.

[12] Since the present writer had some hand in the translation, he feels inhibited from further comment.

The Second Year Course of Readings

~~~~~~

W E HAVE NOW BEEN using the *Divine Office* or the *Liturgy of the Hours* for nearly twenty years and during that time we have become aware of certain defects in the office and a number of desideranda. Some of the former have been ventilated in previous pages (for example the plethora of antiphons) and as to the latter many have found that the lectionaries of the book leave something to be desired. The biblical lectionary is an immense improvement on what we had before but we have become aware that it leaves out a good deal of the Bible even if we take into account the Mass-lectionary. The patristic lectionary is beginning to wear thin, so to say. Certain readings recur with unwelcome frequency and some were not too well chosen in any case.

The reason for this state of affairs is that originally it was intended that there should be two lectionaries for the biblical readings and two for the patristic. So we read in the General Introduction appended to the *Liturgy of the Hours*: 'There is a twofold arrangement for the biblical readings. The first lasts for one year; it is found in the *Liturgy of the Hours*. The second, for optional use, is found in the *Supplement*; this, like the arrangement of the first readings in the ferial Masses "throughout the year" is arranged in a two-year cycle' (no. 145). This 'supplement' will form a fifth volume to the Latin edition of the *Liturgia Horarum*.

Why did the alternative lectionaries never appear? We find the explanation in an article by Mgr Martimort.[1] He writes that at the very moment of going to press with the *Liturgia Horarum* 'it appeared that the insertion of the cycle of two years of biblical readings would give to the four volumes an excessive bulk and would increase the price considerably'. So he and his colleagues, in the heat of a Roman summer (1970), set to work to draw up a new cycle for one year only. 'It is not surprising', he continues, 'that given the conditions they had to work in they had to leave out whole books of the Bible, above all Genesis and the Letter to the Romans.'

Although the *Two-Year Cycle of Scripture Readings* has been in circulation for some years (mostly it would seem in religious houses) it is not easy to use. One has looked for its official publication and it has not come. Mgr Martimort offers as an explanation for the delay the heavy work-load of the Congregation of Divine Worship and the unavailability of the personnel who had worked on the project. Now, it seems, it is being taken up again[2] and the supplementary volume may appear in the next year or two.

It has also been made clear that readings take with them responsories and these have to be composed with great care in order to reflect the substance of the reading. Thirdly, it is intended that the psalm-collects (see above, pp. 104–5) should be included though these too have been available in a booklet for some years. In short, every effort is being made to enrich the content of the Divine Office and to make it a more effective instrument of prayer.

If we would know something of what the alternative biblical lectionary will contain we can glean information from the General Introduction attached to the *Liturgy of the Hours* (GILH, 148–152). In tabulated form we have the following:

> After Christmas to 5 January: instead of Colossians the Song of Songs ('foreshadowing the union of God and human beings in Christ').
>
> Holy Week: instead of Songs of the Suffering Servant read Jeremiah, 'the type of the suffering Christ'.
>
> During Eastertide: Acts of the Apostles instead of e.g. Apocalypse.
>
> 'In Year II readings before Lent are from Genesis, and then (in Ordinary Time) the history of salvation is recounted from the Exile until the time of Maccabees. The later prophets, the wisdom books and the narrative books of Esther, Tobit and Judith have their place in Year II.'

It is clear from these samples that the present lectionary of the office includes some of the readings originally intended for Year II. This will presumably offer another problem for the compilers to solve.

The delay in publishing the *Supplement* has not been without its advantages. The French have provided the references of the biblical readings for the two years for their very popular *Prière du temps présent*. The second volume of the *Neues Stundenbuch* (for German-speaking countries and regions) gives the texts of both years in full and provides them with responsories! A book in Spanish for Mexico, *Liturgia de las Horas*, has also published the two-year cycle. It looks as if English-speaking countries are rather behindhand in this matter.

There has also been movement in the field of patristic lectionaries. Beginning as early as 1969 there was the publication of the *Lectures chrétiennes pour notre temps* from the Abbey of Orval and another from the monastery of En-Calcat. The Germans produced the *Väterlesungen* (Readings from the Fathers), sixteen fascicles from 1977–78, and Dom Henry Ashworth drew up a series, 'A Proposed Monastic Lectionary', published in *Ephemerides Liturgicae* (references only, 1977–78). This was followed by a series of volumes edited by the 'Friends of Henry Ashworth' (who in fact was one of the architects of the patristic lectionary of the *Liturgia Horarum*), the first of which was *Christ Our Light: Patristic Readings on Gospel Themes*, 1, *Advent–Pentecost* (Maryland, 1981). There are yet other lectionaries worked out for and used by monastic communities, Italian, French, German and English.[3] All this would seem to indicate that there is a widespread desire for variety in the office and, in this context, in the readings from the Fathers of the church. A rapid inspection of the lists seems to show that these lectionaries are thoroughly patristic though some few non-patristic writers have been admitted to some of the lectionaries. If this is so (and it is difficult to be sure when only lists of various times and provenance are available to the writer) it means that patristic writings are more acceptable than, say, the occasional extracts from the intensely inward-looking *Imitation of Christ* such as we find in the *Liturgia Horarum*. Even so, there is a certain amount of the patristic material, e.g. 'commentary' on the scriptures, of an allegorical kind. As Mgr Martimort in the article referred to above says when speaking of the very inadequate patristic lectionary of the former office: 'Too often the allegorical commentaries of St Gregory [the Great], the number-symbolism to be found in the works of St Augustine and many other patristic interpretations ... gave an impression of a tiresome anachronism and a false picture of the Fathers' (p. 495).

If then the Fathers of the church are more acceptable in the office than later and especially post-Tridentine authors and if we look to the future, there would seem to be another way.

In the last forty years or more there has been a vast amount of scripture study and innumerable commentaries have appeared. At best these have enabled the non-expert to penetrate more deeply into the meaning of the scriptures not merely in a 'critical' or scholarly way but as a means of nourishing the spiritual life. We have indeed been constantly exhorted to read the scriptures, to make of them our *lectio divina*, somewhat like the monks of the Middle Ages though we cannot put on the mind of the monks of the Middle Ages! It would be immensely helpful if commentaries, written by seasoned scholars, could produce books along the lines of the *Geistliche Schriftlesung*, viz. spiritual reading or rather *lectio divina*. Modern scripture studies have necessarily to be critical and concerned with matters of little interest to the ordinary reader but this work could be the basis of a deeper insight into the word of God. Like the medieval monk we too are time-conditioned, we know more (or can know more) about the scriptures than people did in the Middle Ages – or even than the Fathers – and it is a false simplicity to read them as if nothing has happened since. The spiritual sense of the scriptures based on sound scholarship expounded in books or articles is what I see as a possibility for the future. I am sure there is both a need and a desire for it.

The last matter to be considered is whether the generality of the clergy or indeed religious and lay people who use the office will welcome yet another volume. The English edition, *The Divine Office* (not to mention the *editio typica*, *Liturgia Horarum*, which some of us needed for study), was expensive enough when it appeared years ago and is even more expensive now. Yet another volume would involve yet further outlay. It would seem that the best way for the church authorities to take would be to say that the use of the supplementary volume is not obligatory and at the same time to let the various collections of patristic writings circulate freely (i.e. outside monastic communities) to be used at choice. The main point is not that everyone should read the same extracts from the same Father all over the world but that people should be encouraged to read them, to ponder on them and to feed their prayer with them. If other more modern writers are found to do this, then let them be included.

Notes
~

[1] *Notitiae* 302 (September 1991), 9, p. 492.
[2] See *ibid*. and *Notitiae* 306–307 (January–February 1992), 1/2, pp. 10–167.
[3] See *Notitiae* 306–307, pp. 59–167.

The Celebration of the Divine Office

~~~~~~~

*I*T IS VERY EVIDENT that it is the desire of the church that ordinary people should take part in the prayer of the Divine Office (GI 21, 22, 23, 27), especially Lauds and Vespers (GI 40). This desire and the recommendations that flow from it are firmly based on the teaching of the Constitution on the Liturgy (42) and other conciliar documents about the nature of the church. Even the local community is a manifestation, a sacrament-sign, of the great church spread throughout the world and it is there that the praise and prayer of the Christian community should have a visible presence. Priests and other ministers, if they exist, should meet together with their people to celebrate the prayer of the church whenever it is possible. Priests and clerics living in community and religious of both sexes are urged to celebrate the office in common, especially Lauds and Vespers (26, 27). Likewise, groups of lay people who meet together for whatever purpose should also use the office as far as that is possible, and even families are urged to make parts of the office the substance of their daily prayer (27). There can be no doubt that the church wishes all to make the office their prayer as far as their circumstances allow and it is equally significant that the hours recommended are Lauds and Vespers. These, as we have seen, are the pivots of the prayer of the church, summing up in themselves the essence of that prayer.

This is the ideal set before the members of the church but the reality is likely to be very different. As everyone knows, it has become increasingly difficult to assemble people for anything but eucharistic worship and attendance at that is said to be declining.[1] What then is to be done?

Before discussing practical measures it is necessary to say that Christians and perhaps especially Catholics need to have a greater conviction about the importance of prayer. Catholics particularly have a very strong feeling for the Mass and will (still) go to considerable lengths to ensure that they get to Mass on Sunday. Their appreciation of public prayer seems to be much weaker. This is understandable. Until recently the

~

office was officially in Latin and was regarded as the peculiar exercise of the priest and if it was possible to make something of the Mass in Latin, as millions did for many centuries, the same was not true of the office. In fact for the vast majority of Catholics the office played no part in their Christian lives for over four centuries. It will not be surprising if it takes a very long time to re-integrate it into normal Christian practice. If this is to happen the whole meaning of public prayer as the prayer of the church in which Christ is actively present will have to be brought home to them. The vast teaching of the New Testament and of the Christian writers of all ages urging the necessity of prayer and its importance for Christian living will have to be broken down for them. This will have to go a good deal beyond pulpit exhortations to pray—which have never been lacking—and will have to unfold the meaning of prayer in all its richness if people are to be drawn to it. What is perhaps of even greater practical importance is that they need to be given *examples* of praying communities, or better still, of communities at prayer.

This brings us to the practicalities of the matter. It is pretty certain that Vespers will be the hour that people will be able to attend and this is the first point on which to concentrate attention.

1. Where there is a community of priests and clerics it would seem right and proper that they should recite Vespers in church at whatever hour a number of people can attend. There has been a tendency in the past for religious communities to think of the office as *their* prayer which they may indeed have agreed they were saying *for* the people but that otherwise it was no concern of theirs. When the office was in Latin there was some excuse for thinking like that. But if the church gives a mandate to priests to say the office, it does so so that they may maintain the public prayer of the church which by definition is that of the people also (GI 28ff.). One of the great advantages of a community of priests with a pastoral charge and a public church is that they are able to maintain a presence of public prayer as a normal part of the Christian life.

2. Where there is a number of priests in a parish, the same principle holds good although the practical difficulties may be greater. Priests will have a variety of functions and it may well be difficult to assemble at any given time, but some effort could be made and if only one priest can attend there will usually be a small number of people who will celebrate the office with him. The importance of the matter is not how many people are present but that there should be a fixed hour of prayer and

that the prayer should be seen to go on relentlessly, irrespective of numbers.

3. Where there is only one priest in a parish, the matter becomes more difficult. With the best will in the world he cannot always be in church at the appointed hour. There will be times when he has to be absent or when he is called away. But a celebration of the office does not require the presence of a priest (GI 27) and what we need to do is to build up prayer-groups in our parishes who will undertake to be present on stated occasions and to see that the office is recited whether the priest is there or not. However, it may be conceded that in the smaller parish even this is not possible and then something simpler has to be thought of. If evening prayer cannot be said every night of the week, it may be that Saturdays and Sundays offer an opportunity. The confessional period is still usually kept on Saturday evenings, though less frequented than formerly, and it is possible to use the first part of this period for the recitation of the office. There may only be a few people present but the main point is that the prayer of the church is said. Similarly, on Sundays even if it is not possible to have a full-scale evening service, it is possible to recite Vespers with a few people before the evening Mass. What is important is to establish that there shall be fixed times in the course of the week when the prayer of the church will be celebrated.

These simple celebrations can be enhanced by the addition of singing, first of the hymn, which in the English edition is usually familiar, and secondly of the *Magnificat* in one or other of the psalm-settings that are current. In a parish context it is also useful to make known that the people may add petitions to the intercessions whenever the office is celebrated. But even in these simple celebrations it is important that a longer scripture reading should be used and a commentary, however brief, should be given. The General Introduction suggests the use of the passage from the Office of Readings but this is not always the most apt for a mixed congregation, especially when it is from an obscurer part of the Old Testament. It is better, and I think more profitable, to take a book from the New Testament and use it fairly freely, going through it from the beginning but dwelling on what is more suitable to the group and linking one passage to another. This will ensure that those who have had to be absent for a week will know what has gone before.

It is also possible to link the celebration of the office with certain traditional Catholic devotions. A decade or two of the rosary after

Vespers is acceptable. If time allows, a simple exposition of the Blessed Sacrament concluding with the blessing adds a touch of warmth and familiarity for those who are less accustomed to the austerity of the office. In some places the office is combined with the exposition of the Blessed Sacrament for the Holy Hour devotion. Here the scripture reading(s) and the homily can add depth and richness to the hour of prayer.

There is too the possibility of the house-group envisaged by the General Introduction (27). Here the prayer can be combined with a more extended reading of scripture and the homily could be of a more conversational kind. The intercessions for their part offer the opportunity of a freer kind of prayer which need not be confined to petition. Silences too could be longer so that in one office there would be formal prayer (the psalms), reading, commentary or homily, and the less formal petitions and silences which would allow for the movement of the Spirit. No doubt these possibilities have already been realized here and there and the one benefit the office brings to prayer-groups is objectivity and a wider horizon. All small groups, including sometimes the parish, have a tendency to concentrate on their own concerns and to forget the *oikoumenē*, the great church and the community of mankind.

But it must be confessed that if any of these practices are to become general a considerable change of mind on the part of both the clergy and the people is necessary. The priest, badgered by legislation and long custom, has seen the office as a duty that concerned him and no one else. Notionally he knew that it was the prayer of the community but in actuality this never or only rarely affected his action. The obstacles to the way of communal celebration seemed insurmountable. The office was long and complicated and was in Latin. The Catholic laity were for the most part unfamiliar with the psalms and were not attracted by the little they knew of them. Brought up for centuries on a subjective devotionalism, which even affected their attitude to the eucharist, they were in no position to take to the 'impersonality' of the office. This phase is now passing. The laity read the Bible far more than they used to, they are confronted with a psalm or part of a psalm every Sunday and the devotions of former times seem to have much less appeal. On the other hand, the new office is a very flexible instrument, it is more personal than the old one and there are signs that people take to it once they are given the opportunity. For this purpose there is a single volume containing morning and evening prayer which many have found useful.

~

Instead however of a book of the offices of Vespers and Lauds, a liturgical psalter would go a long way to meet the needs of small communities assembled for the prayer of the church. If we look at the instructions scattered throughout the General Introduction we find that there is more than one way of celebrating the office. The antiphon which need be said only at the beginning of the psalm (123) may be recited or sung by one person, a cantor or someone appointed for the task, and the community can simply listen to it. Obviously no book is needed for the reading, which is best listened to. The responsories both short and long may be replaced by some popular chant so long as it is appropriate or by silence (49). The leader of the group can give out the response to the intercessions and will read the collect. If a hymn is sung at the beginning of the office this can be taken from any authorized source. The advantage of this system is that a psalter arranged according to the offices could be produced for a small sum and would contain what is essential for a full participation in the office.

The Introduction (122) indeed suggests other ways of reciting or singing the psalms: the verses can be alternated by different groups (choir/people) or the responsorial method may be used. This latter method has its attractions and we are already familiar with it in the Mass but unless it is sung it is somewhat dull. However, the Introduction evidently favours considerable flexibility and suggests experimentation. Perhaps as the years go by we shall learn that there are many other ways of singing psalms, ways that are within the capacity of the people.

Still other possibilities are suggested by the Introduction (93–98). Lauds or Vespers may be combined with the Mass. In this case either the introduction of the hour *or* the introduction of the Mass liturgy is used. The three psalms are recited, then the *Gloria* and the collect of the day. The readings (with psalm and Alleluia) follow and on Sundays the Prayer of the Faithful (in the form laid down for the Mass); on week-days the intercessions of the office may be used. The Mass continues as usual until after the communion when the canticle (*Benedictus* or *Magnificat* according to the hour) is sung. The Mass then concludes in the normal way. If the evening Mass of Saturday does duty for Sunday observance this sort of celebration has much to commend it. It brings to the Mass a new element and on festive occasions, such as Pentecost, could provide an agreeable way of celebrating the feast. It is true that the two psalms and canticle of the office with the responsorial psalm of the Mass are rather a lot for one occasion but, given a greater familiarity with the psalms and an ability to sing them, the whole service could be very attractive. The allocation of psalms is balanced by the three readings of the Mass which is a quite traditional arrangement even if the *order* in which they are used is not. There would seem to be no reason why eventually the pattern of the Easter Vigil should not be adopted.

The mid-day office may also be combined with the Mass and substantially that means simply reciting the three psalms after communion. And all these offices may be recited *after* Mass. For Vespers this means that the short reading, the intercessions and the Lord's prayer are omitted and the psalmody and the *Magnificat* are said one after another (97). This does not seem to be a very happy arrangement and it is difficult to know who would find it a convenient one.

Private recitation

Unfortunately private or individual recitation of the office will be the lot of most secular priests for most of the time and in most places. According to the Introduction the clergy, bishops, priests and deacons, 'who represent the person of Christ in a special way', have a mandate to pray 'to God on behalf of all the people entrusted to them and indeed for the whole world' (28). This obligation they will substantially fulfil by reciting the whole of the office but especially Lauds and Vespers, which they will not omit 'unless for a serious reason' (*ibid.*). The recitation of the office then cannot be regarded as an optional extra. Yet there are well-known difficulties. Many large parishes are now understaffed and even in the smaller ones the single priest has many calls upon his time and attention. The form of the office which is obviously meant for a community he sometimes finds unacceptable because unreal. To some much of the psalter is unpromising material for prayer.

What is to be done? Let us put aside the practical difficulties, real or alleged, for the moment. What is required is a radical change of mind and heart. The old Latin office, much of which was incomprehensible to many priests, with the heavy legal sanctions that enforced its recitation, did a great deal of harm to the practice of the prayer of the church. It was a duty to be done, a quota to be got through, rather than a prayer that would nourish the Christian life. If a priest prayed for his people it was during Mass or before or after it that he did so. If he prayed with his people it was in the form of 'devotions' of one sort or another that meant a great deal more to him and the people than anything contained in the office. The first and most fundamental truth we need to grasp is that the office, whatever may be its imperfections, is the prayer of Christ in his church. That is, just as Christ is present (in a special way) in the eucharist, just as he is present in the proclamation of the word and in the celebration of the sacraments, so is he in the prayer of the church: 'He is present when the church prays and sings for he promised: "Where two or three are gathered together in my name, there I am in the midst of them"' (CL 7; Matthew 18:20). Just as the rest of the liturgy engages the action of Christ, so does the prayer of the church. The priest alone in his empty church is in touch with Christ who is the same yesterday, today and for ever and who is ever-living to make intercession for us. Whether we are to think that the prayer of the church has a peculiar efficacy is not the point. That we can leave to God. What is true is that it is the one certain way in which we can pray in union with Christ.

The Introduction (28) states that the bishop and the priest are leaders of the prayer of the communities and because of their special relationship with Christ by ordination they have a special duty of praying for and with their people. As the ancient text of Hippolytus, now again used for the ordination of a bishop, makes clear, prayer for the community is a specifically priestly function: 'May he exercise his priesthood without blame, serving you (*leitourgounta*) day and night that ceaselessly he make you propitious' (to the people). Prayer is as much a priestly function as celebrating the sacraments or preaching the word of God. Even if it seems unsatisfactory, and indeed is, that a priest has to pray so often alone, it is none the less true that when he is engaged in the prayer of the church he is praying in Christ and with the whole church spread throughout the world. But it is also important that at least from time to time he should assemble the parish community to pray with them and to make evident his role as leader of prayer in the local church. It is here perhaps that the combination of an office, say Vespers, with an evening Mass would make the point.

The old office seemed to consist of saying a given quota of words. This notion is explicitly repudiated by the new office (279). Whatever is to be said or done 'Above all, the thing to be achieved is to instil a desire for the authentic prayer of the church and a delight in celebrating the praise of God'. And speaking of different ways of reciting the psalms, the

Introduction remarks 'psalms are not used just to make up a certain quantity of prayer' (121). A reply from the Congregation for Worship heavily emphasizes that in the mind of the church the office is above all *prayer* and affirms that it is not necessary to vocalize the readings, which are to be regarded as nourishment for the soul and the subject-matter of meditation. Nor, it goes on, is it even necessary to pronounce the psalms; in them we should try and catch the echoes of Christ's voice. The purpose of the reform of the office was not to shorten the time of prayer but to give time to pray better. It is not a question of turning over pages or 'getting through the breviary' (*breviarium currendo legentes*) but of personal meditation. The purpose of the office, the note continues, can often be achieved without the oral pronunciation of every word, especially in the reading of the lessons.[2] It may seem odd that the clergy should have to be reminded that the office is prayer but in the past it was often not so regarded. But if it is true that the office is essentially prayer there are certain consequences to be drawn from that truth. We can say some parts of the office more slowly, we can dwell on verses of the psalms if we are so moved, we can ponder on the readings and we need not attempt to say the responsory at all. We can make use of the various devices written into the office to help our prayer. We can use the title of the psalm instead of the antiphon if we so wish. 'For a good spiritual or pastoral reason' (252) we can even occasionally change a psalm or psalms assigned to a particular day for others corresponding to the same hour. This may very well be helpful for the mid-day hour when we can use three of the gradual psalms (which are given in a place apart in the book) instead of what is laid down for the day (e.g. Thursday, Week 3, Psalms 78 and 79). Above all, time is important, not in the sense that we wish to save it but in the sense that we wish to fill it. Wherever we say the office (and given its current brevity there seems to be little excuse for saying it in public places, in aeroplanes or trains), there must be an atmosphere of prayer and experience shows that this is killed if we try and 'fit in' an office in some odd moment which *seems* free – unless of course we are one of those geniuses who can switch off from activity to contemplation at a moment's notice. It should be possible for everyone with a little good will to make the office a real prayer.

Temperaments differ of course and there will be those for whom fixed forms of prayer are difficult. They prefer to follow the movement of the Spirit and are happier in intimate colloquy with God.[3] Granted that is so, it must be affirmed that everyone needs some framework of prayer or it will evaporate into ineffective thoughts and longings. Let us look once again at the structure of the office. The psalms, whatever their difficulties, keep before us the vast history of God's saving work for man and prompt us to raise our minds and hearts to him in gratitude. As almost every writer on the psalms has said, they touch almost every human chord and enable us to express a range of sentiments and needs which would probably not come within our horizon. The danger of unstructured prayer is precisely that it goes round in ever-decreasing circles. Then there are the Bible readings. Sometimes they say little enough to us but in the course of the year the greater part of the Bible is unfolded before us and gives us the opportunity to reflect on God who is revealed there and on his ways with man. Even if the Office of Readings with its longer readings is not used, there are the short ones of the hours from Lauds to Compline and these too offer opportunities for moments of reflection. The Letter of St James may not be everyone's favourite reading but he has some pungent things to say about practical Christianity. Finally, the intercessions again and again remind us that our prayer must have a practical issue and they extend our vision to the whole world and to every need of mankind. It is not often that purely private prayer has so broad a vision.

There is no doubt that the devout Christian in private prayer is praying 'in Christ' but one thing that the prayer of the office does is to enable us to keep in touch with Christ throughout the seasons of the church's year. Through the office (as well of course as in the Mass) we are able to participate in the redeeming mystery of Christ which is unfolded to us in texts of all kinds in a way that is not possible in the eucharist. The whole Christian tradition from the New Testament onwards rises up to show us in this way that, by hymns and antiphons, by readings from the Fathers, by the Christian interpretation of the psalms, we are celebrating the mystery of Christ. The *absence* of all this spells spiritual impoverishment which it is dangerous to tolerate. In urging the extended use of the office for the laity, as well as reminding the clergy of their duty, the church certainly wishes to put an end to that state of affairs.

As far as the pastoral priest is concerned, it is difficult to imagine that he cannot say Lauds and Vespers daily. Even said fairly slowly each office takes little more than fifteen minutes. Presumably too he says some prayer before going to bed. There remains the hour to be said sometime during the day and the Office of Readings which may indeed be said at any time. It may well be that a priest is very busy or moving about, travelling, during the day and then it will be hardly possible to say the day hour. The Office of Readings, which usually is not very long but requires a little quiet and recollection, may be a greater difficulty. But a man has to ask himself: do I ever read the Bible in any consecutive way? If not, he is doing less than his duty. If he does, he simply has to combine that with the three psalms of the office. One advantage of the office lectionary is that it keeps us up to the mark in the reading of the Bible and I do not see that we should have to keep slavishly to the passages printed in the office book. It is better–experience shows–to take the Bible text itself and to look at the context of the extracts and if, as we have said above, we use an edition like that of the Jerusalem Bible (the full one), we shall find that its introductions and notes help us to arrive at a deeper *spiritual* understanding of the text. The Bible readings can indeed become *lectio divina* that will nourish the life of the spirit.

There is of course the moral aspect of the matter, the need of some degree of self-discipline in one's life. This is easier for some than for others, easier for the old than for the young, but everyone's life must have some order (which means discipline) or it will be simply chaotic and however busy-seeming will produce but little. It is quite possible to say Lauds first thing in the morning either before Mass if the priest has to celebrate at that time or as his first duty of the day. It is not difficult to find some period of time for prayer generally and for the office in particular in the late afternoon, before the onset of the evening's work, or before Mass if it is to be celebrated in the evening. The Office of Readings may at times pose a problem. The best time seems to be later in the evening when work is done. If it is left to the morning and has to be combined with Lauds and Mass the amount of material to read and pray about is excessive. The advantage of saying this office the night before is that sometimes the readings are related to the Mass of the next day (GILH, no. 59). This is particularly true of the greater feasts and a knowledge of the office texts helps in the preaching of the homily. But if there are those who find the afternoon a possible time for prayer, the Office of Readings will provide both a framework and subject-matter of the prayer.

However, it may be admitted that the Office of Readings is the one that gives most trouble and on reviewing the whole of the office as it now is, one is inclined to say that it is still not as well adapted for the pastoral life as it might be. Both the Constitution on the Liturgy and the Introduction reiterate that morning and evening prayer are the two most important offices of the day. Great emphasis is laid on this truth and, as we have seen, this is but to recall the ancient practice of the church when these offices were the prayer of the church. For Christians of today, and given the complexities of modern life, prayer in the morning and in the evening is about as much as can be asked of them. For the priest in a busy parish it is sometimes all he can manage. In any future reform of the office it is to be hoped that these factors will be taken into account. What one hopes for is that to morning and evening prayer will be added a course of scripture reading to replace the short readings that exist already. No doubt the arrangement of such a lectionary would be a matter of some complexity but no more complex than the arrangement of the one we now have. The present office lectionary takes some account of the Mass-lectionary, though imperfectly. In Easter time the Acts of the Apostles are read at Mass though with large omissions and never at the office. A re-arrangement here would not be difficult and both lectionaries would benefit. At other times of the year it would be perhaps appropriate that when the Old Testament is read at Mass it should not be read in the office and *vice versa*. Finally, if the material of the Old Testament proved to be too much for one year, we could have a two-year cycle for it as we have a two-year cycle for all scripture readings during the week at Mass. In view of the very considerable omissions from the Old Testament and the 'anthologizing' methods of the compilers in some places, a two-year cycle should make possible a more coherent Old Testament lectionary.

A further refinement is perhaps more disputable. As we have seen in the first chapter of this book, the oldest pattern of Christian prayer is based on the alternation of readings and psalms: the reading provides matter for reflection and the psalm that follows the means for praying about the content of the reading. This, as we know, is the pattern of the Easter Vigil and that was a *popular* service, that is, one in which great numbers of people took part. If morning and evening prayer were extended as suggested above, it is to be hoped that experiments will be made to see if such a pattern is practically possible. It might well mean that the psalm content of these offices would have to be reduced but, as we have also observed, it is possible that there are even now too many psalms in the office. It might mean that the reading would have to be divided and this would demand great skill and discretion. It may well be that there are many who do not find this pattern at all to their liking or a necessary one for liturgical prayer. So be it, but let us not close our minds to the possibilities of such a change. If, as the church desires, at least morning and evening prayer are to become a normal part of every Christian's life, the chances are that the ancient and popular pattern will prove to be the right one. As far as the pastoral priest is concerned, an office consisting of morning and evening prayer with scripture readings and intercessions would give him all that he needs and something that he could incorporate into his daily routine without strain.

The above remarks are no more than the writer's speculations and are to be regarded as such. But one of the features of the reformed liturgy is that it is open-ended and development is not ruled out. The Divine Office has taken many forms in East and West at different times and may do so again in the future. Already new forms of evening prayer are emerging. There is the evening service which includes the ancient rite of the Lucernarium (the lighting of the lamps). The lighted Paschal Candle is carried in procession and placed in the sanctuary where a bowl of incense is burning. A hymn may be sung during this rite. Then comes Psalm 140, the primitive psalm for evening prayer, with its reference to the evening sacrifice, a longer reading with response, an (optional) homily, the *Magnificat*, intercessions, the Lord's prayer, concluding prayer and blessing.[4]

Of the new office as a whole, however, it must be said that the church has put into our hands an instrument of *prayer* and if it is to be judged over-elaborate in some ways, its rules are sane and flexible and it can be used for the purpose for which it was devised.

Notes
~

[1] Here as in all the allegations about a falling church practice we need hard facts, tested figures, and they are hard to come by. What seems to be the case is that the Sunday obligation is no longer regarded as seriously as it once was. This means that on any given Sunday there may be fewer people in church than formerly but it does not mean that there are fewer who are to be described as 'practising'.

[2] *Notitiae* 82 (April 1973), p. 150.

[3] I have even heard people say that formal vocal prayer seems to them unreal and so insincere.

[4] This was drawn up by Paul Inwood (cf. *Evening Prayer*, London, 1986).

Name Index

Subject Index